Subsidies to Chinese Industry

State Capitalism, Business Strategy, and Trade Policy

Usha C. V. Haley

and

George T. Haley

OXFORD
UNIVERSITY PRESS

OXFORD
UNIVERSITY PRESS

Oxford University Press is a department of the University of Oxford.
It furthers the University's objective of excellence in research, scholarship,
and education by publishing worldwide.

Oxford New York
Auckland Cape Town Dar es Salaam Hong Kong Karachi
Kuala Lumpur Madrid Melbourne Mexico City Nairobi
New Delhi Shanghai Taipei Toronto

With offices in
Argentina Austria Brazil Chile Czech Republic France Greece
Guatemala Hungary Italy Japan Poland Portugal Singapore
South Korea Switzerland Thailand Turkey Ukraine Vietnam

Published in the United States of America by
Oxford University Press
198 Madison Avenue, New York, NY 10016

Library of Congress Cataloging-in-Publication Data
Haley, Usha C. V.
Subsidies to Chinese industry : state capitalism, business strategy and trade policy /
Usha C. Haley and George T. Haley.
p. cm.
Includes bibliographical references and index.
ISBN 978-0-19-977374-9 (cloth : alk. paper) 1. Industrial policy—China.
2. Industries—China—Finance. 3. Subsidies—China. 4. Capitalism—China.
5. China—Commercial policy. I. Haley, George T. II. Title.
HD3616.C63H35 2013
338.951′02—dc23
2012038157

1 3 5 7 9 8 6 4 2
Printed in the United States of America
on acid-free paper

Subsidies to Chinese Industry

Many years ago, I learned from one of our diplomats in China that one of the principal Chinese curses heaped upon an enemy is, "May you live in an interesting age." "Surely," he said, "no age has been more fraught with insecurity than our own present time."

Sir Austen Chamberlain, brother of
British prime minister Neville Chamberlain,
quoted by Frederic R. Coudert in
Proceedings of the Academy of Political Science, 1939

We dedicate this book to the working men and women
around the world who soldier on with integrity, dedication,
and commitment in our uncertain age.

THE AUTHORS

USHA C. V. HALEY

Usha Haley is Professor of International Business at Massey University, Auckland, New Zealand, and Research Associate at the Economic Policy Institute, Washington, DC. She has testified on her research on China to the congressionally mandated US-China Economic and Security Review Commission and twice before the Committee on Ways and Means, including on the Nonmarket Economy Trade Remedy Act. She has presented on her research on China before the US International Trade Commission, the US Department of Commerce, and the US Trade Representative, and her research has advised the US-China Joint Commission on Commerce and Trade, the primary trade dialogue between the two countries. Her research on Chinese subsidies has been incorporated into three pieces of antidumping regulation in the European Union.

Her research focuses on the multinational corporation and international strategic management, especially in Asian and emerging markets, including business-government relations, strategic decision-making, sanctions, and subsidies. She has more than 199 publications and presentations including 24 journal articles (in *California Management Review*, *Harvard Business Review* and *Journal of Management Studies* among others), 36 book chapters, and seven books, two of which have been on international best-seller lists. Her books include *Multinational Corporations in Political Environments* (reviewed in the *Wall Street Journal* and *Academy of Management Review*); *The Chinese Tao of Business* (reviewed in the *Wall Street Journal*); *New Asian Emperors* (reviewed in the *Economist*); *Strategic Management in the Asia Pacific*; and *Asian Post-crisis Management*. She is Coeditor in Chief of the new book series *Multinational Investment and Business* for Imperial College Press.

She serves or has served on seven corporate, nonprofit, and governmental planning and advisory boards, sits on five academic journals' editorial boards, serves as Regional Editor (Asia Pacific) for two journals, and has edited four journal special issues on strategic management in the Asia Pacific. She has served on national and international review boards including the Networks of Centers of Excellence, Canada and the Marsden Fund, New Zealand. Her expertise has been profiled numerous times in the international media including the *New York Times*, *Wall Street Journal*, *USA Today*, *Fortune*, *Investor's Business Daily*, *San Francisco Chronicle*, *International Herald Tribune*, CNN, *BusinessWeek*, *Economist*, *Barron's*, *Newsweek*, *Entrepreneur*, *National Business Review*, *Australian*, PBS, CNBC, and NPR.

In 2012, she received the Academy of Management's Practice Impact Award for scholarly impact at the Seventy-Second Annual Meetings, Boston. In 2011, she was featured as "thought leader" on emerging markets at *The Economist*'s flagship High-Growth Markets Summit, London. In 2003, she received a Lifetime Achievement Award from the Literati Club (UK) and a panel of academics, businesspersons, and policymakers for contributions to understanding business in the Asia Pacific. In 2010, she was named an American Made Hero for her work with the US Congress. Her PhD is from the Stern School of Business, New York University. She may be contacted through ChinaSubsidies.com.

GEORGE T. HALEY

George Haley is Professor of Marketing at the University of New Haven (UNH), where he teaches in graduate and executive programs; in summer, he serves as Distinguished Guest Professor of Marketing at the School of Business, ITESM in Mexico. He is founding Director of the Center for International Industry Competitiveness, a Center of Excellence at UNH.

He has conducted policy-analysis seminars on China / emerging markets for the National Intelligence Council / CIA, and the US International Trade Commission, and testified twice before the congressionally mandated US-China Economic and Security Review Commission. He also consults with several multinational companies and governments in Asia, Australia, Latin America, and the United States. He serves or has served as Advisor to the Strategic Planning Board of Rio Tinto, Ltd. (Australia), to the Export Promotion Board (State of Connecticut), and to the Metal Manufacturers' Education and Training Alliance, and as Mentor in the Distribution Business Management Association's Corporate Global Supply Chain Mentoring Program for senior executives of large multinational corporations.

His expertise is in industrial marketing and emerging markets, including the historical, cultural, and legal environments in which marketing strategies are formulated. He focuses on business-to-business marketing, distribution and supply-chain management, product and technology management, strategic marketing, strategic decision-making, Chinese, Latin American, and Asian business, and managing intellectual property in emerging markets. He has over 125 articles, books, book chapters, research reports and presentations, including in journals such as *Harvard Business Review* and *Industrial Marketing Management*. His books include *The Chinese Tao of Business* (recommended by the *Wall Street Journal* as the only book on Asian business to buy) and *New Asian Emperors* (named "an important study" by the *Economist*). His latest books include *Marketing: Planning and Strategy*, 8th ed. (Cengage).

His research has been profiled several times in the major media including the *Economist, Financial Times, Wall Street Journal, Forbes, BusinessWeek, Time, Los Angeles Times*, CNN, *The Lou Dobbs Show* (CNN), *Fortune, Entrepreneur, Christian Science Monitor, USA Today, Voice of America, Industry Week, Investor's Business Daily, Far Eastern Economic Review, Marketing News*, and *Advertising Age*. He serves or has served on the review and advisory boards of eight academic journals and has guest-edited three journal special issues on Business in Emerging Economies and on B2B Marketing. He has been appointed Coeditor in Chief for the new Imperial College Press series on *Multinational Investment and Business*.

In 2009, the American Marketing Association's flagship *Marketing News* named him one of six "Marketing Academics to Watch" based on his research, teaching, and impact. In 2010, AmericanMadeHeroes.com named him a Hero Advocate for his work on behalf of American manufacturers, and he was identified as a "Thought Leader" in Business-to-Business and Industrial Marketing and Manufacturing by *IndustryWeek*. He received UNH's University Research Scholar Award in 2011. His PhD is from the University of Texas at Austin. He may be contacted through ChinaSubsidies.com.

CONTENTS

TABLES

FIGURES

PREFACE AND DETAILED SYNOPSIS

OUR CONTRIBUTIONS

For the past five years or so, we have asked: Why did China frequently move in a couple of years, in capital-intensive industries with no labor-cost advantage, from bit player and net importer to the largest manufacturer and the largest exporter in the world? Why have so many industrialized countries become primarily exporters of commodities and scrap to China? And how is this affecting business strategies and national competitive advantage? This book is an effort to provide some answers to these questions. Economic theories of comparative advantage offered limited insights into these questions that involved Chinese manufacturing subsidies, but we saw that understandings of imperfect markets, state capitalism, business policy, and strategic trade policy could offer more. Our book aims to make several contributions.

First, we provide a complex theoretical explanation for industrial subsidies that in key Chinese manufacturing industries appear in dollar terms to exceed over 30 percent of industrial output. Analyses of manufacturing subsidies have mostly surfaced in economic theories; and economic theories have mostly portrayed subsidies as distortive, redistributing and reallocating resources according to nonmarket criteria and resulting in economically inefficient allocations of these resources. Unless in special circumstances (such as with infant industries), economists have generally ignored the view that subsidies may contribute significantly to aspects of a country's comparative advantage, and not just disadvantage. However, China's state capitalist regime has used subsidies as a tool to promote the governments' and the Communist Party of China's (CPC's) interests. The state has willingly paid the price of economic inefficiency to accomplish the CPC's political, social, economic, and diplomatic goals. Because of China's sudden heft in international trade and manufacturing, these considerations regarding subsidies have an immediacy that abruptly transcends the purely theoretical. Theorists and analysts should therefore explore subsidies as governmental strategic tools, including the potential long-term economic effects on international trade and welfare of using subsidies in this fashion. Again, this book hopes to begin an inquiry into these issues.

Second, we develop independent measures of industrial subsidies using publicly reported data at company and industrial levels and from diverse sources. Generally, researchers have a notoriously hard time measuring subsidies, and Chinese subsidies even more so. As this book describes in several sections, for institutional and strategic reasons, the information on manufacturing subsidies that the Chinese government provides has rampant missing and misreported data; also, few consistent definitions exist for the data. In addition, the Chinese government does not report subsidies to domestic industrial companies, many of whom are major players in their global industries. Yet researchers and analysts as well as governments around the world have depended solely on these Chinese self-reported data for analyses of effects on welfare, industries, and trade. For our analyses, we used data from industrial analysts, nongovernmental organizations, and companies to obtain end-user and reference prices. We gathered data that companies relied on to cost out their products. We analyzed policy statements and reports specifying government subsidies. For many subsidies, we used price-gap analysis to develop our estimates. Though the data are incomplete, for the first time we used multifaceted data that incorporate organizational variables and estimates, not just Chinese governmental reports to measure subsidies.

Third, this book explores the strategic aspect of subsidies for business and governments. It expands on instruments of trade policy to include networks of regulation impacting indigenous innovation, that advance the goals of state capitalism, not of market efficiencies. We separate business strategies into those affected by and shaping consumption and production subsidies. Other theorists have explored businesses and strategic groups' responses to trade policy, including subsidies. We extend their analysis by examining generic market (competitive) and nonmarket (political) strategies that businesses may undertake.

Over the last five years, research in this book on several industries, including steel, glass, paper, auto parts, and solar, has been incorporated into regulation and business strategy both in the United States and in the European Union. The letters from members of the US Congress and the Office of the President in the appendix indicate how some of this research has been used. However, though the practical aspects of our earlier conclusions appeared obvious, we still lacked an adequate understanding of the theoretical context of Chinese industrial subsidies. We see this book as a step in that direction.

CHAPTER OUTLINES

The chapters in this book include a theoretical introduction to subsidies, an overview of the methodology we employed to measure subsidies, four empirical case studies on subsidies to Chinese steel, glass, paper, and auto parts, and finally implications of Chinese subsidies for business strategy and trade policy. The chapters may be read as stand-alone, in-depth inquiries into a topic concerning subsidies or a case that has policy and governmental attention, or in their entirety for an examination into how Chinese subsidies have operated in our global, interconnected business and political environments. A brief outline of each chapter follows.

Chapter 1 asks how subsidies aided China in becoming so competitive in capital-intensive products for which it enjoyed no comparative advantage a decade prior. Economic rationales span the use of subsidies for industrial development (including effective corporate strategy), technology development, and the pursuit of strategic trade goals. These theories mostly portray subsidies as distortive because they redistribute and reallocate resources according to nonmarket criteria, resulting in economically inefficient allocation of resources. Unless in special circumstances (e.g., infant industries), economists have generally not considered that subsidies may contribute significantly to aspects of a country's comparative advantage. Yet without attention to national political contexts, the economic metaphors of free trade, comparative advantage, and efficient allocation of resources appear insufficient to capture the vast changes that have ensued from subsidies and will continue to affect global markets. In several capital-intensive industries with small labor costs and in less than five years, China rose from bit player and net importer to among the largest producers and exporters in the world. Rather than aberrations, in China, subsidies form central parts of "conceptions of control," important ways in which Chinese businesses and governments produce, stabilize, and create common understandings of markets. Subsidies reflect interactions and struggles between critical Chinese actors, including central and provincial governments. Flows of capital serve as important mechanisms for Chinese state control of markets, but few industry studies exist of how these vast flows operate. The opacity and complexity of Chinese government borrowing also hinders accurate assessments. Concepts of state capitalism enunciated as market-transition theory, the multiorganizational Chinese state, and state as paramount shareholder can help to form a prism for more complex and relevant understandings of Chinese subsidies.

Chapter 2 defines subsidies, highlights previous empirical research that identified subsidies in China, surveys the rationales for the variables we used, and covers problems with measurement and data. Here we outline the methodology for the ensuing four sequential industry studies conducted between 2007 and 2011 to identify the growth of subsidies to Chinese manufacturing over time: steel (2000–2007), glass (2004–2008), paper (2002–2009), and auto parts (2001–2011). In all these industries, China had moved from a net importer to one of the largest exporters in the world. In all these capital-intensive industries, labor was between 2 and 7 percent of total costs. In these fragmented industries, the vast majority of firms enjoyed no economies of scale or scope. Although the time periods and some of the industry-specific variables vary because of the availability of data, all studies build on common assumptions and use some common variables. Connections are specified between Chinese policy, trade regulation in the GATT and the WTO, and subsidies. The chapter also surveys research and provides data on major forms of subsidies to Chinese industry including (*a*) free or low-cost loans, (*b*) subsidies to energy (coal, electricity, natural gas, heavy oil), and (*c*) subsidies to key inputs, land, and technology. For our analysis, we included data from companies, nongovernmental organizations, government agencies around the world, think tanks, and industrial analysts to obtain end-user and reference prices. We also analyzed policy statements and reports specifying government subsidies. Though the data are incomplete, for the first time we used multifaceted data that incorporate organizational variables and estimates, not just Chinese governmental reports, to measure subsidies. We discuss data problems we encountered and the price-gap approach we used to measure some of the subsidies. Finally, the chapter presents the 15 equations that we used to calculate subsidies to Chinese industry.

Chapter 3 tracks subsidies to China's steel industry from 2000 to 2007 and the industry's sudden transformation from net importer to the largest producer and exporter in the world. In 2007, China was the largest producer and consumer of steel in the world, with 40 percent of the global market. In 2005, China went from a net steel importer to a steel exporter. In 2006, China became the largest steel exporter in the world, up from fifth largest in 2005. In 2007, energy subsidies to Chinese steel were estimated at approximately $15.7 billion, showing a 3,800 percent increase since 2000. The central government's policies of consolidating the steel industry had failed and the Chinese steel industry had become more fragmented. With no discernible cost advantage, Chinese steel still sold for

25 percent less than US and European steel. From 2000 to midyear 2007, total energy subsidies to Chinese steel reached $27.11 billion, including subsidies to thermal coal of $11.16 billion, to coking coal of $15.29 billion, to electricity of $916.39 million, and to natural gas of $54.12 million.

Chapter 4 documents the Chinese glass industry's explosive growth and exports and the government subsidies that bolstered it from 2004 to 2008. In 2009, with over 31 percent of global glass production, China was the largest producer of glass and glass products, had the greatest number of glass-producing enterprises, and had the largest number of float-glass production lines in the world. China was also the largest consumer of glass. However, because of existing and planned production capacity, glass exports from China were expected to outpace greatly projected increases in domestic demand. Since 2003, glass production in China has more than doubled. Concurrently, production capacity in China has also doubled since 2003 and increased more than threefold since 2000. China's glass industry enjoyed no economies of scale or scope. The industry also displayed geographic fragmentation, with manufacturers in 29 of the 32 provinces. Because of poor data, analysis took place at the level of the flat-glass sector that received approximately $4.8 billion in subsidies from 2004 to 2008. Extrapolating to the glass industry as a whole, we determined that China's glass and glass-products industry received at least $30.3 billion in subsidies from 2004 to 2008. The subsidies spanned heavy oil, coal, electricity, and soda ash and grew steadily in this period, reaching about 35 percent of gross industrial output value of glass in 2008.

Chapter 5 covers China's rapid rise in the global paper industry, fueled by over $33.1 billion in government subsidies from 2002 to 2009. Since 2000, China tripled its paper production. In 2008, China overtook the United States to become the world's largest producer of paper and paper products. China's paper industry has limited economies of scale or scope and is geographically fragmented, operating in 30 provinces. China also has among the smallest forest bases in the world per capita. Consequently, it is the largest importer in the world of major industrial inputs, including pulp and recycled paper. Labor makes up about 4 percent of the costs in this industry; in contrast, imported recycled paper and pulp comprise over 35 percent of the costs. Yet Chinese paper sells at a substantial discount compared to US or European paper. Governmental policies have systematically aimed to reduce China's dependence on imported raw materials and to subsidize the paper industry's restructuring. Subsidies measured from 2002 to 2009 include those for electricity ($778 million), coal ($3 billion), subsidy income reported by companies ($442 million), and loan-interest subsidies ($2 billion); from 2004 to 2009 they include those for pulp ($25 billion); and from 2004 to 2008, they include subsidies for recycled paper ($1.7 billion). Missing data prevented calculation of pulp or recycled-paper subsidies in 2002, 2003, and 2009.

Chapter 6 highlights how from 2001 to 2011, the Chinese auto-parts industry received $27.5 billion in subsidies, helping to make it one of the largest producers and exporters in the world. As a "pillar industry," auto parts have received strong support from the Chinese government. The industry has grown more than 150 percent since 2004 but remains highly fragmented with more than 10,000 registered and 15,000 unregistered manufacturers. US global auto strategy has centered on manufacturing in China and exporting back home. Consequently, China's exports of auto parts to the United States are three times those of its next highest trading destination, Japan. Specific subsidies included $2.3 billion reported by 73 companies (2001–2009); $1 billion for coal (2001–2010); $0.6 billion for electricity (2002–2010); $0.3 billion for natural gas (2004–2010); $1.6 billion for glass (2004–2010); $3.2 billion for cold-rolled steel (2003–2010); and $18.4 billion for technology development and industrial restructuring (2001–2011). For the next decade, the government has committed an additional $10.9 billion in subsidies for restructuring and technology development.

Chapter 7 analyzes how subsidies to Chinese industry have affected and are affected by business strategy and trade policy. Our findings contradict the widespread belief that China's enormous success as an exporting nation derives primarily from low labor costs and deliberate currency undervaluation. The subsidy practices we covered have impact beyond the four industries on which we focused. We explore the implications of these subsidies for firms, for the global economy, and for future research. Business strategies include lobbying for subsidies, advocating for protection from subsidized foreign competitors, and adroit managing of supply chains to guard against the whiplash effects generated by uncoordinated subsidies. Free trade may lead to suboptimal outcomes, and protectionism can increase national income by raising firms' profitability in imperfect markets. With an open US market and closed China market, Chinese firms could achieve more efficient scale via sales volume domestically and abroad, while squeezing US competitors into a portion of their domestic market. Once foreign firms fall behind, recovering profitability becomes unlikely, and so strategic trade policy should rationally become managers' top priority. Business strategies alter in response to production or consumption subsidies and include market or competitive as well as nonmarket or political strategies. Understanding trade-policy instruments can explain some patterns of specialization ensuing from trade with China, and we cover three government policies broadly focusing on domestic consumption (antidumping and countervailing duties) or domestic production (indigenous innovation). Subsidies to Chinese manufacturing have many implications for firms, including manufacturing location and technology development. For the global economy, regular boom-and-bust cycles may now become the new normal, and these call for informed negotiation via trade blocs and bilaterally. Chinese government subsidies will continue, contributing substantially to their firms' competitiveness in global markets.

ACKNOWLEDGMENTS

The opinions we express in this book are ours alone. However, we could not have written a book of this nature without the support and advice of numerous people. Among them, the following stand out for their help and friendship through this project: Mike Wessel (US-China Economic and Security Review Commission and Wessel Group), who introduced us to the hidden problem of Chinese subsidies and, with his hands-on knowledge of trade, economics, and international law, provided much advice and guidance as we analyzed these four industries; Scott Paul (Alliance for American Manufacturing) and Rob Scott (Economic Policy Institute), who funded some of our research on subsidies and commented on many revisions of our empirical reports, but refrained from trying to influence the results.

We also thank the many academics, managers, government officials, governmental representatives, trade representatives, trade lawyers, industry analysts, students, coauthors, and reporters in the United States, China, Australia, the EU, New Zealand, Mexico, India, Taiwan, and Hong Kong who tirelessly listened to our ideas and generously gave of their time and insights. These include participants of the US International Trade Commission's Industry Seminar Series in Washington, DC, for initial feedback on the variables used in this book and their measurement. Special thanks also to senior policymakers and analysts in the United States International Trade Commission (USITC), United States International Trade Administration (ITA), United States Department of Commerce, and the United States Trade Representative (USTR), Washington, DC, for regular and helpful feedback through the various industrial studies. Specific industrial studies in this book also benefited from insights, data, or both from John Bonnell (JD Power Asia Pacific), Scott Boos (Alliance for American Manufacturing), Tim Brightbill (Wiley Rein), Robert Carr

(USITC), Vince DeSapio (USITC), Elizabeth Drake (Stewart & Stewart), Per Ekander (Arctic Paper), Jake Handelsman (International Forest & Paper Association), Dawn Heuschel (USITC), Ambassador Alan Holmer (Department of Treasury Special Envoy to China and the Strategic Economic Dialogue), Gerald Houck (USITC), Jennifer Kelly (United Auto Workers, Michigan), Thomas Klier (Federal Reserve Bank of Chicago), Stephen Koplan (Wessel Group), Jamie Milnes (MEPS International, UK), Keith Romig (United Steelworkers), Tim Stratford (China Affairs, USTR), the Trade Working Group of the US Congress, and, Timothy Weckesser (SinoConsulting).

Our industry study on steel subsidies draws on our earlier unpublished Alliance for American Manufacturing report; and our industry studies on glass, paper, and auto-parts subsidies draw on our earlier Economic Policy Institute briefing papers to inform the trade debate. These industry studies have benefited from reviews from academics and also from policymakers, US senators and representatives, trade lawyers, labor-union leaders, managers, and industry and country analysts.

Finally, we owe special thanks to our editor, Terry Vaughn at Oxford University Press, who believed in this project, provided suggestions, and in good humor gave us extra time when problems acquiring Chinese data invariably affected our schedules. We also thank Catherine Rae and Cathryn Vaulman at Oxford University Press for her help with our manuscript.

To all the above mentioned who helped shape our writing, we owe our gratitude.

CHAPTER 1
The Hidden Advantage of Chinese Subsidies

China provided "easy access to capital," Michael McCarthy, director at Evergreen Solar, told us on a wintry February morning as the company started moving all production of solar panels from Massachusetts to a joint venture (JV) in Wuhan, China. "We need capital to expand and grow. That is fundamental." Earlier, in January 2011, Evergreen Solar had closed its main US factory and laid off 800 workers. In the previous three years, with the Massachusetts government's loans and tax credits and its proprietary technology, Evergreen had become the United States' third-largest solar-panel manufacturer. The company cited plunging solar-panel prices worldwide, coupled with much higher Chinese government subsidies (financial transfers from the government that provided benefits) as reasons for its move.[1]

The Chinese had become the largest manufacturers and price setters in the nascent solar photovoltaic industry, accounting for over half the world's production in 2010. World prices had fallen by two-thirds in the last three years. Evergreen's CEO, El-Hillow, told the *New York Times* that the Chinese governments' and state-owned banks' considerable subsidies had helped Chinese manufacturers to keep costs very low (Bradsher 2011a). In 2010, the top five solar companies in China had received over $31.3 billion in loans from the state-owned China Development Bank alone (Mercom).[2] El-Hillow said that the Chinese were now offering him similar massive subsidies that would keep Evergreen competitive; these subsidies, rather than low Chinese labor costs, influenced his move, he elaborated, as labor formed just a tiny part of his manufacturing costs. China's real advantage, he said, lay in the ability of solar-panel companies to partner with local governments and to obtain loans at very low interest rates from state-owned banks. Evergreen, with its partners, the Wuhan municipal and Hubei provincial governments, borrowed two-thirds of its Wuhan factory's costs (as compared to less than 5 percent of its US factory's costs from the Massachusetts government) from two Chinese state-owned banks at very low interest rates with no principal or interest payments due until the end of the loan in 2015. "Therein lies the hidden advantage of being in China," El-Hillow said (Bradsher 2011a).

This book provides a theoretical basis and an empirical analysis for understanding the hidden advantage of Chinese production subsidies with practical implications for world industry. Rather than aberrations, in China subsidies form central parts of what Fligstein (2001) called "conceptions of control," important ways in which Chinese businesses and governments produce, stabilize, and create common understanding of their markets. Flows of subsidies reflect interactions and struggles between critical Chinese actors such as central and provincial governments and state-owned enterprises (SOEs) with different resources, interests, and visions of markets. As we describe in later chapters, Evergreen's story has resurfaced across other industries, including steel, glass, paper, and auto parts. In all these capital-intensive industries where labor costs play minor roles, and in the space of approximately five years, China rose from a net importer to among the largest producers and exporters in the world. How did subsidies aid China in becoming so apparently competitive in capital-intensive products for which it enjoyed no comparative advantage[3] a decade prior? What are the implications for firms and other countries in the face of this hidden advantage? Table 1.1 indicates the growth of three measurable subsidies to Chinese private firms and SOEs in the form of research-and-development (R&D) funds, subsidies to loss-making SOEs, and additional appropriations for SOEs' circulating capital, as reported by China's National Bureau of Statistics (NBS). From 1985 to 2005, these reported subsidies totaled $310.18 billion.

China's modern global rise began more than three decades ago in 1976, when Deng Xiaoping took over as China's paramount leader after Mao Zedong. Deng's vision for China's restructuring included "socialism with Chinese characteristics," where the state continued to retain ultimate control of China's economic and political environments as it opened up to the world (Communist Party of China 2007). Analysts and researchers have credited Deng's policies as transforming Mao's restrictive and failed state-control model into one that could operate effectively in a global, capitalist economy (Spence 1997). In December 2001, in line with Deng's reforms, and after 15 years of diplomatic negotiations, China became a

Table 1.1. REPORTED SUBSIDIES TO CHINESE MANUFACTURING ENTERPRISES, 1985–2005 (BILLIONS OF DOLLARS)

	Innovation and technology subsidies	Subsidies to loss-making SOEs	Subsidies for SOEs' circulating capital	Total
1985	3.52	17.27	0.49	21.28
1986	3.76	9.41	0.29	13.46
1987	3.36	10.11	0.32	13.79
1988	4.06	12.00	0.26	16.32
1989	3.89	15.91	0.32	20.12
1990	3.22	12.10	0.23	15.55
1991	3.40	9.59	0.25	13.24
1992	4.06	8.07	0.19	12.32
1993	7.31	7.14	0.32	14.77
1994	4.82	4.25	0.20	9.27
1995	5.92	3.93	0.42	10.27
1996	6.29	4.06	0.52	10.87
1997	7.76	4.45	0.63	12.84
1998	7.75	4.03	0.51	12.29
1999	9.25	3.50	0.68	13.43
2000	10.45	3.37	0.86	14.68
2001	11.98	3.63	0.27	15.88
2002	11.70	3.14	0.23	15.07
2003	13.21	2.74	0.14	16.09
2004	15.03	2.63	0.15	17.81
2005	18.25	2.36	0.22	20.83
Total	158.99	143.69	7.50	310.18

Source: Compiled from China Statistical Yearbook; Girma et al. 2009.

member of the World Trade Organization (WTO) (*BBC News* 2001). In a front-page editorial, China's state-owned newspaper, *People's Daily*, labeled WTO membership as a "historic moment in China's reform and opening-up and the process of modernization" with prophetic hopes that China's manufacturing and exports would become even more competitive globally. In 2009, China surpassed Germany to become the world's largest exporter (Haley 2010). In 2010, China became the second-largest producer in the world, overtaking Japan. In 2010, Chinese foreign-exchange reserves also topped $2.85 trillion, the largest in the world (Bradsher 2011b). In December 2010, only the United States and Japan exceeded China's patent filings; with 16.7 percent annual growth from 2006, in 2011 China surpassed the United States to become the top patent filer in the world (Yee 2011; Zhou and Stembridge 2010).

In 2011, Chinese labor wages, though rising, still constituted about one-fifteenth of labor wages in the United States and other industrialized countries.[4] Yet China's economic growth has speedily transcended its historical base of labor-intensive industries to capital-intensive industries. Rodrik (2006) showed that China's exports have significantly more sophistication and contain more high-tech goods than pure comparative-advantage arguments predict. He argued that China's industrial policies of "promotion and protection" shaped its industrial structure and exports. Much of China's economic prowess has manifested in the space of a decade, with many Chinese products selling for about 30–50 percent less than comparable products from industrialized nations. Economic theories of cost advantages from efficiencies and technological breakthroughs fail to explain fully these cost advantages: As the industry studies in this book indicate, Chinese industries remain highly fragmented, with most companies having no economies of scale or scope and using antiquated technologies. The next section highlights some of the unique characteristics of Chinese state capitalism. The ensuing sections provide brief reviews of economic and sociopolitical reasons for subsidies to enable moving beyond pure comparative advantage as an explanation for China's economic rise and global economic effects.

STATE CAPITALISM WITH CHINESE CHARACTERISTICS

State capitalism refers to situations where states play significant and visible roles in markets. Polanyi (1944; Polanyi, Arensberg, and Pearson 1957) identified states and markets as the two central, interconnected pillars of modern capitalism. Subsequent research elaborated on the state's roles in modern industrialized societies (e.g., Wallerstein 1979; Hobson 1997; Weiss 1998; Evans, Rueschemeyer, and Skocpol 2002). Focusing on Japanese institutional arrangements, Johnson (1995) confirmed the capitalist developmental state's significance in industrialization through emphasizing growth, productivity, and competitiveness and using an elite bureaucracy. Other research in Korea (e.g., Amsden 1992), Taiwan, and Singapore (e.g., Deyo 1987; Wade 1990; Wong 2004) amplified states' roles in industrial development.

Chinese state capitalism has commonalities with other Asian variants that have strong governments to direct investment and to suppress labor (Fligstein and Zhang 2011). Indeed, the Chinese government deliberately learned from Japanese, Korean, and Singaporean developmental experiences. In the late 1990s, Beijing tried to reorganize SOEs into big business groups similar to those in Japan and Korea (White et al. 2008). The State-Owned Assets Supervision and Administration Commission (SASAC) of the State Council learned about asset management from Singapore's Ministry of Finance and Temasek. But in Japan, Korea, and Singapore, elite families have always controlled private, large firms (see Haley, Haley, and Tan 2009); in China, the state, rather than elite families, controls firms in the core Chinese economy.

Lin (2011) identified state capitalism as varying across two dimensions: the extent of the state's ownership of production; and the extent of the state's coordination with other enterprises. Among nation-states, China uniquely synchronizes party, government, military, and economy. The Chinese state freely creates and maintains enterprises, holds a majority of the shareholdings, controls critical personnel decisions, and supplies capital (Haley, Haley, and Tan 2004). SOEs compete with other enterprises in the market, and its elites enjoy capitalist rewards. However, the elites ultimately answer to the state rather than to boards of directors, shareholders, or other stakeholders. The market asymmetrically favors SOEs for capital and other resources. Some SOEs become national champions as the state restricts their competitors and encourages their mergers and acquisitions. Along with control of rewards and incentives for personnel and organizations, Lin (2011) identified control of capital as one of the distinguishing facets of Chinese state capitalism.

The Chinese central and provincial governments direct all the major financial institutions (Lin 2011). The State Council's vice premier manages all major banks. Seventeen institutions control four-fifths of the banking system's assets; the government appoints and controls their managers' mobility. Consequently, financial institutions fully cooperate with state's directives in disbursing capital. Despite provincial tussles, the Chinese state, financial institutions, and SOEs appear seamless in trade and foreign investment. For example, in trade agreements, the Chinese government almost always commits to infrastructural construction and natural-resource explorations, which it allocates as no-bid contracts to SOEs. The SOEs also receive financing from the Chinese state-owned banks. Table 1.2 indicates the extent of governmental ownership of bank assets in China.

Flows of capital serve as an important mechanism for Chinese state control of markets, but few industry studies exist of how these flows operate. Additionally, the opacity and complexity of Chinese government borrowing hinders accurate assessments of the state's liabilities and capital flows. In 2010, the Chinese central government had official treasury debt of less than 20 percent of GDP. However, using official government sources,

Table 1.2. GOVERNMENTS' SHARE OF BANK ASSETS IN CHINA, 2009

Full state control (63.4%)	Partial state control (22.1%)	Least state control (14.5%)
Large commercial banks (51.3%)	Joint-stock commercial banks (14.9%)	Rural credit cooperatives (10.9%)
Policy banks (8.7%)	City commercial banks (7.2%)	Nonbank financial institutions (1.9%)
Postal service banks (3.4%)		Foreign banks (1.7%)

Source: Compiled from Dean, Browne, and Oster 2010.

Batson and Zhang (2011) estimated public debt load as 82 percent of GDP in 2010. They attributed this debt to the myriad fiefdoms within China's large public sector that freely borrowed money to finance provincial, including industrial, ambitions (also see Shih 2008). As table 1.3 shows, local governments' debt rose from 0 percent of GDP in 1998 to 27 percent in 2010. Most of this lending originated from public-sector entities such as the China Development Bank, Ministry of Railways (MOR), and

Table 1.3. OFFICIAL CHINESE PUBLIC DEBT AS A PERCENTAGE OF GDP, 1998–2010

Year	Official domestic debt	Foreign debt	Central bank bills	Policy bank bonds	Ministry of Railways	Local govt. debts	Bank restructuring costs	Contingent NPL liabilities	Total
1998	9%	4%	0%	6%	2%	0%	3%	52%	76%
1999	12%	4%	0%	7%	2%	5%	7%	49%	86%
2000	13%	4%	0%	7%	2%	5%	15%	30%	76%
2001	14%	4%	0%	8%	2%	4%	15%	26%	73%
2002	16%	3%	1%	8%	2%	6%	14%	23%	74%
2003	17%	3%	2%	9%	1%	7%	12%	18%	70%
2004	16%	2%	7%	9%	1%	7%	13%	12%	67%
2005	17%	1%	12%	10%	1%	12%	17%	8%	77%
2006	16%	1%	15%	11%	2%	15%	14%	6%	80%
2007	19%	1%	14%	11%	2%	16%	11%	5%	80%
2008	17%	1%	15%	12%	2%	16%	12%	2%	77%
2009	18%	1%	12%	13%	3%	23%	11%	2%	84%
2010	17%	1%	10%	13%	4%	27%	9%	1%	82%

Source: Batson and Zhang 2011.

local-government investment corporations (LICs). Credit rating agency Fitch Ratings (2010) reported that Chinese banks were increasingly engaging in complex deals that hid the size and nature of their lending, obscuring hundreds of billions of dollars in loans. The report also said that Chinese regulators understated loan growth in the first half of 2010 by 28 percent, or about $190 billion—real loans were closer to RMB 5.9 trillion than the reported RMB 4.6 trillion. Many banks continued secretly to shift loans off the books, creating a "pervasive understatement of credit growth and credit exposure." In 2009, lending by state-run banks comprised one of China's most aggressive forms of stimulus (Barboza 2010).

In 2011, China's first national audit of regional finances confirmed that local governments owed RMB 10,700 billion ($1,650 billion) or about 27 percent of China's GDP, again easily outstripping the central government's official debt figures. The audit confirmed a rise of 62 percent in local governments' debt after the 2008 financial crisis. In 2011, other estimates put the government's contingent liabilities at over 150 percent of GDP when they included SOEs' debt implicitly backed by the state (Rabinovitch and Anderlini 2011). In contrast, the United States had a debt-to-GDP ratio of 93 percent, and Japan's ratio hovered at over 225 percent. The audit revealed that Chinese provincial governments had created over 6,576 arm's-length financing vehicles to circumvent central banking rules for easier access to RMB 4,971 billion in loans. But previous estimates had put the total debt load at closer to RMB 14,000 billion. The discrepancy arose because the audit only included loans to financing vehicles with explicit guarantees from local governments, rather than state land or other collateral that the governments mostly used instead.

Provincial governments' policies drive much of China's capital flows into fixed-asset investments, or investments in plant, equipment, infrastructure, and real estate. For example, in the fourth quarter of 2008, the Chinese central government allocated about two-thirds of its economic-stimulus package, or approximately RMB 2.7 trillion, for provincial governments' expenditures. However, the provincial governments' stimulus spending ballooned to nearly RMB 10 trillion, about four times the central government's contribution. The local governments borrowed cheaply or at no cost from state-owned banks to bridge the gap and invested this capital in industrial and infrastructural projects built by locally supported SOEs with materials purchased from other SOEs (Meyer 2011). China's fixed-asset investments jumped 33 percent in the first five months of 2009, the most in five years (*Bloomberg*, June 22, 2009). Table 1.4 shows the continued rise of fixed-asset investments in China from the 1990s. Figure 1.1 shows that fixed-asset investments grew from about 24 percent of GDP in

Table 1.4. FIXED-ASSET INVESTMENTS IN CHINA, 1990–2010

Period	Fixed-asset investment (RMBbn)	Fixed-asset investment nominal growth (%)	Fixed-asset investment real growth (%)
1990	451.7	2.4	-5.2
1991	559.5	23.9	13.2
1992	808.0	44.4	25.2
1993	1,307.2	61.8	27.8
1994	1,704.2	30.4	18.1
1995	2,001.9	17.5	11.0
1996	2,291.4	14.8	10.4
1997	2,494.1	8.8	7.0
1998	2,840.6	13.9	14.1
1999	2,985.5	5.1	5.5
2000	3,291.8	10.3	9.1
2001	3,721.4	13.0	12.5
2002	4,350.0	16.9	16.7
2003	5,556.7	27.7	25.0
2004	7,047.7	25.8	19.1
2005	8,860.4	25.7	23.7
2006	10,987.0	24.0	22.2
2007	13,732.4	24.8	20.1
2008	17,229.1	25.5	15.2
2009	22,484.6	30.1	33.3
2010E	27,656.0	21.0	16.9

Source: Dragonomics.

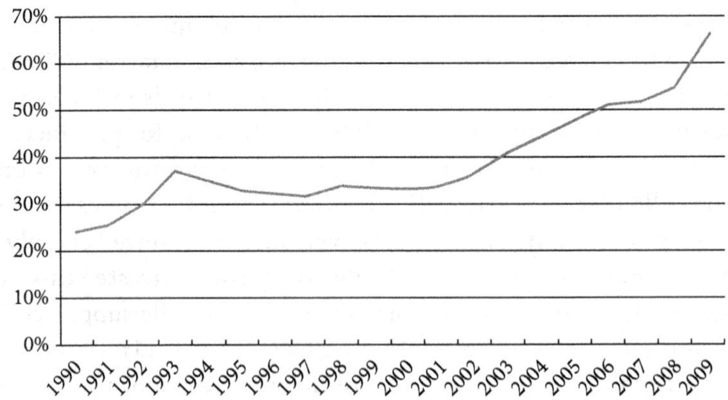

Figure 1.1
China's Fixed-Asset Investment as a Percentage of GDP, 1990–2009
Source: Dragonomics.

1990 to 66 percent of GDP in 2009. The next section provides economic rationales for subsidies.

ECONOMIC RATIONALES FOR SUBSIDIES

Economic rationales do not deal specifically with China but span the use of subsidies for industrial development (including effective corporate strategy), for technology development, and for the pursuit of strategic trade goals. A selective review of some theories as they explain the use of subsidies follows. Economists distinguish between general social expenditures (such as those on infrastructure) and specific subsidies to industries. General expenditures do not, in theory, affect resource allocations among industries or sectors. Conversely, economic theories mostly portray specific subsidies as distortive because they redistribute and reallocate resources according to nonmarket criteria, resulting in economically inefficient allocation of said resources. Except in special circumstances (such as with infant industries), economists have generally ignored the view that subsidies may contribute significantly to aspects of a country's comparative advantage, and not just disadvantage (Trebilcock et al. 1982).

According to classical free-trade theory, in domestic markets, subsidies can reduce either manufacturers' or consumers' costs for products. In either case, the country will produce or sell more of the subsidized products than in efficient markets without the distortive subsidies. Consequently, subsidies divert resources from efficient manufacturers (where the resources yield the highest returns through the market) to subsidized manufacturers (where they yield artificially high returns). The subsidizing country will become poorer by not using resources efficiently and through taxing its efficient producers (thereby increasing their net costs and reducing their market share of goods and investment) to pay for subsidizing inefficient manufacturers (Behboodi 1994).

Economists assume that in countries with representative governments, key interested parties decide on the costs and benefits of subsidies. Consequently, one can wrongly argue that if country A subsidizes production or exports, the resulting economic distortions become principally country A's misfortunes. Importing countries' consumers can enjoy the cheaper goods made possible by country A's subsidies (Hufbauer and Erb 1984) and expanded market share. Indeed, using panel data covering 325 manufacturing industries from 1997 to 2006, Auer and Fischer (2010) demonstrated that imports from nine low-wage countries (including China) resulted in strong downward pressure on prices. When low-wage country A captures a 1 percent share of a US sector, producers' prices in that sector decrease by 2.35 percent (Auer and Fischer 2010). But despite apparent gains to consumers in importing countries, country A's subsidized producers may drive out other countries' producers, capture their markets, and later make good any losses through monopolistic pricing (Dixit 1983). Other countries may also emulate the subsidies, creating spirals of wasteful distortion and overinvestment. In this fashion, subsidies can reduce world economic efficiency and thereby the gains of international exchange to all countries. Economists therefore propose that unbridled and competing national subsidies can undermine world prosperity.

Economic theory provides guidance on using subsidies as one of many efficient means of attaining government-articulated objectives. Economists have analyzed the role of subsidies in building infrastructure, helping struggling or infant industries, promoting the development of new knowledge through research and development, redistributing income, helping poor consumers, and meeting a range of other social-policy objectives.

As WTO debates reveal, governments view some public-policy objectives, such as national security, cultural heritage, and diversity, as crucial to national identities and to transcending narrow economic-maximization objectives. Sectors in which national security considerations figure prominently include subsidies to food and energy production (World Trade Organization 2006). WTO discussions on subsidies as they relate to increasing agricultural production include concepts of "multifunctionality." For example, agricultural production results in commodities such as food and fiber and "noncommodities" that exhibit the characteristics of positive externalities and public goods. Noncommodities include landscape, cultural heritage, biodiversity, rural employment, food security, and animal welfare. WTO debates have centered on the least-costly policy alternatives, including subsidies, to attain multifunctional objectives.

Economic analysis can show how governmental subsidies help when the market allocation of resources appears inconsistent with social objectives. Analysis can also reveal whether subsidies provide the best policy among alternatives. However, when governmental decisions to grant subsidies have little to do with efficiency considerations, as in China, economic analysis based on welfare analysis offers few insights (see World Trade Organization 2006). Subsequent sections review how subsidies affect industrial development, knowledge acquisition, and strategic trade policy, as well as where economic theories fall short.

Industrial Development

Governments may justify subsidies as ways to overcome information barriers and coordination problems. In infant industries and undeveloped capital markets, subsidies may help producers, consumers, and lenders overcome informational barriers to market entry and enhance learning spillovers. Subsidies may aid coordination of interdependent investments corresponding to vertical linkages in production, large-scale economies, and restrictions to trade. Governments have used the prevalence of informational asymmetries in capital markets to justify credit subsidies. However, subsidies can only enhance efficiencies under specific assumptions regarding information asymmetries; under alternative assumptions, interventions become interest-rate taxes. Coordination failures also provide poor economic arguments because all relevant investments will necessarily result in profitable industries. Pure coordination may yield better results. Empirical research on industrial-development policy, including studies of the East Asian miracle from the World Bank, has left room for competing interpretations on the success of subsidies and the other factors that have contributed to successful industrial development.

Porter (1990) has argued that through consistent, long-term investments, governments can shape comparative industrial advantage to become more than a function of classical advantages (deriving from basic human, physical, and capital resources). By judicious and well-planned investments in infrastructure and key economic sectors, governments may enhance natural endowments and develop others. Government policies toward the capital market and education affect factor conditions. Governments can affect buyers' demands through regulation and shape producers' strategies through large-scale purchases. Thereby, governments can improve or detract from national advantage.

Porter's analysis has a distinct role for corporate strategy and rests on the premise that firms, not countries, compete in international markets. According to Porter, internationally successful firms locate each aspect of their activities in the country best suited to advance particular industrial interests. Even if a firm locates its entire production line in one country, it must take advantage of state-industry synergies for international success. Despite short-term benefits for firms, Porter (1990) argued that government subsidies detract from true competitive advantage. Subsidies delay industrial adjustment and innovations. Most subsidies also come with explicit or implicit strings, such as limits on where firms can locate plants or how many jobs they can eliminate, thereby constraining firms' flexibility. Ongoing subsidies dull incentives and create an attitude of dependence. Firms' managers focus attention on renewing subsidies rather than creating true competitive advantage. Subsidized industries propagate their noncompetitiveness as subsidies to one ailing industry encourage others to seek them.

Porter identified tax incentives as better vehicles to upgrade industry than subsidies: tax incentives force firms to undertake projects only when they perceive economic returns. Direct subsidies may also provide more economic benefits when they cover modest fractions of firms' costs and governments use subsidies as signals of appropriate firms' behavior. He proposed that indirect government subsidies for education, infrastructure, and research universities sustain competitive national advantage and that consumer subsidies create fewer distortions than direct payments to firms.

Rather than through higher levels of output, countries may also achieve higher standards of living for their populations through low output in high-wage industries. Some economists have encouraged subsidies for higher-value-added production or for industries that pay higher wages (Katz and Summers 1989). Growth in these products will cause a shift of resources (including workers) from low-wage industries to higher-paying ones. Consequently, economists have argued that the subsidization of high-wage industries, such as the steel or aircraft industries, should result in shifts of resources and expansion of high-paying production that allow low-wage workers to move up and to collect industrial rents.[5] This argument rests on the economic premise that in open economies, the greater the world price of the subsidized, high-wage, value-added product, the greater the marginal welfare gained per dollar of subsidy. Economists such as Porter have contended that industrialized countries cannot compete with Mexico, China, and India for low-wage products and should not aim to do so. A strategically sound industrial policy would then divert subsidies from low-wage industries to more advantageous ones.

Knowledge Acquisition

Some theories suggest that societies and consumers may gain from governmental subsidies to industries where large investments in R&D constitute barriers to entry. Governments may also use R&D subsidies to capture positive spillovers inherent in knowledge creation. The social benefits of new knowledge may exceed the benefits that private investors in R&D may be able to appropriate. R&D may therefore generate positive externalities, and government subsidies may supplement resources devoted to creating knowledge (World Trade Organization 2006).

Rather than provide subsidies, governments can capture the spillover effects of R&D by granting firms temporary monopolies through intellectual-property regimes that encourage knowledge creation. A patent, for example, can guarantee the inventing firm the sole use of its invention over a specific period. This monopoly ensures higher returns on firms' investments in knowledge creation. Once the patent expires, other firms can benefit from the underlying knowledge. In the global economy, intellectual-property regimes need to protect patents across countries to maintain incentives for R&D investments. Lax intellectual-property regimes, such as China's (Haley, Haley, and Tan 2004), may modify or eradicate R&D externalities and the benefits of governmental subsidies. Consequently, the nature of worldwide intellectual property regimes should help shape policies on how firms may benefit from their research, positive externalities for other firms, and the country's optimum allocation of subsidies to private R&D.

Economists have acknowledged that governments may also subsidize firms to secure national advantage and to shift rents in industries characterized by economies of scale and imperfect competition, which may occur in R&D intensive industries: R&D intensity and other entry costs may lead to economies of scale in production processes. One can view subsidies for national champions, such as in China, as policies supporting such rent-shifting programs. Though these subsidies are likely to hurt trading partners' manufacturers in the same or similar industries, they may benefit consumers and importers of the manufactured products as increased competition lowers prices (World Trade Organization 2006). However, economists also highlight the risks of strategic subsidy schemes: the more governments enter into competition, the more likely that capital dissipates in excessive entry, eventually leading to higher than necessary consumer prices, as none of the subsidized firms can produce at efficient scale.

Some economists have argued that R&D subsidies may encourage firms to devote more resources to R&D activities and thereby increase the long-run rate of economic growth (Aghion and Howitt 1992; Romer 1990). Furthermore, because R&D subsidies may promote growth, many other public policies that indirectly affect R&D incentives for firms can also affect long-run growth. However, Segerstrom's (2000) analysis showed that the effects of general R&D subsidies on growth may vary by the static rates of vertical and horizontal innovation. Firms engage in vertical R&D to improve the quality of existing products, and in horizontal R&D to increase the number of industries in the economy (create entirely new products). Segerstrom (2000) assumed that firms that innovate and become industry leaders earn temporary monopoly profits as rewards for their R&D efforts. Additionally, each innovation dimension (horizontal or vertical) has its own degree of static, diminishing returns to R&D expenditure. In the long run, a general R&D subsidy should increase innovation in the dimension in which diminishing returns set in more slowly. To summarize, general R&D subsidies should decrease long-run growth if they promote vertical innovation (horizontal R&D expenditures have greater diminishing returns), and horizontal innovation serves as the stronger engine of growth (R&D difficulty increases rapidly as product quality improves). General R&D subsidies should also decrease long-run growth if they promote horizontal innovation (vertical R&D expenditures have greater diminishing returns), and vertical innovation serves as the stronger engine of growth (R&D difficulty increases slowly as product quality improves). General R&D subsidies increase long-run growth in the opposite cases.

Strategic Trade Policy

The effects of subsidies on trade depend on the size of the subsidizing country and if its production becomes large enough to affect world prices. If production remains small, quantities in the market will change, but not prices. In large countries, both import-substituting and export-promoting subsidies will result in price declines. Many economists view subsidies for export promotion as preferable to those for import substitution because countries may choose those industries in which they have comparative advantages; and as many countries account for subsidies in national budgets, the costs of subsidies may be more transparent than those of tariffs, a generally preferable and more focused policy measure.

Brander and Spencer (1985) presented a theoretical analysis based on imperfect competition to demonstrate that export subsidies benefit subsidizing countries. Subsidies provide advantages to countries to capture large shares of the production of profit-earning, imperfectly competitive industries. Export subsidies thereby allow governments to carry out profit-shifting policies of industrial development. Brander and Spencer argued that in a world of imperfect information and imperfect governments, national motives for subsidies may open the door for various kinds of socially wasteful rent-seeking, jointly suboptimal for all producing nations. However, countries perceive themselves as competing for profitable international markets. In this global world, the credibility of governmental support for industries, and specifically export subsidies, can confer strategic advantages on domestic firms. In particular subsidies can advantageously position domestic firms in noncooperative rivalries with other firms and allow them to expand their market shares. The terms of trade will move against the subsidizing country, but as price still exceeds the marginal resource cost of exports, the resulting expansion of exports can raise domestic welfare. Consequently, although producing countries have cooperative incentives to agree not to use export subsidies, they also have incentives to cheat on any resulting agreements, suggesting that international regulations that attempt to discourage subsidization, such as the General Agreement on Tariffs and Trade (GATT) or WTO, are likely to require regular reinforcement and scrutiny to survive.

Political Limits of Economic Rationales

Drawing primarily on studies of Western democracies, researchers have argued that governments rarely survey all appropriate policy instruments before relying on subsidies. Rather, subsidies emerge through political processes in which politicians and administrators act according to their own preferences and within constraints sets by lobbyists and labor groups (Spencer 1988). Political processes result in suboptimal economic systems in which individuals and groups further their own economic interests. Political actors appear as entrepreneurs selling subsidization policies for votes (Reynolds 1993), and firms appear as rent-seekers. Partisan political actions cause allocative inefficiencies and ethical problems, by encouraging firms to engage in rent-seeking or by reallocating tax revenues to small organized groups that aim to appropriate economic rents. Subsidies comprise wealth transfers from poorly organized social elements who cannot resist demands to well-organized groups pressing for them. Large enterprises, politically strategic regions, powerful industrial organizations, trade unions, or other highly concentrated interests benefit from subsidies, and small or newly established enterprises, consumers, or nonunionized wage-laborers pay for them. Firms' rent-seeking behaviors include lobbying, efforts to obtain valuable import licenses or quotas, donations to political parties, the promise of jobs and perquisites to policymakers, blackmail and bribery, and eventually increased corruption.

Subsidies comprise just one part of the complex socioeconomic structure of a country. The economic metaphors of free trade, comparative advantage, and efficient allocation of resources involve more than just deregulation of markets and removal of trade barriers. Without attention to the national political contexts in which these decisions have occurred, these economic metaphors also appear insufficient to capture the vast changes that have ensued in global markets. Hudec (1990) observed that the market produces a better allocation of resources only if one assumes that resource allocation should proceed according to the desires of the consumers who make up market demand. However, in market economies, and especially in nonmarket economies such as China (U. C. V. Haley 2007), a multitude of actors make allocative and distributive decisions, ostensibly for economic, but probably also for political, moral, or social reasons. Which externalities they want to capture, the nature of their ideal markets, which social goods they want to protect or advance, and the types of industrial economies they want to foster comprise value choices that policymakers make through unique sociopolitical, and not necessarily economic or consumer-driven, channels. The next section views subsidies through the lens of state capitalism.

SOCIOPOLITICAL RATIONALES FOR CHINESE SUBSIDIES

Models in economics form metaphors and, far from value-free, reflect social assumptions (see Ziliak 2011). Using the dominant metaphor of market economics, Adam Smith's (1776) invisible hand (of self-regulating markets), many theorists have argued that free trade between rational, self-interested people and countries leads to greater wealth; others have concluded that collective attempts such as those by the Chinese government to steer economic outcomes through subsidies will naturally backfire because they benefit fewer individuals. Yet Chinese economic policies have historical precedents not in free-market but in Confucian metaphors, where individual utility subsumes in harmonious fashion to administrative utility (see Haley, Haley, and Tan 2004). Theories of market transition, multiorganizational states, and state as shareholder shed light on the Chinese context for policy decisions on subsidies, with implications for Chinese and global welfare.

Market Transition Theory

Market Transition Theory owes its formal exposition to Victor Nee. Examining socialist economies that were opening up in the 1980s, especially China, Nee (1989) argued that shifts from planned to market economies change social stratification and erode the administrative elites' relative powers. According to Nee (1989, 663), "The transition from redistributive to market coordination shifts sources of power and privilege to favor direct producers (i.e., entrepreneurs) relative to redistributors (i.e., cadres)." Nee identified three processes that transform socialist economies: market power, market incentives, and market opportunity. He assumed that markets favor human over political capital and direct production over redistribution. Using data from a 1985 survey in Fujian, Nee (1989, 1996) presented a clear theory on the role of markets and individual-level incentives in social transformations and, implicitly, on the trajectory of China's economic reforms: Markets would diminish the state's power, and individual freedom in market exchanges would fundamentally change China. He argued that the economic pursuits of power and plenty would drive economic reforms in China. As the Chinese government undertook reforms, Chinese and Western capitalist development would converge: markets would shape human capital, governmental position, and geographic development in both sets of societies. Nee also implied that individual-level economic indicators, such as household income, and returns to education could measure the degree of marketization in China (Guthrie 2000).

Market Transition Theory assumes that the Chinese state has aimed at creating a market economy based on private ownership, but political obstacles have blocked governmental reforms and implicitly have spawned production subsidies. The theorists have assumed that for short-term political expediency, Chinese policymakers settled for next-best alternatives to achieve a market economy, including semiprivatizing SOEs, subsidizing some industries, introducing foreign competition, and encouraging entrepreneurship. In these perspectives, subsidies serve as stopgap approaches to grease and to realign the wheels of burgeoning Chinese free-market capitalism. Yet facts belie these primarily Western assumptions: the power of the state is expanding in China. Figure 1.2 shows that since 1996, the ratio of private to government consumption has been falling rather than rising, as free-market theories would have us believe should happen in overtly successful economies. Trade has enabled the Chinese government to increase its share of both economic consumption and production. In May 2010, in the *Financial Times* annual ranking of the Global 500, a Chinese SOE, PetroChina, overtook Exxon Mobil as the world's most valuable company by market capitalization. Other Chinese companies in the top 15 included the state-run banks Industrial and Commercial Bank of China (ICBC) and China Construction Bank, and China Mobile (officially headquartered in Hong Kong).

Other data also belie Nee's predictions. For example, Huang (2008) convincingly argued against a gradualist trajectory of Chinese economic

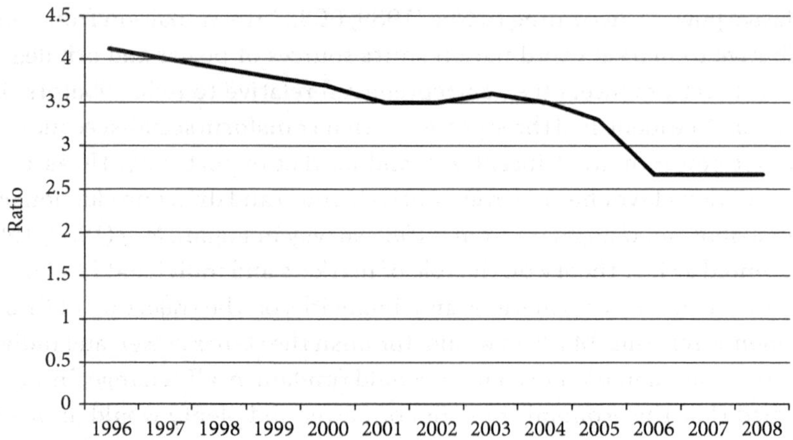

Figure 1.2
Ratio of Private to Government Consumption in China, 1996–2008
Source: Economist Intelligence Unit; OECD.

transformations that should have begun with small steps in the 1980s and then accelerated in the 1990s. Through analysis of Chinese government documents in town and village enterprises (TVEs), Huang (2008) showed that in the 1980s, bottom-up entrepreneurship and liberalization occurred on many fronts in China. However, in the 1990s, a substantial reversal of reforms took place. China's growth did not derive from conventional growth mechanisms, including private ownership, property rights, financial liberalization, and reforms of political institutions. In the 1990s, China reversed many highly productive rural experiments and policies and centralized rural administrative management. Chinese policymakers poured investment and credit into cities and heavily taxed rural sectors to finance state-led urban growth. In the 1990s, policy change drew on technocratic industrial policy with a heavy urban bias. Credit constraints on rural entrepreneurship, including private TVEs, rose substantially. Individual-level indicators corroborate the growth of administrative and urban elites. As Huang (2008) argued, in the 1990s, rural household income grew half as much as in the 1980s, and rural business income fell precipitously. Simultaneously, the size of government, measured as head counts of officials and the value of fixed assets they controlled, expanded enormously.

Huang (2008) listed several welfare implications from the policy reversals in the 1990s. Although GDP grew rapidly during both the 1980s and 1990s, household income grew much faster in the 1980s. The share of labor income to GDP rose in the 1980s but declined in the 1990s. Total factor productivity growth since the late 1990s either slowed down from the 1980s or collapsed. The majority of China's poverty reduction occurred during the entrepreneurial era (1980–1988) rather than during the state-led era (1989–2002). In the 1990s, income disparities worsened substantially and have continued to worsen. Indeed, in 2011, income inequality in China ranked as the highest in the world, with the Gini index jumping from .28 in the mid-1980s to .4 twenty years later (*Economist* 2011).[6] In the 1990s, land grabs and political corruption greatly increased. Additionally, despite vaunted increases in R&D, between 2000 and 2005 the number of illiterate Chinese adults increased by 30 million, reversing decades of progress in basic education (Huang 2008).

The Multiorganizational Chinese State

Rather than a unified political entity, the Chinese state consists of decentralized organizational sets that often pursue their own interests (Fligstein 1996; Shih 2008). Provinces in China have always enjoyed strong traditions of autonomy from the central government (Haley, Haley, and Tan 2004). In this context, Nee (1998) elaborated that formal (contracts, property rights, laws) and informal (norms, networks) constraints combine to shape organizational and economic environments in China. When the center's formal rules contradict powerful provincial preferences, a decoupling occurs of informal norms and practical activities from the formal rules. This decoupling "enables organizations to maintain standardized, legitimating, formal structures, while their activities vary in response to practical considerations ... [and] day-to-day business" (Nee 1998, 88).

Walder (1992) provided some of the institutional context for Chinese subsidies. He highlighted that to understand China's economic transformation, one had to understand also the hidden and conflicting budgetary processes that straddled central and local governments. Local governments and the firms they controlled had differing abilities to extract revenues from the center. The further from the central government a firm lay, the more power and control local governmental jurisdictions had over revenue extraction and firm management. Local officials ran their jurisdictions as they would industrial firms—local officials as industrial managers, governmental jurisdictions as industrial firms. As Walder (1992, 528–29) explained, "China's national budget is a nested hierarchy of independent budgets—each government unit exercises property rights over firms under their financial jurisdiction.... This bureaucratic economy, far from being a monolith, is composed of thousands of government jurisdictions of varying sizes, each of which seeks to expand its revenues by capturing investment, subsidies, and grants."

As owners of enterprises, Chinese local and central governments also pursue objectives other than profitability (Kornai 1990; 1992); these objectives in turn influence choice of subsidies as policy instruments. Local and central governments' objectives include supplying scarce inputs for other enterprises, maintaining full employment, funding pensions, and providing medical insurance, housing, and social services. Government officials' nonfinancial objectives conflict with their interests in firms' strong financial performance. Governmental abilities to redistribute funds from profitable enterprises to subsidize those that are unprofitable also bolster their nonfinancial objectives (Walder 1995). Shirk (1993) observed that provincial governments often redistribute stronger firms' retained profits and governmental revenues to bolster weaker firms through "scientific research subsidies," or *keyen butie*; "reserve funds," or *jidong jijin*; and other subsidies—as well as use these funds for personal bonuses.

The governments' nonfinancial interests in firms, and the firms' dependence on governments for bailouts and subsidies, create mutual dependence. Walder (1995) referred to this situation as one of bilateral monopoly or extreme asset specificity. Suboptimal regimes of bargaining arise with soft budget constraints and incentives for firms to hoard and to overinvest. The governments' dependence upon firms for output, employment, and social welfare constrains their abilities to discipline firms or to shut them down. Firms' managers also conceal resources in their constant bargaining over more resources and more favorable financial terms. Simultaneously, governments faced with large numbers of firms to monitor encounter informational problems.

Walder (1995) concluded that in China, physical-output indicators did not provide information on the efficiency of firms, and financial indicators would prove inaccurate unless prices reflected market realities. Local bureaucracies have complicated monitoring by creating numerous competing principals that further impede or distort the flow of information back to the central government. Principals for SOEs include bureaus of taxation, finance, labor, and prices, as well as industrial bureaus. Each of these bureaus makes slightly different demands, many counter to the demand for strong financial performance, and contributes a layer or two of bureaucracy. Some bureaus, especially industrial bureaus, collude with firms to conceal slack resources and work at cross-purposes with other bureaus that monitor financial performance (Walder 1992). Under these relatively invariant Chinese institutional conditions, moves toward market mechanisms and increased efficiencies will backfire without divesting the state of ownership (Kornai 1992).

Case studies confirm that provincial governments deploy massive subsidies to support favored business groups and further provincial rather than central objectives or efficiencies. For example, Xu and Yeh (2005) observed that in Guangzhou city, soft budget constraints allowed the municipal government to undertake investments without conforming to market logic or considering profits and costs. Liu (2008) observed similar patterns with the Shandong government. In July 1993, Shandong published "opinions on accelerating development of local business groups" and quickly selected 136 large groups for direct supervision. In 1996, Shandong identified eight groups as "provincial champions" and aimed to transform them into conglomerates similar to their chosen exemplar, South Korea's Samsung. For the provincial champions and other privileged businesses, the Shandong government constructed individual business plans, transferred old loans into state shares, upgraded enterprises with imported technology, supplied water, electricity, land, and transportation at discounted rates, and extended financial support as preferential tax rates, profit-retention schemes, and low-interest loans. For example, the Shandong government forgave merged enterprises' loan interest when those enterprises lost money within three continuous years and failed to pay loans for two years. With the "bank and enterprise hand in hand" policy, Shandong gave big groups priority access to bank loans and financial services. These subsidies created inefficient SOEs but also provincial champions, some of which became national leaders, like the Haier Group and the Qingdao Brewery Group.

The State as Paramount Shareholder

As indicated in the previous section, in state capitalism, the state, with its myriad interests, plays the leading role in national economic development. In China, state interests equate to those of the Communist Party of China (CPC) which has ruled China since 1949. The CPC forms the center of the Chinese state, military, and media, and the Chinese constitution guarantees its powers (McGregor 2010). The CPC's paramount interests have a big hand in shaping the policy environments around subsidies. In 2004, Hu Jintao succeeded Jiang Zemin as top leader of the fourth generation of leadership of the CPC, and therefore paramount leader of China. In 2003, he had assumed the lesser role of president. In China, political factors matter at least as much as, and often more than, economic factors for firms' and markets' performance and therefore for the dispensation of subsidies (Haley, Haley, and Tan 2004).

From 2003 to 2012, Premier Wen Jiabao chaired China's State Council, the country's main administrative authority and the nerve center of China's state capitalism. The State Council includes the heads of all central ministries and important bureaucracies, including the National Development and Reform Commission (NDRC), which guides macroeconomic planning, intervenes in markets, sets prices for many products, and influences SOEs. In a CNN interview, Wen (2008) elaborated on the role of the Chinese state in markets: "The complete formulation of our economic policy is to give full play to the basic role of market forces in allocating resources under the macroeconomic guidance and regulation of the government. We have one important piece of experience of the past 30 years, that is to ensure that both the visible hand and invisible hand are given full play in regulating the market forces." Chinese policymakers have built an economic system to ensure that market forces serve primarily the CPC's development goals.

Bremmer (2010) has attributed the rise of Chinese state capitalism to the fall of the Soviet empire in 1991. He has argued that the CPC recognized that if it failed to generate prosperity for the Chinese people, it would similarly lose its control. To protect their monopoly on political power, the CPC's leaders endeavored to ensure that the state controlled as large a share as possible of the wealth that Chinese markets generate. Haley, Haley, and Tan (2004) have conversely argued that the Chinese never significantly changed their historical style of operation. Indeed, Chinese Communism approximated or emulated Soviet Communism far less than it did imperial administrative dynasties. A continuity of Chinese administration and management styles, including administrative and economic control, has existed from imperial through Maoist and modern times. This continuity emerged in the party manifesto issued after the fall of the Soviet empire, which stated, "The party must grasp not only the gun, but the asset economy as well." The managing of Chinese SOEs and business environments also reflects this continuity. Table 1.5 compares imperial and Maoist bureaucracies as they affected rent collection and center-province relations.

In the early 1990s, Chinese policymakers carefully studied Korean and Japanese development of large-scale indigenous firms that could compete in global markets; for Beijing, the lessons supported the subsidization of strategic industries. Policy discussions in Beijing referenced the nurturing role of the state in Korea and Japan (Thun 1994). As Vice Premier Wu Banguo stated in 1998: "In reality, international economic confrontations

Table 1.5. COMPARING IMPERIAL AND MAOIST BUREAUCRACIES

Imperial bureaucracy	Maoist bureaucracy
Small policymaking core in capital	Small policymaking core in capital
Decentralized implementation by trained/semitrained local elite—the scholarly/gentry class	Decentralized implementation by trained/semitrained local elite—the local Communist cadres
Local bureaucracies beholden to the rulers, not to the ruled—imperial stated goals must be attained or surpassed	Local bureaucracies beholden to the rulers, not to the ruled—central government's stated goals must be attained or surpassed
Strong provincial governments following the center's lead—tended to go their own way when center was weak	Strong provincial governments following the center's lead—tended to go their own way when center was weak
Minimum standards of taxation contributed to center and set by center; local gentry set actual taxes collected from populace	Minimum standards of taxation collected for center and set by center; local cadres set actual taxes forwarded to center in names of cadres
Effect: Excessive taxes collected to amass personal wealth for local elites and enhance social standing and power	**Effect:** Excessive rents collected at provincial levels to impress superiors with performance and enhance personal political position and power

Source: Compiled from Haley, Haley, and Tan 2004.

show that if a country has large companies or groups it will be assured of maintaining a certain market share and a position in the international economic order. America, for example, relies on General Motors, Boeing, Dupont and a batch of other multinational companies. Japan relies on six large enterprise groups and Korea relies on ten commercial groupings. In the same way now and in the next century our nation's position in the international economic order will be to a large extent determined by the position of our nation's large enterprises and groups" (cited in Nolan 2001, 17). Korean policymakers joined symposiums in Beijing to explain how the Korean government promoted the development of large firms (see Ministry of Machinery 1994, 11). Chinese policymakers concluded that by supporting targeted firms with low-interest loans and subsidies, preferential taxation, and exemptions from tariffs on imported equipment, they could advance the state's interests in the new economic order (Thun 2004).

Subsidies also helped when the Western financial crisis and global recession deprived China of many major customers, thereby threatening China's political stability (Bremmer 2010). In November 2008, Beijing used a $586 billion stimulus package to subsidize the export sector's survival, to prevent factory closings, and to minimize the risk of unemployed migrant workers generating civil unrest (European Chamber 2009; Komesaroff 2009). In 2009, China's central government used an additional $19 billion to subsidize exports and factories. Despite diplomatic pressure from the United States (Krugman 2010), the Chinese government has also depressed the value of China's currency to spur exports and to increase foreign reserves that Beijing has used to make acquisitions around the world. Management consulting firm Accenture estimated that from January 2008 to June 2010, China's overseas acquisitions in America, Canada, Europe, and developing countries in Asia, Africa, and South America totaled over $91.4 billion. Many of these acquisitions have attempted to secure long-term subsidized supplies of oil, gas, metals, minerals, and other commodities that China needs to continue economic expansion, to generate prosperity at home, and to safeguard the CPC's political future. Table 1.6 shows the rise of China's foreign-exchange reserves from $11.1 billion in 1990 to $2.8 trillion in 2010.

SOEs serve as the primary vehicles for Chinese state capitalism. According to China's Ministry of Finance, in 2008 SOEs' total assets approximated $6 trillion, equal to 133 percent of annual economic output that year. Beijing sets non-profit-oriented goals for the SOEs to accomplish and thereby uses SOEs to further its industrial policies. Formed in 2003, SASAC manages the CPC's efforts to control China's SOEs while increasing the SOEs' economic returns and maintaining the government's political returns (G. T. Haley 2007). Through SASAC, the state's economic and political goals become operational. A total of 141 SOEs under SASAC made net profits of $101.96 billion in 2008 with $613 billion in revenues in the first five months of 2009 (*China Daily*, June 29, 2009). However, as George Haley (2007) testified before the US-China Economic and Security Review Commission (USCC), Chinese expectations of acceptable profitability do not necessarily correspond to Western expectations. Chinese policymakers view firms' bottom lines differently than do Westerners: technology acquisition provides a key goal in Chinese firms' operations, even at the expense of surrendering profitability.[7] Chinese policymakers also view successful use of SOEs as instruments to obtain foreign-policy goals as part of the SOEs' profits. Historically, any Chinese SOE, especially a major one, could rely on substantial government subsidies and bailouts whenever it encountered losses.

To handle information streams emanating from the state's multiple bureaucracies, the Fifteenth CPC Congress formulated the "grasping the large, and letting the small go" policy (G. T. Haley 2007). Premier Zhu

Table 1.6. GROWTH OF CHINA'S FOREIGN-EXCHANGE RESERVES, 1990–2010

Period	Foreign exchange reserves (US$bn)	Additions to foreign exchange reserves (US$bn)[a]	Growth
1990	11.1	n.a.	
1991	21.7	10.6	95.5%
1992	19.4	-2.3	-10.6%
1993	21.2	1.8	9.3%
1994	51.6	30.4	143.4%
1995	73.6	22.0	42.6%
1996	105.0	31.4	42.7%
1997	139.9	34.9	33.2%
1998	145.0	5.1	3.6%
1999	154.7	9.7	6.7%
2000	165.6	10.9	7.0%
2001	212.2	46.6	28.1%
2002	286.4	74.2	35.0%
2003	403.3	161.9[a]	40.8%
2004	609.9	206.7	51.2%
2005	818.9	208.9	34.3%
2006	1066.3	247.5	30.2%
2007	1528.2	461.9	43.3%
2008	1946.0	417.8	27.3%
2009	2399.2	453.2	23.3%
2010	2847.3	448.1	18.7%

Source: Dragonomics.

[a] Additions to foreign-exchange reserves are adjusted to account for $45 billion transferred to Bank of China and China Construction Bank on December 31, 2003.

Rongji had proposed the slogan as pragmatic recognition that in the more complex world that China had entered, the state could not control "the small" details and should focus on controlling the most important details, that is, "the large." SOEs serve as the primary agencies for state control of industrial development in China. During the financial crisis beginning in 2008, massive governmental stimulus spending strongly favored SOEs through a government policy known as *guo jin min tui*, or "the state advances, the private sector retreats." In the first half of 2009, small and medium-sized enterprises (SMEs) received only 8.5 percent of the $1.1 trillion of Chinese government loans; yet SMEs created and supported

70 percent of urban jobs in China (*China Daily*, January 20, 2009). In 2010, many SOEs with subsidized balance sheets were buying smaller private-sector competitors and extending the reach of the state.

In the hierarchy of SOEs, pillar or key industries serve as China's national champions, with access to priority funding, including subsidies. China chooses pillar industries on the following criteria (G. T. Haley, 2009): (1) defense, (2) job creation, (3) technology acquisition, and (4) competitive advantage. Several industries fall under more than one criterion. Fifteen industries constitute pillar industries for China, as promulgated in China's Tenth and Eleventh Five-Year Plans: (1) aerospace, (2) autos and auto parts, (3) banking and insurance, (4) biotechnology, (5) computer chip design and manufacture, (6) computing and computer hardware, (7) information technology, (8) iron and steel, (9) logistics, shipping, and storage, (10) machinery and mechanical equipment, (11) oil and petrochemicals, (12) software, (13) telecommunications and telecom equipment, (14) utilities and power equipment, and (15) wholesaling and retailing. Individual provinces also have their own SASACs and may anoint their own pillar industries for provincial development from the central list; as indicated in the previous section, the provinces often support their local champions from extrabudgetary sources of revenue that they do not share or divulge to the central government. Consequently, many firms in pillar industries receive subsidies from both central and provincial sources.

In October 2010, the CPC Central Committee's Proposal for Formulating the Twelfth Five-Year Program for China's Economic and Social Development (2011–2015), stated that over the next five years, Beijing planned to nurture an additional seven new strategic industries and to develop these into pillar industries. The industries included (1) new-generation information technology, (2) energy-saving and environment protection, (3) new energy, (4) biology, (5) high-end equipment manufacturing, (6) new materials, and (7) new-energy cars. The proposal indicated that to develop these industries, Beijing would increase available R&D funds; implement fiscal, tax, and financial policies to support major state-level science and technology projects; promote indigenous innovation to improve industry core competitiveness and economic efficiency; and "adjust" tax and pricing systems for land, water, and electricity so that their share of GDP would rise from less than 2 percent in 2011 to 8 percent in 2015.

Cheap loans from state-controlled banks and other subsidies have contributed not just to the extraordinary rise in fixed-asset investments outlined in table 1.4, but also to enormous excess capacity in China. From 2003 to 2008, the overall ratio of China's gross industrial output almost doubled to 160 percent of GDP, while the relative size of heavy industrial production in the economy nearly tripled (Komesaroff 2009). As has become apparent in solar-panel production, China exported its excess production, depressing international prices and driving down global industrial efficiencies (Haley and Haley 2012). National Bureau of Statistics data show that in 2009, China's steel industry, already the world's largest, had the capacity to produce 660 million tons per year, with excess capacity of 22 percent; yet another 70 million tons of capacity was under construction. True excess capacity in this industry appears even higher, as recent central government audits have identified many small, unapproved mills with a combined capacity of 30 million tons. Thus by the end of 2010, China likely had steel capacity of around 760 million tons—far in excess of annual steel demand, which is now running at about 574 million tons. China's surplus capacity of almost 200 million tons looms larger than total output from Japan, the world's second-largest producer (Komesaroff 2009). Similarly, China is the world's largest producer of polysilicon for solar panels, but has excess capacity of over 80 percent in this industry. As the industrial case studies in this book highlight, overcapacity extends across the board in China. Besides steel, polysilicon, and solar panels, China is also the world's largest producer of aluminum, autos, cement, plate glass, coal, chemicals, wind power equipment, ships, crushed soybeans, and fertilizer; according to the State Council, all these industries also suffer from great overcapacity (Komesaroff 2009).

Researchers have isolated underpriced distorted factor inputs, predominantly cheap capital that subsidizes production and investment, as a primary cause for China's extraordinary growth and excess capacity (Huang and Wang 2010). Excess capacity in Chinese heavy industry has contributed to global economic imbalances. Heavy industrial exports accounted for 39 percent of China's total exports in 2008, up from 29 percent in 2002. As a European Chamber (2009) report described, China's growth model requires that external demand from the European Union (EU) and the United States continue to absorb the overcapacity it produces. Despite the impact of the financial crisis on these major global consumers, investments in excess capacity continue unabated in China.

Theories of subsidies drawing on international trade and international law fail to explain fully the modern economic rise of China. Developed in times when state capitalism did not constitute a major player in the global economy, they provide skeletal, sometimes misleading guidance on corporate or governmental policies. During the thirteenth century, professors at the University of Paris decided to investigate if oil would congeal if left out overnight. For them, research meant searching through Aristotle's writings. However, as Aristotle had never addressed the issue, they declared the question unanswerable (Starbuck 2006). Rather than declaring China's hidden advantage as unanswerable and somewhat magical, we propose viewing the issue through the prism of state capitalism and subsidies. In chapter 2, we review some empirical evidence on the effects of subsidies and delineate the methodology in our industry studies.

NOTES

1. In August 2011, Evergreen Solar filed for bankruptcy in the United States, stating that it could not compete with Chinese competitors without reorganization.
2. According to Mercom, the top five loan subsidies from China Development Bank to Chinese solar companies included those to LDK Solar (credit $8.9 billion), Suntech (loan $7.3 billion), Yingli Green Energy Holdings (loan $8.3 billion), JA Solar Holdings (loan $4.4 billion), and Trina Solar (loan $4.4 billion).
3. In economics, comparative advantage results from differing endowments of the factors of production (capital, land, labor) entrepreneurial skills, power, technology, etc. The concept owes its origins to David Ricardo (1772–1823) and his work on comparative costs. For trade, comparative advantage implies that a country should specialize in producing and exporting only those goods and services that it can produce more efficiently (at lower opportunity costs) than other goods and services (which it should import). Ergo, free trade benefits all countries, because each can gain (the gains from trade) if it specializes according to its comparative advantage.
4. For example, according to statistics from Nomura International, the minimum monthly wage in Beijing rose from about RMB 200 in 1994 to RMB 1,200 in 2011.
5. Economic rent refers to excess distribution to any factor in a production process above the amount required to draw the factor into the process or to sustain the current use of the factor.
6. The Gini index is the most common measure of inequality. A score of 0 means perfect equality and everyone earns the same. A score of 1 means that one person gets everything. The United States has the second-most unequal society, with a Gini index that rose from 0.34 in the 1980s to 0.38 in the mid-2000s.
7. Huang (2003) also emphasized that SOEs' primary objectives include qualifying for state allocation of foreign exchange to finance technology acquisition.

CHAPTER 2
Measuring Subsidies to Chinese Industry

This book draws on four sequential industry studies conducted between 2007 and 2011 to identify the growth of subsidies to Chinese manufacturing over time: steel (covering the period 2000 to 2007), glass (2004 to 2008), paper (2002 to 2009) and auto parts (2001 to 2011). In all these industries, China has moved from a net importer to one of the largest, if not the largest, exporters in the world. In all these capital-intensive industries, labor comprised a small part, between 2 and 7 percent, of total costs. In these fragmented industries, the vast majority of firms enjoyed no economies of scale or scope. Although the time periods and some of the industry-specific variables vary because of the availability of data, all studies build on common assumptions and use some common variables. This chapter defines subsidies, highlights previous empirical research that identified subsidies in China, indicates problems with measurement and data, and covers the rationales for the variables and methodologies we used.

SUBSIDIES AND CHINESE POLICY

In 1947, the GATT's original drafters paid little heed to the trade issues associated with subsidies; in 1995, the GATT was subsumed by the WTO, which has reflected the perceived need to discipline subsidies in an increasingly integrated world. For instance, the GATT, including the Tokyo Round Subsidies Code resulting from negotiations in 1979, contained no definition of the term "subsidy." However, the WTO's Agreement on Subsidies and Countervailing Measures (SCM) formally identified subsidies for the first time as unrequited transfers from governments to enterprises, including direct payments, tax concessions, contingent liabilities, and the purchase and provision of goods and services (World Trade Organization 2006). Part I of the SCM agreement classified a "subsidy" as a "financial contribution by a government," in the form of (1) a direct transfer of funds, (2) a decision to forgo revenue that is "otherwise due," (3) the provision of goods and services (except general infrastructure), or (4) an income or price support scheme, if the financial contribution confers a "benefit."[1] The requirement that subsidies confer benefits underscores that not all government programs qualify as subsidies: if a government provides goods and services at market prices, for example, no benefit arises and thus no subsidy exists. This definition also excludes regulatory measures or other policies, such as border protection, without transfers of government resources (Sykes 2005). China has defined subsidies more narrowly as unrequited direct payments from governments to enterprises, including the returning of value-added tax (VAT) (Girma et al. 2007). We use the broader WTO definition.

Since January 1, 2000, the SCM has classified subsidies into two categories, prohibited (irrefutably presumed to distort trade) and actionable (permitted, but potentially subject to action). Actionable subsidies could be subject to trading partners' remedial actions (including countervailing duties or CVDs) if they could demonstrate that these subsidies led to adverse trade effects—namely serious prejudice, injury to the industry of an importing member, or nullification or impairment of benefits. As with GATT, the SCM prohibits two types of subsidies: (1) export subsidies and (2) local-content or import-substitution subsidies. Export subsidies are contingent, in law or in fact, whether solely or as one of several conditions, on export performance. Local-content subsidies are contingent, whether solely or as one of several other conditions, upon the use of domestic over imported goods.

In her testimony before the US-China Economic and Security Review Commission, Usha Haley (2006) identified industrial subsidies in China as deriving from governmental dominance of the economy and from various factors including the central, provincial, and municipal governments' strategic goals and patronage. The subsidies include direct and indirect components that affect firms' top and bottom lines and exports. State subsidies flow into state-owned enterprises (SOEs), although some well-connected private firms also benefit from indirect subsidies. Subsidies exist in all industries that the Chinese state and provincial governments consider economically or militarily strategic.

In its Protocol of Accession to the WTO, China agreed to eliminate subsidies to loss-making SOEs by 2000. Nonetheless, these subsidies have continued. The WTO requires annual notification from members on subsidies they maintain and encourages additional, needed information on subsidies. The Chinese government has not acknowledged the presence of any subsidies to domestic producers in its declaration to the WTO. On April 13, 2006, China, a WTO member since 2001, submitted an overdue subsidies notification to the WTO identifying 78 subsidy programs from 2001 to 2004. The WTO specifies that members should provide sufficient information "to enable other members to evaluate the trade effects and to understand the operation of notified subsidy programs." China's report stated that several central government ministries and agencies distributed and monitored subsidies, and extensive legislation in China supported the subsidies. Yet no statistical data existed in China to assess the trade effects of any subsidy or even the total annual amounts budgeted to these subsidies. Foreign-invested enterprises (FIEs) / foreign equity joint ventures and agriculture / animal husbandry appeared as the primary beneficiaries in China's notification. China's notification concentrated on subsidies to FIEs to invest in key strategic Chinese sectors and ignored most subsidies that reduce local producers' operating and production costs vis-à-vis foreign producers.[2] The notification also focused only on subsidy programs supported by the central government (rather than from provincial and municipal governments) and ignored commercial banks' lending policies or other financial preferences for SOEs and favored producers.

From public records, researchers have found that SOEs appear highly subsidized with implications for production, exports, and social stability. The Chinese central and provincial governments routinely subsidized SOEs before China joined the WTO. For example, Brandt and Zhu (2000) found that by 1993, the Chinese government annually transferred more than 3 percent of GNP to SOEs to support their wage payments, capital expenditures, and other operating costs exclusive of any tax or interest liabilities. According to Liu (2001), subsidies to SOEs as a percentage of GDP were 6.5 percent in 1992, 5.3 percent in 1993, and averaged 4.9 percent between 1990 and 1994. However, these researchers excluded from their estimates bank loans at preferential rates, which currently serve as a major subsidy to SOEs. Girma et al. (2009) found that between 1995 and 2005, subsidies totaled $310.1 billion, with about $151.1 billion directed at SOEs, of which 95 percent were making losses. The Chinese government subsidized SOEs to dampen unemployment rates and to prevent social riots that could arise from SOEs' bankruptcies (Luo and Golembiewski 1996). Subsidies to SOEs accounted for more than one-third of the SOEs' total profits between 1998 and 2004. Lin and Jiang (2011) noted that Chinese governments often kept subsidies "off-budget," for political reasons. Indeed, vested interests often motivated financial subsidies, which generally compromised the accurate modeling of any subsidy framework.

Policies regarding subsidies become difficult to unravel as the Chinese state encompasses central and local governments, with competing and often conflicting agendas, and different bureaucratic and political factions at the national level. Subsidies and the policies behind them reflect this fragmentation and conflict. Thousands of warring units that cohabit under the Chinese state's umbrella control the SOEs. Consequently, SOEs enjoy direct subsidies stemming from state directives and elicit varying degrees of support. Generally, despite stated policies, outsiders cannot ascertain the true policies that underlie subsidies. A secretive and authoritarian organization with unclear aims, closed to scrutiny and debate, controls the Chinese state.

More effectively placed subsidies appear in the SOEs that the Beijing central government has classified as global champions. However, recent examples illustrate their complexity. CNOOC is a Hong Kong–listed firm 70 percent owned by an unlisted parent company, all of whose shares are owned by the central government agency, SASAC. Beijing has helped CNOOC to acquire contracts to control foreign-energy reserves, and the company heavily relies on subsidized financing from SASAC. Local governments control other SOEs. These include white goods maker Haier (owned by the Qingdao city government) and the municipally owned Shanghai and Nanjing car companies. These companies also receive subsidies in line with Beijing's stated goals of creating state-owned multinationals and retaining domestic control over key sectors, such as autos. The demands of both the central government, which sets industry policy, and their local government overlords, whose interests may conflict with Beijing's industrial-policy goals, shape the subsidies the SOEs receive, as well as the SOEs' evolution, strategies, and policies. Huawei, a maker of telecom-network equipment, illustrates a third level of policies and subsidies. Huawei is ostensibly privately owned, although many of its shares are owned by the local state-telecom authorities to whom it has sold equipment. It enjoys a $10 billion low-interest credit line from the China Development Bank, whose mission includes making concessional loans in support of the state's policy goals. Huawei also has strong ties to China's military.

MAJOR FORMS OF CHINESE SUBSIDIES

Anecdotal evidence and some research indicate that subsidies to Chinese industry probably exist in every knowable form. This chapter identifies major and measurable forms of subsidies, including loans, subsidies to energy, and subsidies to key inputs and to technology.

Free or Low-Cost Loans

The government exercises a strong grip on banks, stock markets, and bond issuance and these translate to the ability to make grandiose loans. In three years from 2002 to 2004 after China joined the WTO, loans increased by 58 percent, or $785 billion. In 2003, new lending equaled almost one-quarter of GDP. Half of all bank loans went to SOEs, and most will never be repaid. However, data from China's central bank, the People's Bank of China (PBC), show that the real growth occurred in various forms of off-balance-sheet lending, which exploded to RMB 3.8 trillion in 2010, more than doubling from RMB 1.6 trillion in 2009 and exceeding the RMB 3.1 trillion total from 2003 to 2008 (table 2.1). The PBC's figures cover three main types of such lending: bankers' acceptances (*yinhang chengdui huipiao*), designated or entrusted loans (*weituo daikuan*), and loans by trust companies (*xintuo daikuan*) (Zhang 2011).

Table 2.1. CHINA'S SHADOW FINANCING, 2002–2010 (TRILLIONS OF RENMINBI)

	Fund-raising by nonfinancial firms in China								
	2002	2003	2004	2005	2006	2007	2008	2009	2010
Insurance	0	0.1	0.1	0.1	0.2	0.1	0.1	0.1	0.1
Capital markets	0	0.1	0.1	0.2	1.0	1.0	1.9	1.9	1.9
New RMB & FX loans	2.0	3.0	2.4	2.4	3.6	3.8	5.0	10.4	8.2
Off-balance-sheet loans									
Designated loans	0	0	0.35	0	0.15	0.35	0.15	0.4	1.1
Trust loans	0	0	0	0	0.05	0.15	0.3	0.44	0.39
Bankers Acceptance	0	0.25	0	0.05	0.2	0.7	0.4	0.7	2.3
Total off- balance-sheet loans	0	0.25	0.35	0.05	0.4	1.2	0.85	1.6	3.8

Source: Compiled from Dragon Week, February 28, 2011, and independent research.

Bankers' acceptances consist of promises of future payment by banks' customers made from deposits at the banks and that the banks guarantee. This form of financing surged to RMB 2.3 trillion in 2010, 10 times the average of RMB 224 billion per year from 2003 to 2009. For designated or entrusted loans, nonfinancial companies lend money directly to each other, with banks acting as intermediaries. The banks earn fees for these transactions, but the loans stay off their books. Designated loans also jumped to RMB 1.1 trillion in 2010, versus an annual average of RMB 264 billion from 2003 to 2009. According to the PBC, loans issued by trust companies amounted to only RMB 386 billion in 2010, versus RMB 437 billion in 2009. This low figure does not take into account the securitization of lending that took place when trust companies repackaged and sold bank loans as wealth-management products (Zhang 2011). According to Fitch, these products' value soared to RMB 2 trillion in 2010, versus RMB 400 billion in 2009. Consequently, real off-balance-sheet lending is probably much larger than the PBC's estimates.

Several researchers have found that central and local governments have directed banks to provide loans to SOEs to further the state's goals. As the governments report most of these loans as unpayable, they burden the banking system (see Cull and Xu 2003); however, no public information exists on the magnitude of these loans. Eckhaus (2006) found that at least through 2003, provincial governments' bank loans encouraged SOEs' exports in the important, exporting provinces. Claro (2006) also argued that the Chinese governments provide SOEs with preferential access to credit at the expense of more profitable projects. By lowering the costs of capital, subsidized credit supports the coexistence of SOEs with low productivity and nonstate firms with higher productivity in China. Ferri and Liu (2009) found that from 2001 to 2005, SOEs received about 65 percent of total loans from state-owned commercial banks (SOCBs) and paid significantly lower financing costs than other companies—indeed, paying market interest rates would have entirely wiped out their existing profits. SOEs' losses contributed greatly to SOCBs' nonperforming loans and resulted in repeated capital injections from the government into the SOCBs, restarting the subsidy process. A 2011 study by the Beijing think tank Unirule Institute of Economics found that SOEs paid an average annual interest rate of 1.6 percent from 2001 to 2008, while private companies during the same period paid 5.4 percent.

Favored, government-linked firms listed on international stock exchanges also have free access to bank loans. In June 2011, Standard & Poor's (S&P) withdrew its long-term corporate-credit rating for Chinese paper company Nine Dragons' debt, citing "insufficient access" to management, transparency and governance, and the company's "aggressive debt-funded growth appetite." S&P stated that without sufficient access to management it "cannot fully understand the company's strategy and financial management or assess its future credit risks" (Law and Chiu 2011). Earlier that month, a short seller had published reports alleging problems with the reporting of financial transactions, including loans and grants by Sino-Forest Corporation, a Hong Kong–based tree-plantation company listed in Toronto. Nine Dragons' gearing ratio, a key measure of debt, stood at about 90 percent at the end of December 2010. An earlier Citigroup report stated the company had doubled its capital expenditure to RMB 9.2 billion ($1.42 billion) for the fiscal year ending June 30, 2011, to fund new plant construction and to acquire a paper mill in Hebei Province. Nine Dragons' deputy general manager Benjamin Ng said that the S&P decision would have no impact on the company's relationships with banks and ability to get loans (Law and Chiu 2011).

In the paper industry, loan-interest subsidies are special Chinese government funds allocated from the central budget or raised from treasury bonds to finance plantations or renovations in paper-mill technology. These subsidies provide capital reimbursement or the loan-interest amount as start-up capital for qualifying projects. The standard subsidy term is two years. For enterprises on China's "top enterprises" list, the subsidy term is three years. However, exceptions take place, and Shandong Chenming received a five-year loan-interest subsidy in 2004. In 2009, the Ministry of Commerce announced that for forestry clients, the maximum term for forestry and agriculture loans would be 10 years; the maximum term for instant forest, ecological construction, and follow-up industrial development 20 years; and the maximum term for forest paper-processing projects 12 years (State Forestry Administration 2009).

Subsidies to Energy

In 2009, according to the International Energy Association, China overtook the United States to become the largest consumer of energy in the world. China consumed 2.3 billion tons of oil equivalent in that year, about 4 percent more than the United States, which burned through 2.2 billion tons of oil equivalent. The oil-equivalent metric represents all forms of energy consumed, including crude oil, nuclear power, coal, natural gas, and renewable sources such as hydropower (Swartz and Oster 2010). Industry accounts for over 70 percent of final energy consumption in China, while the residential, commercial, and transportation sectors account for 10, 2, and 7 percent, respectively (CEIC database). The Chinese government heavily subsidizes energy: While China's corporate energy-price index doubled between 2002 and 2008, the world energy-price index rose by more than 400 percent during that period. China's oil, water, and industrial electricity tariffs are about one-third to one-half of the world's averages and even lower than many developing countries' (European Chamber 2009). In China, energy subsidies arise as the government artificially holds the price below the full economic costs of usage or production. Yet researchers have had great difficulty accessing public information to ascertain the existence of energy subsidies. The International Energy Agency's (1999, chap. 5) sole comprehensive study on China's energy subsidies indicated an average subsidy rate of 10.9 percent in 1998, with social-welfare losses equivalent to 0.36 percent of GDP. Lin and Jiang (2010) also examined Chinese subsidies to coal, oil products, natural gas, and electricity. They found that in 2007 China's energy subsidies equaled 1.43 percent of GDP, or RMB 356.73 billion. Subsidies to industry (nonresidential subsidies) approximated 0.55 percent of GDP, or RMB 136.82 billion.

Despite its importance, researchers and analysts have had trouble deciphering China's energy consumption and attendant effects on industries. Energy consumption of Chinese industries fluctuates constantly and presents a fusion of governmental plans and market forces, formal regulation and seat-of-the-pant remedies, central intentions, and local interests. Local governments control more than 40 percent of energy generation, a substantial proportion of coal production, and a fair amount of electricity dispatch. Depending on the exact structure of ownership of coal and energy assets in any locality, local governments can exercise decisive control over both pricing and dispatch. National security considerations and SOEs' habits of secrecy also obscure many key metrics. While the National Development Reform Commission (NDRC), the country's top economic-planning agency, sets price guidelines, the actual costs and subsidies vary greatly across China since local regulators influence the prices. In a recent white paper, the Information Office of the State Council (2007) admitted that "China's energy market system is yet to be completed, as the energy pricing mechanism fails to fully reflect the scarcity of resources, its supply and demand, and the environmental cost." Local influences on pricing, dual supply chains for companies, and arrears can obfuscate assessments of what the firms pay for coal, electricity, oil, or natural gas.

In September 2007, a draft version of China's Energy Law included the suggestion that China establish a unified institution, such as a Ministry of Energy, to supervise the country's energy industry (*Shanghai Security News* 2007). Currently, multiple ministries and commissions govern China's energy industry, including the NDRC, the State Electricity Regulatory Commission (SERC), the Ministry of Land Resources, and the Ministry of Commerce (MOFCOM). The Energy Bureau, an NDRC bureau in charge of supervising the energy industry, has a full-time staff of only 100 people; in contrast, the US Energy Department has a staff of 110,000 (Kahn and Yardley 2007). Furthermore, companies such as the China National Petroleum Corporation (CNPC) and the China Petroleum and Chemical Corporation (Sinopec), both of which originally comprised one ministry before being converted to SOEs in the 1980s, still retain the same hierarchical rank as ministries in the government, putting them higher than the bureau that is charged with supervising them. The proposed institution would have a higher rank than these companies. However, experts have argued that the establishment of such a Ministry of Energy would involve the interests of too many parties, leading to potential bureaucratic conflict, and the plan would stall, as similar plans have in the past.[3]

Coal. China is the world's largest coal producer and has the world's largest coal market, double the size of the United States'. While down from a postreform high of 76 percent in 1990, coal still meets over two-thirds of China's energy needs. China consumed about 2.58 billion tons in 2007, about 69.5 percent of its energy mix. Intermediate consumption (66.9 percent for power generation, 21.3 percent for coking, and 7.9 percent for heating) made up about 75 percent of China's coal consumption, with end-use consumption (78 percent by industry) contributing to the rest.

Over 75 percent of the demand growth in the post-WTO years has come from the power sector, as electricity demand boomed and alternative fuel sources (hydro, natural gas, wind, and nuclear) for generating that electricity failed to keep pace. Of the 50 percent of coal not consumed by the power sector, the majority sells directly to industry for use in boilers, coking ovens, and on-site ("inside the fence") power generation. Households' coal consumption, which accounted for 20 percent of total demand in 1985, dropped to 4 percent as China's residents moved into homes equipped with gas and electricity for cooking and heating. In 2004, the iron and steel industry accounted for around 13 percent of total coal consumption in China (International Energy Agency 2006).

In 2009, China swung abruptly from being a net exporter to a net importer of coal with total imports tripling to 127 million tons and net imports a massive 100 million tons. In 2010, Chinese coal imports accounted for over 20 percent of global, seaborne coal trade. Transportation and quality considerations, as well as huge increases in industrial capacity, prompted this shift. China's eastern provinces accounted for over 75 percent of national electricity generation and hence thermal-coal demand; but over 70 percent of China's total proven coal reserves lie in three northwestern provinces, Shanxi, Shaanxi, and Inner Mongolia. Costly and unreliable transportation from these mines raises coal prices. Chinese coal also has on average lower calorific content and higher sulfur and ash content than Indonesian, Australian, or Russian coal. To produce the same energy output as a ton of imported coal, a Chinese power producer may have to use a ton and a half. China imports almost all its coking coal for steel production.

Since the 1980s, China has gradually liberalized coal pricing. As with many other Chinese goods, a two-tiered price system emerged, the first set by the NDRC for plan-allocated quotas and the second set by the market for other demand. Over the last two decades, the amount of coal produced for other demand has grown. At the beginning of 2007, the Chinese government abolished the two-tier system, and both contract and spot coal must now be negotiated at market rates; however, legacy behaviors linger among the companies.[4]

As the government continues to control electricity tariffs, indirect governmental influence affects coal prices in China. Government interventions allocate thermal coal through administrative persuasion of state-owned coal mines and through allocations of transportation capacity, which can represent up to 25 percent of coal price (Lin and Jiang 2011). Consequently, thermal-coal pricing, though undergoing several reforms, currently endures highly imperfect market conditions.

Electricity. Like the coal used to generate it, industry consumes the majority of the country's electricity. Rapid economic growth has led to dramatic growth in China's electricity demand. In 2007, China consumed 3271.18 TWh[5] of electricity, of which industry consumed 75 percent, agriculture 3 percent, transportation 2 percent, and construction 1 percent. Household consumption accounted for approximately 11 percent, down slightly from a high of 12.5 percent in 2001 (CEIC database). Electricity pricing constitutes a highly sensitive issue, and the government firmly controls it (Lin and Jiang 2011).

China generally has set electricity tariffs lower than supply costs and lower than developed countries' tariffs. Industries also have had higher tariffs than residences. According to the SERC and *China Electric Power Yearbook* (2008), in 2007, the average residential customer paid CNY 470.88 per MWh,[6] industrial customer CNY 514.18, and commercial customer CNY 851.79.

Electricity prices for Chinese industry appear high. However, conversations with industry analysts indicated that many companies do not bear the full costs indicated by national average figures from the

NBS. Subsidies or "price adjustments" permeate the system, and some of these price adjustments occasionally become declassified. The NDRC sets electricity tariffs province by province based on the recommendations of local pricing bureaus that answer to local officials. Local social and economic concerns often impede the NDRC's efforts to rationalize energy pricing and to reduce overall energy consumption. For example, the Chinese steel industry's energy-intensive firms consume about 20 to 40 percent more energy per ton of output than their competitors in the OECD (Wan 2006), and are therefore sensitive to electricity-price increases. The provinces that support their inefficient steel companies have resisted the NDRC's efforts to raise prices for steel, and nonpayment has become an important issue.

The NDRC on April 16, 2007, required 14 provinces to halt immediately their preferential electricity-price policy for local, high-energy-consuming enterprises, in an attempt to curb these industries' development (*Asia Pulse* 2007). To restrain high-energy-consuming industries, China had previously introduced in September 2006 differentiated electricity prices for such industries as steel, electrolytic aluminum, ferroalloy, calcium carbide, caustic soda, cement, yellow phosphorus, and zinc smelting. The provincial governments failed to implement the policies uniformly. Consequently, the NDRC, together with the SERC, ordered locals to rectify their misbehavior by the end of April 2007.

Yet provinces continue to subsidize routinely the costs of electricity for steel, glass, paper and auto-parts production. In 2006, when Beijing announced its nationwide campaign to raise electricity prices to energy-consuming industries, officials in Ningxia Province worked to evade the requirements. Fearing the impact on the local economy, the provincial government brokered a special deal for the Qingtongxia Aluminum Group, which accounted for 20 percent of the province's industrial consumption and 10 percent of its GDP. Provincial officials removed the company from the national electricity grid and supplied electricity directly to it, exempting it from expensive fees. Consequently, Qingtongxia continued to get its electricity at the lowest price available (French 2007).

Electricity prices overtly remain tightly controlled by the NDRC's Price Bureau. Unlike the developed countries, China has no separately determined transmission tariffs. The NDRC determines both the price at which the generators can sell power to the grid and what the grid can charge different categories of users. When setting these prices, the NDRC tries to accommodate provincial stakeholders' interests. Provincial officials lobby for end-user pricing low enough to keep their industries viable and citizens happy. The power generators lobby for on-grid tariffs high enough to cover their fuel costs and to ensure profits for future investments. And grid companies lobby for margins to finance expansions such as the $130 billion they asked to expand China's transmission network between 2006 and 2010 (Rosen and Houser 2007). Complex and opaque end-user pricing and transmission costs obfuscate the allocation of rents across the electricity-value chain. Because this study relied solely on published prices and the NDRC's disclosures on provinces that had subsidized their steel, glass, paper, and auto-parts industries, the subsidies to electricity are probably underrepresented.

The demand surges after 2004 shrank coal inventories and doubled spot prices. In response, the NDRC enacted a price pass-through mechanism whereby electricity tariffs could be raised by 75 percent of coal-price increases. Yet electricity prices have only risen by 20 percent on average since the beginning of 2004. The gap between the published national average on-grid price and end-user prices indicates that the grid should make huge profits. However, the reported transmission industry-wide data show meager 2006 profits of 4 percent, up from 1.6 percent in 2004. Further investigation has revealed that the grid can collect less from end users such as steel companies (either because of reduced rates or nonpayment) than the published rate tables suggest (Rosen and Houser 2007).

Reflecting the dominance of coal in China's electricity fuel mix, substantial growth in electricity output has increased demand for thermal coal. Coal consumption by the electricity sector increased at an average annual rate of around 21 percent between 2002 and 2004 following an increase of 5.6 percent in 2001. Many coal and power-generation companies have public listings, but considerable government control and ownership remains in both industries. The government is increasingly linking electricity prices with coal costs, and linking electricity consumption with the introduction of more transparent pricing mechanisms. For example, two-part tariff rates have been introduced to curb electricity consumption by energy-intensive industries, and retail electricity charges have also risen recently to reflect higher coal prices (Australian Bureau of Agricultural and Research Economics data).

In mid-2004, the price of electricity was increased on average by 0.08 cents per kWh.[7] A further increase of 0.27 cents per kWh was introduced in the eastern, northern, central, and southern grids to pass on additional costs of transmission. In 2005, the State Council approved the implementation of a new pricing mechanism to link electricity charges to coal costs. An increase in the coal price is passed on to electricity consumers when the average coal price changes by more than 5 percent over six months. If the change in the average coal price is less than 5 percent in six months, the percentage price change carries over to the next six months. However, as table 2.2 reveals, the central government simultaneously offers a subsidy to the electricity-generation industry, in effect since 2005, to offset the higher electricity prices; this subsidy is then passed on to electricity's customers, including the industries we cover in this book.[8] The fuel-input adjustment in 2005 and the attendant increase in subsidy responded to a significant increase in thermal-coal prices in 2004 (Ni 2006). In June 2006, electricity charges were increased in response to higher coal costs, additional adjustments for new generation and transmission projects' higher construction costs, and relocation compensation and support for the development of renewable-energy projects. Simultaneously, a subsidy to industry was added to "adjust" for the increased prices.

Natural gas. China's central government has tightly controlled natural-gas prices and has attempted to keep gas prices for industry competitive with other developing countries. But this approach failed to

Table 2.2. SELECTED SUBSIDIES FOR ELECTRICITY IN CHINA

	Price changes and subsidies US cents/kWh
Average regional increases in sales prices	
Eastern China	0.22
Central China	0.36
Southern China	0.37
Northeastern China	0.17
Average increase (all regions)	0.30
Subsidies for state government projects	
Relocation compensation for new projects	0.78
Support for the development of renewable energy projects	0.0125
Subsidies for power-generation projects	
Compensation for losses caused by the rise in coal cost and transport fees	0.122
Compensation for installation of desulphurization facilities	0.03
Subsidies for grid construction	
State power-grid construction	0.026
Rural power-grid construction	0.007
Subsidies for local government projects	
Subsidies to small hydropower projects, gas-fired projects, wind-power projects, and WEP projects	0.016

Source: Derived from data provided by Australian Bureau of Agricultural and Research Economics, *Interfax China Energy Weekly*.

induce the development or importation of sufficient quantities of natural gas to meet burgeoning demand. Consequently, natural-gas prices have increased. Although Beijing sets natural-gas prices, they vary by province and sector. In most provinces, residential users pay the highest price, followed by chemical producers, power generators, and fertilizer manufacturers.[9]

Historical reasons add to the confusion surrounding natural-gas pricing in China. End-user prices basically consist of three parts: production costs, pipeline-transmission costs, and city-distribution costs. The government makes the production cost (or factory price) uniform for a particular gas source. Pipeline transmission and city distribution costs, however, also depend on the pipeline network's length, city-distribution characteristics, and consumers' income in addition to locations (Lin and Jiang 2011). Unable to estimate government costs, Lin and Jiang (2011) used American Henry Hub's natural gas price as the benchmark for domestic production costs.

China has a long history of using natural gas. Yet, in 2000, because of underdeveloped gas markets and institutions and the lack of an integrated, national gas-pipeline network, the share of gas in the fuel mix remained at a low 3.0 percent. The chemicals and fertilizer industries, and the oil and gas sector, served as primary consumers of natural gas. In 2000, only 0.5 percent of electricity generation in China was gas fired.

As figure 2.1 from the NDRC reveals, the Chinese price of natural gas is based on Cost-Plus rather than Net-Back pricing, where

Cost-Plus Pricing = Wellhead Regulated Price + Pipeline Mark-up Cost + Local Distribution Mark-up Cost = Sales Price to Consumer

and

Net-Back Pricing = Market Value of Gas Based on Price of Consumer's Competing Fuel – Distributor Charges – Pipeline Transportation Charges = Net-Back Price at the Well Head.

On December 22, 2005, the NDRC announced that it had changed the natural-gas pricing system and would allow a natural-gas price hike of 8 percent per annum (Yeh 2005). Despite the government's proposal of hiking prices by 8 percent a year, it could be the year 2016 before China's domestic-gas prices synchronize with international averages (HSBC projections). Because of pricing controls on natural gas, China's wellhead gas price trades 60 percent lower on average than international prices,

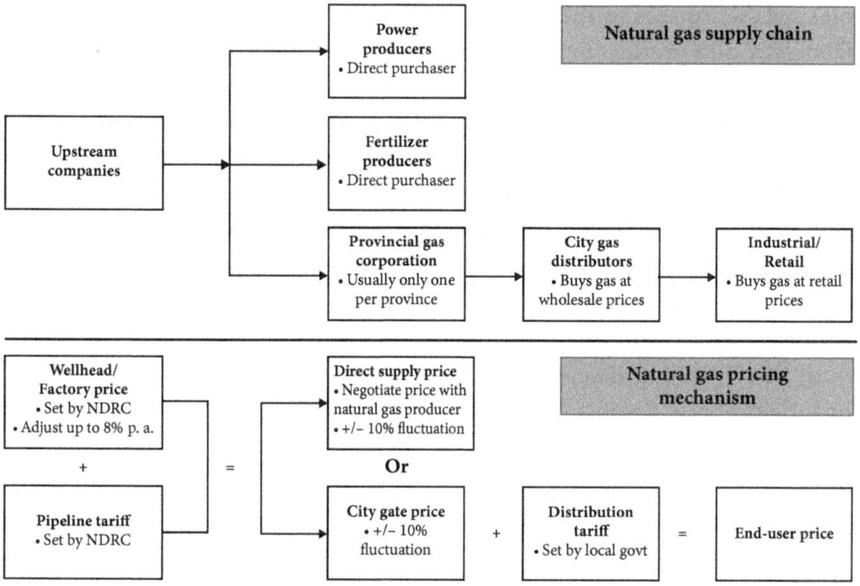

Figure 2.1
Natural Gas Supply Chain and Pricing Mechanisms in China
Source: National Development and Reform Commission through HSBC.

providing a significant subsidy. The EBITDA[10] margin on the domestic wellhead price is 16 percent against the 60 percent of major international benchmarks. These artificially low gas prices reduce the financial burden for end users, including firms in the steel and auto-parts industries.

Despite the low usage of natural gas in Chinese industrial cost structures, firms benefited in 2005 from artificially low prices. However, as natural-gas prices have risen 8 percent per annum, many of these gains appear to have eroded. Also, a tight gas market creates an incentive for CNPC and Sinopec to supply residential customers at the expense of industry. Several firms have had difficulty ensuring reliable supply at the government-stipulated price, and prices have risen in response.

Heavy oil. China's two oil giants, China Petroleum and Chemical Corporation (Sinopec) and China National Petroleum Corporation (CNPC), receive subsidies for their operations from the NDRC and the Ministry of Finance. Specifically, while world-market prices dictate crude prices in China, the administration sets oil-product prices and also issues rebates. Theoretically, oil-product prices in China are pegged to the weighted average of the Brent, Dubai, and Minas crude-oil prices, taking into account processing costs, distribution costs, and refineries' profit margins. However, because of inflation concerns, rarely does the NDRC permit domestic oil's product prices to move with the fluctuations of international prices. Domestic oil's product prices lag behind international prices, and domestic refineries dependent on imported feedstock operate at a loss when international crude prices surge. All of China's crude imports—more than 3.3 million barrels a day as China imports about half its oil—are processed by the refineries of Sinopec and CNPC, with Sinopec handling 80 percent of the total (Bo 2007; Stanway 2009). Chinese oil demand has been rising at about 8 percent annually; virtually every incremental barrel of Chinese oil demand must be met by imports. In 2009, China was the biggest single contributor to the annual increase in global-oil demand.

In 2007, Beijing disclosed a total of RMB 60 billion in oil subsidies, of which about RMB 5 billion went to the main refiner, Sinopec. This amounted to 1.2 percent of government expenditure, 0.2 percent of GDP, or about one-third of total taxes paid by the state-run oil companies. In the first quarter of 2008, Sinopec got RMB 7 billion to compensate for first-quarter refining losses. Beginning in April 2008, the government also began rebating 75 percent of the value-added tax paid on imports of crude oil by Sinopec and PetroChina's parent company, CNPC (the VAT rate on crude imports was 17 percent). This translated into a disclosed subsidy payment of RMB 7 billion for April 2008; total recorded refiner subsidies probably exceeded RMB 70 billion in 2008. Adding in user subsidies (which should not change much given that retail prices are fixed), Beijing probably paid out at least RMB 130 billion in subsidies in 2008, or about $20 billion, more than double the 2007 figure. The gross cost approximated 2.1 percent of budgeted 2008 government expenditure.

Subsidies to Inputs, Land, Technology

The Chinese government has also provided a range of industry-specific subsidies for inputs into production, land, and technology to firms that the central and provincial governments perceive as strategically important. SOEs and favored companies can purchase inputs such as components and raw materials below cost and directly from each other, affecting the competitiveness of certain sectors in the global economy. Land subsidies arise as the government artificially holds the price of land below the full economic cost of usage for firms in key strategic sectors. Technology subsidies provide support for R&D, brand development, and technology acquisition.

A report from the Specialty Steel Industry of North America (2008) described how the Chinese government provides raw materials to producers in key industries at preferential, subsidized prices. Testimony in

2007 before the US-China Economic and Security Review Commission (USCC 2007, 40) also concluded that "provincial and municipal governments subsidize purchases of... raw materials... by requiring other SOEs or pressuring their own suppliers to provide these inputs at below-market or even below-cost prices" (G. T. Haley 2007). In 2008, in countervailing duty investigations of products imported from China, the US Department of Commerce found that the Chinese government conferred substantial countervailable subsidies upon producers of downstream products for the provision of raw-material inputs at below-market prices (Specialty Steel Industry of North America 2008, 51).

For the glass industry, subsidies that we could identify and measure include those for soda ash; for the paper industry, pulp and recycled paper; and for the auto-parts industry, glass, cold-rolled steel, and technology. As measurement and rationales for these subsidies are inextricably linked to government policies aimed at these industries, we explore each of these subsidies in depth in their industrial context and in subsequent chapters.

DATA PROBLEMS

A report on Chinese subsidies by the Specialty Steel Association of North America highlighted some problems with obtaining valid and reliable data on the issue.

> Obtaining information regarding the nature and type of assistance received by Chinese producers is complicated, because corporate reporting in China is limited and often unavailable, particularly from SOEs. Indeed, a report issued by the Office of the US Trade Representative has described the difficulty of obtaining information regarding Chinese support measures as follows: "China's subsidy programs are often the result of internal administrative measures that are not publicized. Sometimes they take the form of income tax reductions or exemptions. They can also take a variety of other forms, including mechanisms such as credit allocations, low interest loans, debt forgiveness, and reduction of freight charges." Accordingly, due to the lack of publicly available information in China, the beneficiaries of subsidies granted by the Chinese government are not identified, in most instances, in this report. (Specialty Steel Association of North America 2008, 33)

Institutional reasons (including poor infrastructure to gather data) and strategic reasons (such as using data to create an informational black hole to confuse competitors) hinder the collection of high-quality data in China.[11] Researchers and analysts have found energy subsidies particularly hard to measure because of problems with the quality of energy statistics and accounting data.[12] In China's case, the country's size, its rapidly shifting quasi-market system, and the tendency of provincial officials to disguise statistics to boost their political fortunes magnify the problems of data quality.[13] Chinese central and provincial governments also covertly and overtly use many policy instruments to reduce industrial costs. For example, analysts from the International Energy Agency (IEA) noted major problems with energy statistics submitted by China, including the substantial discrepancy between coal supply and demand arising from poor data on stock changes. Consequently, the IEA started compiling its own statistics to estimate Chinese coal production based on demand-side statistics (International Energy Agency 2007).

Lack of regular and rigorous surveys also clouds other official statistics on energy. China's official statistics are riddled with inconsistencies. For example, the numbers reported on growth in both GDP and fixed investment, as well as between investment and savings, are incompatible. Services are poorly covered in national-account measures, and consumption of all kinds, including industrial consumption, is probably grossly underestimated (*Economist* 2002, 2006).

Accounting data in China are particularly opaque. Despite Beijing's avowed goal of adopting international accounting standards, certain activities, such as "related-party transactions," are not consistent with international standards, so officials and managers fudge. Under international accounting norms, managers should clearly disclose deals between companies with overlapping ownership. But because overlapping ownership permeates China and the government still owns majority shares in every large steel and auto company (Wiley Rein 2007), detailing individual transactions would overwhelm financial reports. Consequently, "pure state-controlled enterprises" have no disclosure requirements.[14] For the research in this book, many of the companies' annual reports did not reveal standard accounting data such as "bad debts" and did not define terms such as "payables to the government." Cash inflows from some companies' operations exceeded the sales reported on the income statements, with no clarification.

Because of limitations attending the quality, completeness, and quantity of glass industry-level data,[15] the analysis began with subsidies to the flat-glass sector of the Chinese glass industry, which were then extended to the entire Chinese glass and glass-products industry. Despite efforts to close inefficient and small plants, policymakers within China generally do not perceive the glass industry as a strategically important or pillar industry. Consequently, less systematic and comprehensive operational data exist for glass than for pillar industries such as steel and autos. Also, two-thirds of the sales revenues in glass come from small and medium-sized enterprises, whose operations are difficult to track in China. Only the 10 largest enterprises release systematic accounting data, and about a third of revenues come from "unknown or other" enterprises. Because it serves as a major supplier to strategic industries such as construction and automobiles, the flat-glass sector provided the most complete data and also data from a variety of sources. The latter factor was important because official surveys of the industry were found to be flawed. For example, data approved by the NBS listed thousands of employees in the flat-glass sector and hundreds of thousands of yuan of gross industrial output of flat glass for 11 provinces—with zero companies. The aggregate data were cross-checked with semi-independent industrial sources, and the data on the specific numbers of companies in each province were not used.

For the paper industry, current and recent data on forests and agriculture in China are particularly thorny to obtain from official sources. Haley, Haley, and Tan (2004, 139–40) discussed how for several years China had routinely released misleading data showing high stocks of fish, thereby allaying fears of dwindling global fish reserves—until the United Nations Organization's observers noted increasing unrest in Chinese fishing villages because of fish shortages. Independent sampling revealed serious shortfalls in China's fish reserves, with many species on the verge of extinction. Yet the Food and Agricultural Organization (FAO), year after year, released rosy official data on China's extremely high stocks of fish. Currently, the FAO uses its own estimates on China's forestry reserves and businesses. These estimates often contradict China's official statistics. Because of the problems identified, the analyses of the paper industry often used FAO statistics.

Global political debates surrounding China trade have increased impediments to obtaining high-quality Chinese data on subsidies. For example, since 2005, data on China's paper industry have been hard to gather following the consideration of antidumping actions by the US Department of Commerce. Also, 88 percent of the total companies in China's paper industry are small, while 12 percent are medium-sized: the operations of these small companies were difficult to track in China. Only the 10 largest companies released systematic accounting data.

Data on prices for domestic (rather than imported) pulp and recovered paper were also challenging to obtain, and we relied on estimates from investment houses on domestic companies' operations. Our analysis used subsidy income reported in annual reports from 212 of the largest companies in China's paper industry. Yet most of these companies did not release annual reports or systematic and complete accounting statements.

Without consistent disclosure requirements, many of the companies appeared to file detailed annual financial statements only sporadically.

For all four industries, subsidies to and from large SOEs or collectives were difficult to identify because of accounting practices. For example, the large Chinese state-owned oil companies appeared to be reporting government subsidies as profits or revenues. In 2008, PetroChina announced that its profits for the year were mostly from government subsidies and import-tax rebates (Interfax 2008b). Similarly, in March 2008, Sinopec announced that it would receive a government subsidy of $1.74 billion. Some of the subsidy ($693.6 million) would be included as part of the company's revenues for 2007; the rest of the subsidy ($1.05 billion) would be counted as revenue for the first quarter of 2008 (Interfax 2008a). SASAC reported that dividends paid by 122 central SOEs would reach RMB 60 billion in 2010, almost double the RMB 32 billion in 2009. Companies controlled by the central government reported big profits in 2010, which grew 39 percent from the previous year to RMB 1.1 trillion; dividend payments also rose from 5.3 percent of after-tax profits in 2009 to 7.1 percent in 2010. With the stated aim of imposing greater financial discipline, the government was hiking SOEs' dividend payout rates to 10–15 percent of profits in 2011. However, simultaneously, the government was also returning these dividend payments to SOEs as subsidies and either not listing them as government revenues (Dragonomics, February 2011) or reporting them with minus signs under government revenues (Eckhaus 2006).

Given the monumental issues associated with getting valid and reliable data from China, our research used data from multiple reliable sources across China, the United States, Taiwan, India, and Australia, including Chinese government agencies (such as the NDRC), US government agencies (such as the International Trade Commission), international agencies (such as the IEA), international investment houses (such as BNP Paribas), and industry associations (such as the American Iron and Steel Institute). Data were also obtained from individual Chinese companies. Data were cross-checked across at least two sources when possible, and when discrepancies arose, the most conservative data were used. Estimates were checked against accounting data provided by individual companies and interviews with managers. Ill-defined data were discarded. For example, the China Iron and Steel Association's (CISA's) Financial Assets Department had recorded subsidies to steel companies and disclosed in publicly available accounting statements that subsidies to the industry were included in various industry-level calculations. However, the CISA's accounting figures were incompatible across variables. Inquires revealed that the department officially defined only two terms that it published—"pretax profit" and "recovery rate of payment." Third parties were not entitled to define the terms that the CISA published. Consequently, the data were not used in the analysis.

THE PRICE-GAP APPROACH

In cases of murky data, analysts commonly adopt the price-gap approach to measure subsidies (World Bank 1997; International Energy Agency 1999). We used price gap to estimate subsidies to coal, natural gas, and heavy oil. According to the price-gap approach, subsidies to consumers lower end-user prices and result in higher consumption levels. End-user prices are compared to reference prices to measure the price gap. The reference price represents the efficient price that would prevail in a market undistorted by subsidies and corresponds to the opportunity cost of the last unit consumed. The reference price is usually taken as the border price adjusted for transportation and distribution margins and any country-specific taxes in the case of traded goods or the long-run marginal cost of production in the case of goods that are not significantly traded. The approach is designed to capture the net effects of all the different policy instruments that affect a good's price (World Bank 1997; International Energy Agency 1999). The price gap can be represented as a dollar value of subsidy per unit of subsidized good or as a percentage of the reference price.

Price-gap has the advantage of conceptual and analytical simplicity and serves as the most pervasive approach in analyzing energy subsidies (see Lin and Jiang 2011). Corden (1957) proposed the theoretical foundation of the price-gap approach, assuming that subsidies to consumers of energy lower the end-user prices of energy products, leading to more consumption than would occur in their absence. McCrone (1962) undertook an early application to agriculture subsidies in the UK. OECD (1998) applied this method to analyze fossil fuels' effects on the environment, whereas IEA (1999, 2008), and Coady et al. (2010) used this method to estimate the magnitude of energy subsidies in other countries. However, the price-gap approach also has limitations: among them, the approach only captures the subsidies on end use and only identifies static effects. These characteristics suggest that the approach may underestimate the impact of energy subsidies (IEA 1999) and should therefore provide a lower bound rather than an average.

Several issues and assumptions shape the calculation of subsidies through price gap. The estimation of the reference price plays a key role in the calculation of the price gap and therefore in the size of the subsidy.

Different reference prices can produce very different subsidy estimates. The choice of exchange rate used to compare domestic and international prices also assumes importance. The use of official exchange rates may give very different results from the use of purchasing power parities (PPP), as end-user prices can differ significantly across countries in nontraded goods.[16] Multiple prices in one economy (as exist in China) can also affect the estimation of end-user prices. This study used official exchange rates for the years in question; the reference prices were industry-specified world prices for thermal coal, coking coal, and natural gas as indicated by the international industry associations for steel, glass, paper, and auto parts. The end-user price corresponds to the actual price to energy consumers without transportation costs. We omitted transportation costs, as they varied widely within industries and interviews with both managers and policymakers revealed that stated, official transportation prices were routinely subject to price adjustments of over 25 percent by both provincial and central governments, none of which we could access through public records.

EQUATIONS TO MEASURE SUBSIDIES TO CHINESE INDUSTRY

The equations we used to measure subsidies in the four Chinese industries follow.

Loan and Reported Subsidies

1. Reported subsidies (T_{rs})—Paper industry

$$T_{rs} = \sum_{i=1}^{n} Co_i,$$

where:

T_{rs} = Total subsidies reported in annual reports of 212 Chinese paper companies in each year

Co_i = Subsidy income reported in Chinese paper company's annual report in each year

2. Loan-interest subsidies (A_{lis})—Paper industry

$$A_{lis} = \sum_{i=1}^{n} Co/Yr,$$

where:

A_{lis} = Total loan-interest subsidies paid to Chinese paper industry from 2002 to 2009[17]

Co = Reported loan-interest subsidies

Yr = The number of years over which the loan-interest subsidies are projected to be paid

3. Subsidies reported in 73 companies' annual reports, CS_{ap}—Auto-parts industry

$$CS_{ap} = \sum_{i=1}^{n} (SI_i + GG_i + TR_i),$$

where:

CS_{ap} = Total subsidies reported in auto-parts companies' annual reports from 2001 to 2009

SI_i = Subsidies reported as subsidy income in auto-parts company's annual reports

GG_i = Subsidies reported as government grants in auto-parts company's annual reports

TR_i = Subsidies reported as tax refunds (less VAT tax refunds) in auto-parts company's annual reports

Energy Subsidies

4. Provincial-electricity subsidies (PEs)—steel, glass, paper, and auto-parts industries

$$PE_s = \sum_{i=1}^{n} (Skwh_i (EU_i \times SEU_i)),$$

where:

PE_s = Total benefits to a Chinese industry by provinces' electricity subsidies

EU_i = Total electricity usage in a Chinese industry in each year

SEU_i = Percentage of value produced by a Chinese industry in electricity-subsidizing provinces in each year

$Skwh_i$ = Subsidy rate in each year

And SEU_i is determined by

$$SEU_i = \sum_{i=1}^{n} ((6((TS_i - TSIP_i)/Pr) + TSIP_i)/TS_i),$$

where:[18]

TS_i = Total industry production in all Chinese provinces producing in specific industry in each year

$TSIP_i$ = Total industry production in eight Chinese provinces identified as paying electricity subsidies in each year

Pr = Number of provinces producing in each industry, less the eight provinces identified as paying electricity subsidies

5. Electricity coal-price increase subsidy (CPI_s)—steel, glass, paper, and auto-parts industries

$$CPI_s = \sum_{i=1}^{n} (S_i (EU_i \times SEU_i)),$$

where:

CPI_s = Total benefits to a Chinese industry for coal-price subsidy paid to electricity-generation industry

EU_i = Total electricity usage by industry in each year

SEU_i = Percentage of electricity usage by a Chinese industry in each year

S_i = Coal-price-increase subsidy rate in each year

6. Thermal-coal subsidies (TC_s)—steel, glass, paper, and auto-parts industries

$$TC_s = \sum_{i=1}^{n} ((WPT_i - CPT_i)\, KT_i),$$

where:

TC_s = Total subsidies paid to a Chinese industry for thermal coal

WPT_i = World price of thermal coal in each year

CPT_i = Chinese price for thermal coal in each year

KT_i = Ton usage in a Chinese industry of thermal coal in each year

7. Coking-coal subsidies (TCC_s)—steel, paper, and auto-parts industries

$$TCC_s = \sum_{i=1}^{n} ((WPC_i - CPC_i)\, KC_i),$$

where:

TCC_s = Total subsidies paid to a Chinese industry for coking coal

WPC_i = World price of coking coal in each year

CPC_i = Chinese price for coking coal in each year

KC_i = Ton usage in a Chinese industry of coking coal in each year

8. Natural-gas usage subsidies (NG_s)—steel and auto-parts industries

$$NG_s = \sum_{i=1}^{n}((USP_i - CP_i)\,SG_i),$$

where:

NG_s = Total natural-gas subsidies paid to a Chinese industry.
USP_i = World price of natural gas in each year
CP_i = Chinese price of natural gas in each year
SG_i = Natural-gas usage by a Chinese industry in each year

9. Heavy-oil subsidies (HO_s)—glass industry

$$HO_s = \sum_{i=1}^{n}((WPHO_i - CPHO_i)\,THO_i),$$

where:

HO_s = Total subsidies paid to Chinese flat-glass sector for heavy oil
$WPHO_i$ = World price of heavy oil in each year
$CPHO_i$ = Chinese price for heavy oil in each year
THO_i = Metric ton usage in the Chinese flat-glass sector of heavy oil in each year

Input Subsidies

10. Soda ash subsidies (SA_s)—glass industry

$$SA_s = \sum_{i=1}^{n}((WPSA_i - CPSA_i)\,SAU_i),$$

where:

SA_s = Total soda-ash subsidies paid to flat-glass sector
$WPSA_i$ = World price of soda ash in each year
$CPSA_i$ = Chinese price of soda ash in each year
SAU_i = Soda-ash usage in Chinese flat-glass sector in each year

11. Pulp subsidies (TP_s)—paper industry

$$TP_s = \sum_{i=1}^{n}((WPP_i - CPP_i)KP_i),$$

where:

TP_s = Total subsidies paid to Chinese paper industry for pulp
WPP_i = World price of pulp in each year
CPP_i = Chinese price for pulp in each year
KP_i = Ton usage in the Chinese paper industry of pulp in each year

12. Recycled-paper subsidies ($TOCC_s$)—paper industry

$$TOCC_s = \sum_{i=1}^{n}((WPR_i - CPR_i)KR_i),$$

where:

$TOCC_s$ = Total subsidies paid to Chinese paper industry for OCC
WPR_i = World price of OCC in each year
CPR_i = Chinese price for OCC in each year
KR_i = Ton usage in the Chinese paper industry of OCC in each year

13. Glass subsidies (GS_{ap})—auto-parts industry

$$GS_{ap} = \sum_{i=1}^{n} GU_i(CGC_i - WGC_i),$$

where:

GS_{ap} = Total glass subsidies to auto-parts industry
GU_i = Glass usage in years 2004 to 2010
CGC_i = Chinese costs per tonne of flat glass in each year
WGC_i = World costs per tonne of flat glass in each year

14. Cold-rolled steel subsidies ($CRSS_{ap}$)—Auto-parts industry

$$CRSS_{ap} = \sum_{i=1}^{n} CRSU_i(CCRSP_i - WCRSP_i),$$

where:

$CRSS_{ap}$ = Total cold-rolled steel subsidies to auto-parts industry.
$CRSU_i$ = Cold-rolled steel usage in each year
$CCRSP_i$ = Chinese costs per tonne of cold-rolled steel in each year
$WCRSP_i$ = World costs per tonne of cold-rolled steel in each year

Technology Subsidies

15. Government tech-policy subsidies TPS_{ap} (general formula)—auto-parts industry

$$TPS_{ap} = \sum_{i=1}^{n}(TPSAC_i + TPSAL_i),$$

where:

TPS_{ap} = Total reported government technology and production enhancement grants for auto-parts industry

$TPSAC_i$ = Technology and production enhancement grants announced by central government for auto-parts industry

$TPSAL_i$ = Technology and production enhancement grants announced by local governments for auto-parts industry (seven local governments' reported subsidies have been traced)

NOTES

1. SCM Agreement, Article 1.1.
2. On November 29, 2007, after negotiations with the United States, China agreed to terminate a dozen more subsidies and tax rebates. However, the agreement mostly affected exports by Chinese companies that have foreign investors or are JVs with foreign companies. See Wesiman (2007).
3. *Interfax China Energy Weekly* (2006), various issues.
4. For discussions of China's coal sector see Melanie et al. (2002); and Melanie and Austin (2006).
5. Terawatt hours.
6. Megawatt hour.
7. Kilowatt hour.
8. *Interfax China Energy Weekly* (2006), various issues.
9. For the role of natural gas see Schneider et al. (2003).
10. Earnings before interest, taxes, depreciation, and amortization.
11. For a discussion of the informational black hole see Haley and Tan (1996); and Haley, Haley, and Tan (2009).
12. Wiley Rein (2007) found no systematic evidence of energy subsidies to the Chinese steel industry but presented anecdotal evidence of an electricity subsidy to Baosteel.
13. For a discussion of problems surrounding data collection in China and interpretation of official Chinese statistics see Haley, Haley, and Tan (2004).
14. For a discussion of research on obtaining valid information in Asia see *The Economist* (2001); and for a discussion of Chinese accounting see *The Economist* (2007).
15. This concern was shared by six Chinese government agencies in guidelines for the Chinese glass and glass products industry released in 2008.
16. For a discussion of the problems surrounding using PPP to understand China's economy and prices see *The Economist* (2007).
17. The NDRC specified loan-interest subsidies of $2.13 billion to 13 paper projects out of the 43 announced to receive these subsidies. The subsidies reported in this book were to be paid over the eight-year period of this study. The formula seeks to reflect the annual benefits of the subsidy, not just the total benefit paid.
18. Six provinces are paying electricity subsidies but have not been specifically identified by the NDRC; 22 provinces have not been specifically identified as paying electricity subsidies by the NDRC.

CHAPTER 3
Steely Commitment: Subsidies to China's Steel Industry

This chapter analyses energy subsides to Chinese steel from 2000 to 2007 and the policies that led to China's becoming the major driver for the global steel industry.[1] The global steel industry has undergone significant restructuring since the 1970s. China's share of world steel production rose from 15.7 percent in 1999 before WTO membership to 47 percent in 2011. As the largest steel producer in the world, China has significantly impacted international steel prices and supply of raw and finished materials. Since 2005, the growth of China's steel industry has outstripped Chinese government predictions, indicating the unpredictable role of subsidies and local governments. For example, China's output of crude steel reached 706 million metric tons in 2011, far exceeding the prediction of 660 million tons made at the beginning of that year (China Iron and Steel Association).

In 2007, China was the largest producer as well as consumer of steel in the world, representing 40 percent of the global market. Much had changed for China's steel industry in the previous five years. In 2003, China imported 43.2 million tons of semifinished and finished steel products, or about 13 percent of the global steel trade flow. In late 2005, China went from a net steel importer to a steel exporter. In 2006, China became the largest steel exporter in the world by volume, up from fifth largest in 2005. In 2006, China claimed 34 percent of the global steel production of 1.24 billion tons, displaying a six-year compounded annual growth rate (CAGR) of 23 percent and enormous ramping up of domestic supply.[2] The calculation of subsidies for this study ended in the first nine months of 2007; at that time, China produced 308 million tons of crude steel and 337 million tons of finished steel. Since then, the industry and the subsidies that fueled it have experienced unabated growth. In 2009, China produced 567.8 million metric tons of crude steel and accounted for 46.4 percent of world steel production of 1,226.5 million tons (CEIC, Mysteel). In June 2012, China's share of world steel production remained steady at 47 percent, accounting for nearly half of total world production, while the United States ranked fourth at 6 percent. China's share loomed larger than the combined production of the largest historical producers of steel, the United States, the EU 27, Russia, and Japan (International Trade Administration).

The Chinese steel industry as it exists today stems from government intervention, oversight, and subsidies. Previous reports have documented the off-the-book and on-the book subsidies that permeate Chinese steel (Haley 2006; Wiley Rein 2007). This report concentrates on energy subsidies (coal, natural gas, and electricity) to the Chinese steel industry from 2000 to 2007. Drawing on published research and public data sources, many from the Chinese government, the research shows that energy subsidies fell in 2002 and 2003, immediately after China joined the WTO; however, the subsidies surged in 2004 and have continued to grow exponentially since then, corresponding to China's rise as the largest producer and exporter of steel in the world.

Figure 3.1 traces how energy subsidies to Chinese steel have continued to rise along with the industry's growth and exports. By 2006, total energy subsidies to steel had grown by 1,365 percent over 2000. Energy subsidies to steel exceeded $7.8 billion in the first half of 2007, growing 25 percent since 2006. In 2007, energy subsidies to Chinese steel were estimated at approximately $15.7 billion, showing a 3,800 percent increase since 2000; similarly, in 2007, Chinese production of steel and Chinese global steel exports (including to the United States) were calculated to have grown by 289 percent and 1,276 percent from 2000.[3] As indicated in chapter 2, the Chinese government has not acknowledged the presence of energy or any other subsidies to its domestic steel producers in its declaration to the WTO.

CHARACTERISTICS OF THE STEEL INDUSTRY IN CHINA

In July 2005, the National Development and Reform Commission (NDRC) released the China Iron and Steel Industry Development Policy highlighting steel as a strategic and pillar industry. The policy announced the central government's aim of consolidating and modernizing the industry, with

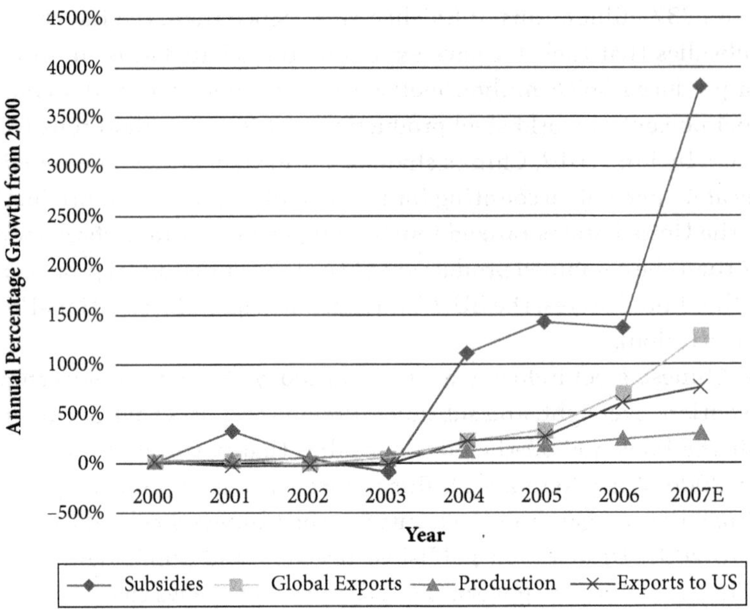

Figure 3.1
Growth of China's Energy Subsidies, Crude Steel Production, and Steel Exports, 2000–2007
Sources: *Business Standard*, Citigroup Global Markets, Iron and Steel Statistics Bureau, Mysteel, United States International Trade Commission, authors' estimates.

the specific goal of "strategic reorganization." The policy also announced the creation by 2010 of two 30-million-ton annual capacity producers and several "internationally competitive" companies at the 10-million-ton level. The steel industry easily surpassed these goalposts. By 2009, China's largest steel producers included Hebei Iron and Steel (producing 40.2 million tons annually), the Baosteel Group (38.9 million tons), and Wuhan Iron and Steel (30.3 million tons); Hebei and Baosteel also ranked as the second and third largest producers in the world. Seven other companies produced between 10 and 30 million tons. However, after the 10 million-ton-production level, a sharp drop-off occurred, and most of the industry consisted of small and inefficient firms.

In October 2005, in a joint statement to the WTO Transitional Review Mechanism on China's accession, the United States, Canada, and Mexico noted that two articles on the state's role in implementing policy could violate WTO antisubsidy rules. Specifically, article 16 of the Chinese policy provided for various types of state support in developing and modernizing the industry. Also, article 18 "encouraged" the Chinese steel industry to use domestically produced equipment and to import equipment only if domestically made equipment was insufficiently advanced, unavailable, or in short supply (Cooney 2006).

Taube and in der Heiden (2009) sketched the multilayered system of alliances that underpin the Chinese steel industry's development. At the national level, the major strategic groups that comprise the steel industry include the NDRC, the China Iron and Steel Association (CISA), SASAC, and the top management of China's leading steel firms. At the provincial levels, local governments and smaller steel firms form local alliances to promote the development of local industry in the face of often adverse central-government policies. This has resulted in political failures reinforcing market failures and has led to large increases in annual production capacity, which Taube and in der Heiden (2009) estimated at over 100 million tons a year, as well as widespread government subsidies. They concluded that the cost structures and sales prices of China's steel firms reflect not real market constellations and scarcities but political patronage. In general, China's steel firms operate at artificially depressed cost levels.

The central government has repeatedly announced its intention to control and to direct the steel industry. For example, in its Steel Policy of 2005, China banned foreign acquisition of large steel mills. The Eleventh Five-Year Plan for National Economic and Social Development of the People's Republic of China also reiterated the principle of using central control to eliminate the obsolete, to restructure, to upgrade industrial products, and to lower consumption of raw materials.[4] Provincial governments have resisted and openly flouted these policies. Consequently, in 2007 as in 2012, the Chinese steel industry was characterized by overcapacity and fragmentation and served as an arena of political struggles between the central and provincial governments.

Fragmentation

Beijing had learned that fewer producers can lead to stronger pricing power in the global markets, and its policy objectives aimed in that direction. The Steel Policy of 2005 emphasized the government's proclaimed determination to avoid inefficient use of resources, including capital, energy, and raw materials (such as iron ore and coking coal), and to protect both intangible (such as environmental) and tangible assets. Raising the equity requirements for steel plants also highlighted the central government's efforts to curb excess capacity. These attempts at consolidation synchronized with Beijing's policy of building 150 state-owned enterprises (SOEs) as global champions (G. T. Haley 2007).[5]

As mentioned earlier, the central government's policies of consolidating the steel industry failed. As figure 3.2 shows, the top 15 producers controlled 48 percent of domestic production in 2004, but their aggregate share dropped to 43 percent in 2006. These data indicate that the central government strongly influenced the major producers' expansion, yet production shifted out of Beijing's radar and weakened the major producers' market power. The Chinese steel industry continued to become more fragmented, while the rest of the world moved toward more concentrated production.

The major Chinese steel producers' production rankings during the period under study bring the industry's fragmentation into sharper focus. Although China had the world's largest steel industry, in 2004 only one Chinese producer, Shanghai Baosteel, ranked among the world's 10 largest producers. Only two Chinese producers, Shanghai Baosteel and Anshan (now Anben), produced more than 10 million tons in that year, while eight reached that level in 2005. In 2005, 25 Chinese producers ranked in the top 80 in the world. Yet these producers accounted for less than 40 percent of total Chinese production (ISI Emerging Markets Analytics).

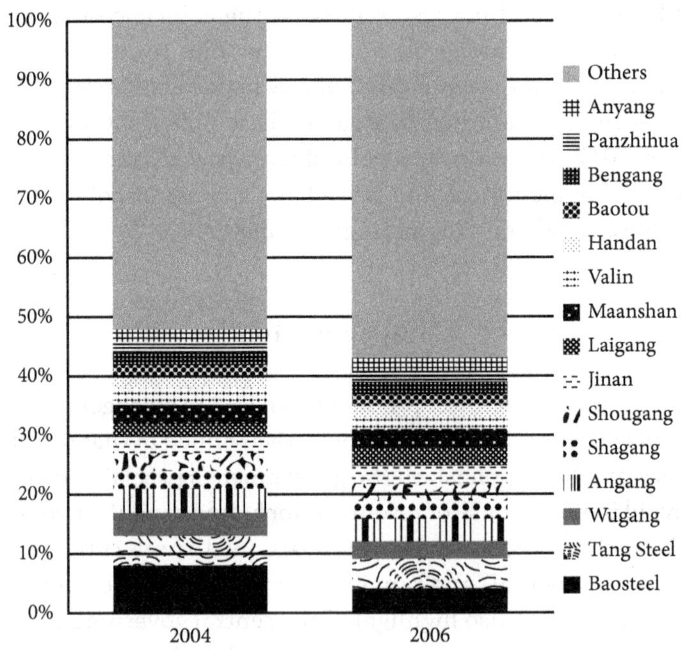

Figure 3.2
Firm Share of Chinese Steel Production in 2004 and 2006
Source: BNP Paribas.

The structure of the Chinese steel industry also reflects the Chinese central and provincial governments' ongoing roles. The Chinese steel industry continued as primarily state-owned. Although minority positions in some of the larger producers were privately owned, the Chinese central and provincial governments held majority interests in every major Chinese steel producer. Every province and every region seemingly wanted its own steel mill, and local governments were providing lavish benefits to build or to keep their steel industries (Directorate for Science Technology and Industry Steel Committee 2006).

Consequently, the Chinese steel industry was also fragmented geographically. While steel production was concentrated in the northeast, no province accounted for more than 18 percent of China's annual production. Moreover, several provinces had annual production of less than five million metric tons per year. Figure 3.3 shows annual production of finished steel in China, by province, in 2005.

In 2005, Hebei province ranked highest among China's provinces for steel production. By September 2006, Hebei earned $2.04 billion for the export of iron and steel products, up by 46.3 percent from the previous year. The number of profitable steel producers in Hebei Province rose by 178 from the corresponding period in 2005 to 904.[6] This trend has

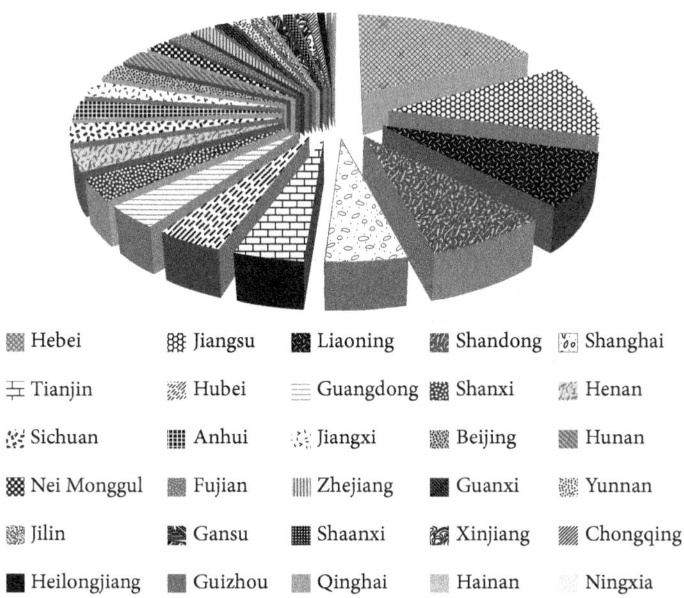

Figure 3.3
Chinese Steel Production by Province, 2005 (millions of tons)
Source: China Steel Industry Association; CEIC.

continued. From 2008 to 2010, Hebei Province continued as the largest steel producer in China. At end of the first eight months of 2010, Hebei Province produced 121 million tons of iron and steel products, up by 27.9 percent from the previous year, and represented 22 percent of China's total steel production. In 2010, the next largest steel producers, Jiangsu and Shandong Provinces, accounted for 11.3 percent and 8.4 percent of China's steel production. As with previous years, every province wanted to encourage steel production. In production growth, Shaanxi Province topped the list with growth of 79.5 percent, followed by Tianjin and Zhejiang with respective growths of 36.9 percent and 36.4 percent.

Supply and Demand

Despite its strategic and political importance, lack of government statistics has obfuscated a systematic understanding of the Chinese steel industry, including trends in domestic supply and demand (Haley 2003; Rawski 2001). Steel demand in China grew at 19.9 percent per annum from 2000 to 2005.[7] Over 50 percent of the steel demand in China came from long products such as rebar and H-beam, which were primarily used in the property and construction sectors. Conversely, in most industrialized countries, over 50 percent of steel demand has come from flat products such as steel sheets and plates. Steel demand from construction had been slowing down because of the central government's efforts to cool down this overheated sector. The construction sector's steel-consumption growth rate declined from 33 percent in 2003 to 9 percent in 2005.[8] Overall, China's population growth rate had also decelerated to a stable 0.6 percent per annum since 2000. Based on assumptions of stable population growth and governmental control of overheated sectors, it was estimated that steel demand would demonstrate a 15.7 percent year-on-year increase. Applying a 15 percent growth rate, China reached steel consumption per capita of 853 pounds and 981 pounds in 2007 and 2008, respectively. In contrast, the more industrialized countries consumed between 550 and 1,320 pounds of steel per capita.

Although demand has been increasing in China, supply surges from China have posed the biggest concern for the global steel industry. The NDRC's estimate of crude-steel capacity increases in 2007 ranged from 10 percent to 15 percent year on year. However, independent research showed that total crude-steel capacity in China reached 499 million tons in 2007, up 19.3 percent year on year.[9]

Extensive anecdotal evidence supports the provincial drive behind excess capacity in Chinese steel (Price et al. 2007; Rosen and Houser 2007). Chinese steel mills across all provinces have aimed to increase their size and thereby increase their chances of survival. Aside from cost efficiencies and economies of scale, local governments have supported these expansions as they support provincial officials' career advancements and perquisites: large-scale steel operations can translate to higher employment and tax revenues for local authorities. As a result, while the NDRC's Steel Policy encouraged consolidation by phasing out furnaces smaller than 300 cubic meters by 2007 (translating to crude-steel capacity of 357,000 tons per annum) a different trend has emerged. Instead of spontaneous and guided mergers among the steel companies to form larger entities, each small mill appeared to have been defending its position through organic growth by increasing output. The stated need for the central government's approval did not hinder creeping excess capacity from de-bottlenecking, and this additional capacity amounted to as much as 20 percent of current capacity. In 2007, some small steel producers had suggested that they were adding one to two million tons of crude steel, which did not require the central government's approval. The NDRC had extended the deadline for the closure of small plants to 2010, which also removed some pressure to consolidate.

As of the writing of this book, Beijing continues to fight its losing battle to shut down outdated production facilities. In July 2011, the Ministry of Industry and Information Technology issued a document requiring 154 iron and steel companies nationwide to eliminate combined outdated iron-making capacity of 31.22 million tons within the year, higher than the target of 26.53 million tons the Ministry had set in May (Xinhua News Agency 2011). The 154 companies included 58 companies with 27.94 million tons of outdated steelmaking capacity. Policymakers in Beijing have rationalized that as the Twelfth Five-Year (2011–15) Program is in its initial phases, local governments have faced less pressure to meet elimination targets and therefore have failed to push hard to shut down outdated capacities in steel, reported *China Business News*, quoting an unnamed source from a privately owned steelmaker. However, the government-owned Xinhua News Agency (2011) concluded that local governments also lacked sound supervision and monitoring in slashing outdated capacity, as the steel sector played a central role in regional GDP contributions and employment.

The larger steel companies such as Baosteel, Wugang, and Angang had the central government's steadfast and visible support for their expansion; but even the small companies expressed confidence in their ability to obtain financing—through their connections or through convertible bonds. For example, in December 2006, Panzhihua New Steel and Vanadium, a Shenzhen-listed arm of Panzhihua Iron and Steel Group (Pangang), announced it would issue convertible bonds to raise RMB 3.2 billion ($406.63 million) to buy assets from Pangang. Net proceeds from bond placements amounting to RMB 3.107 billion ($394.82 million) were to be used to acquire Pangang's steel and mining assets, including a cold-rolling plant with a 1.3-million-ton capacity of cold-rolled plates and galvanized plates a year, and the first phase of a Baima iron-ore mine, which was scheduled to start operation in December 2006 and to reach designed capacity by 2008.[10]

As a result of the policies outlined above, rapid growth of steel production has outstripped consumption since the second quarter of 2004, when the central government announced measures to control construction activities. The large gap between demand and supply led to even more Chinese steel flooding the world markets. Taking the steel consumption per capita and the central government's policy measures and cross-checking these figures with other industrial data and economic indices, the forecast growth of Chinese steel supply in 2007 was 19.3 percent, compared to 25.0 percent and 26.4 percent in 2005 and 2006, respectively.[11] Figure 3.4 sketches supply and demand of Chinese steel from 2000 to 2006 and shows the calculated projected increase from 2007. Although calculations vary depending on data sources, the analyses invariably reveal that supply of Chinese steel exceeded demand during the period of study. Other calculations estimate that between 2002 and 2007, world steel production grew at

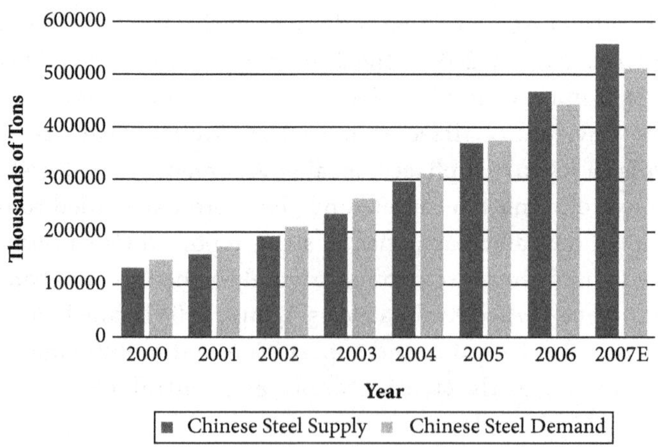

Figure 3.4
Supply of and Demand for Chinese Steel, 2000–2007
Source: BNP Paribas; authors' estimates.

a CAGR of 7 percent, against production in China at a CAGR of 18 percent (ISI Emerging Markets).

Cost Structure

Eighty-seven percent of China's crude-steel capacity comes from blast furnaces (BOF), the highest percentage in the world. The process of making steel influences the choice of raw materials and thereby determines the steel producers' cost structures. The more the steelmakers integrate upstream, the more cost efficient their production. BOF steel production on average has lower costs per ton of crude steel, given its integration with iron ore. The raw materials for BOF steel production (iron ore, coking coal, and thermal coal) form the principal components of steel-manufacturing costs and represent 50 percent to 70 percent of the cost of goods sold for Chinese steel producers.

The authors' research shows that Chinese steel producers' costs are generally 20 to 25 percent lower than those of American and European producers.[12] Quality differentials contribute to overall differences in costs, as China has focused on low-end steel.[13] However, even if we assume the same quality, factors such as the production process and costs of raw materials and electricity/utilities reduce costs. As the analysis later highlights, subsidies have significantly reduced the costs of raw materials and electricity for Chinese steel factories.

Transportation costs associated with raw materials also affect steel producers' costs, but they vary widely in China. Low-cost producers such as Baosteel are located at harbors, whereas others, such as Wugang, rely on inland transportation to get raw materials from ports to mills, adding additional costs. Compared with steel mills located inland, plants located by harbors can save about RMB 20 to 30 per ton on time and costs associated with inland transportation. Producers with their own fleets also have lower freight costs for imported raw materials such as coking coal and iron ore than those that depend on external ships. For instance, the prevailing rate to transport coking coal from Australia to China was $16 per ton; but, Baosteel paid only $6 per ton as shipping took place on its own vessels.[14]

Figure 3.5 compares production costs for steel in China and India, another large Asian emerging-market country. For the Chinese steelmaker, Baoshan, raw materials form a greater proportion of the cost structure than for the Indian steelmaker, Tata; but labor and fuel each comprise a smaller proportion of the costs.

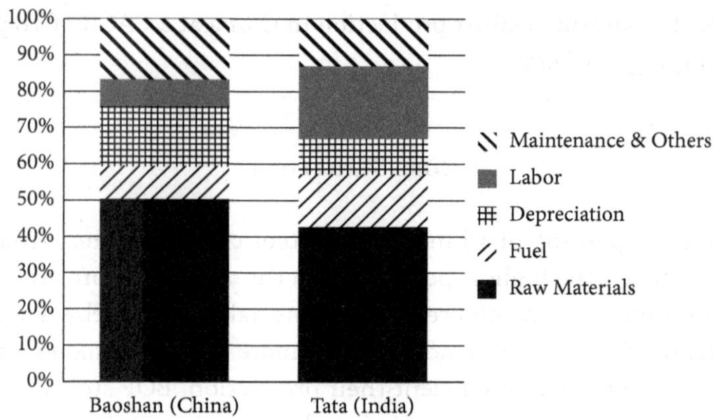

Figure 3.5
Breakdown of Steel-Production Costs in China and India
Source: BNP Paribas; Yuanta Core Pacific Securities; authors' estimates.

Exports

In 2007, China already commanded a share of 20.7 percent of global steel exports, making it by far the largest exporter of steel in the world. Previous research has shown a relationship between China's exports and subsidies to SOEs (Girma et al. 2007). Other research has shown that a large portion of the subsidies to steel have come from local and provincial governments to enhance regional exports (Eckaus 2006; Taube and in der Heiden 2009).

China's elevation to the largest exporter of steel in the world has accompanied fragmentation in the steel industry, ramped-up production, destocking of steel products, and a significant slowing of demand growth (Macquarie Research 2007). Lower prices for Chinese steel also served as drivers for exports. The cost structure of the Chinese steel industry, and the US and European companies' strong pricing power, elevated steel prices in the two markets above steel prices in Asia, particularly in China. In 2006, Hot Rolled Coil (3.0 mm) was priced at $602 per ton and $633 per ton in the United States and Europe, respectively, compared to $505 per ton in Asia and $424 per ton in China (excluding value-added tax). With shipping freight at $60 to $70 per ton, Chinese steel could still sell at an 18.8 percent discount to domestic products in the United States, the largest steel importer.[15]

In tandem with the rise of Chinese exports, US imports of finished steel products from China more than doubled in 2006, increasing from 2.3 million tons in 2005 to 5.35 million tons in 2006. This rate of increase continued in 2007. In the first half of 2007, US imports increased 23.8

percent over the same period in 2006. China's total finished-steel exports surged to 33.8 million tons in the first half of 2007, up nearly 100 percent compared to the same period in 2006.[16] In 2007, Chinese steel exports to the United States alone grew by 610 percent from 2000 (US International Trade Commission). Growth of Chinese steel exports to the United States may have decelerated relative to the rest of the world because of the declining value of the dollar in 2007.[17] In 2008, Chinese steel exports to the United States grew by 73 percent from the previous year. Chinese steel exports declined substantially in 2009 and 2010 because of the recession in the United States, but picked up again in 2011 with a rise of 83.3 percent from the previous year. From 2000 to 2011, the United States has experienced a trade deficit on steel with China for every year but 2003, when it experienced a surplus of $8.8 million. In 2011, the US trade deficit with China on steel approximated $1.36 billion, a rise of 142 percent from $564 million in 2000. Since 2009, noting that Chinese steel costs between 20 and 30 percent less than steel from industrialized countries depending on costing assumptions, the United States and the EU have filed trade complaints and slapped tariffs against various Chinese products made from steel (see Tang 2010). We cover the strategic rationales behind some of these complaints in chapter 7.

To summarize, under true market conditions, China would probably have had a large and diverse steel industry, but not one that grew to account for about half of total world steel production within a decade of joining the WTO. The Chinese steel industry in its current form is the creation of the Chinese government. It has benefited from massive direct and indirect subsidies, many of which violate the WTO's Subsidies Agreement, China's obligations under its WTO accession agreement, or both. As described earlier, the Chinese government has also adopted an official policy that requires it to continue to provide the steel industry with massive subsidies.

MEASURING ENERGY SUBSIDIES IN CHINA

This study identifies and measures energy subsidies to the steel industry in China, specifically to coking coal, thermal coal, natural gas, and electricity. A detailed examination of the methodology including definition and measurement of variables, as well as problems attending the measurements, is presented in chapter 2.

This research shows that though some subsidies have fallen, total energy subsidies to steel have increased overall and most dramatically since 2004, corresponding to the sharp increase in exports. Figure 3.6 summarizes subsidies to thermal coal, coking coal, electricity, and natural gas; table 3.1 provides the detailed figures. Using the conservative data and methods outlined in chapter 2, this study determined that total energy subsidies to Chinese steel from 2000 to midyear 2007 reached $27.11 billion. Total energy subsidies in 2006 approximated $5.84 billion, and from January through midyear 2007 reached a record high of $7.84 billion.[18] Energy subsidies to Chinese steel since 2002 (immediately following China's WTO entry) through midyear 2007 approximated $25.07 billion.

Subsidies to coal. In 2004, the iron and steel industry accounted for around 13 percent of total coal consumption in China.[19] Using the data and methods outlined in chapter 2, this study determined that subsidies for thermal coal to the Chinese steel industry from 2000 to midyear 2007 reached $11.16 billion. Subsidies to thermal coal in 2006 fell to $731.25 million, as coal prices tended to converge toward market prices. However, from January through midyear 2007, subsidies to thermal coal rose to an all-time high of $5.88 billion, as provincial subsidies may have kicked in to bolster steel production. Thermal-coal subsidies to Chinese steel from 2002 (immediately following China's WTO entry) through midyear 2007 approximated $10.21 billion.

Similarly, coke prices continued to converge upward with world prices since 2004, leading to increased provincial subsidies. The Chinese coke

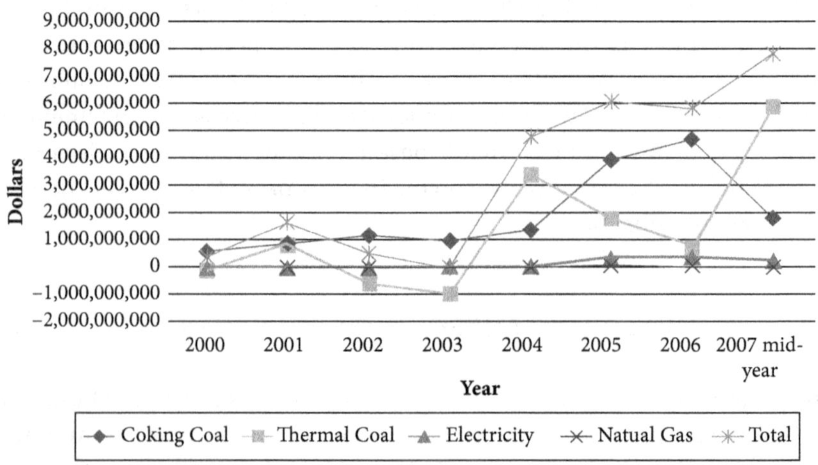

Figure 3.6
Energy Subsidies to Chinese Steel, 2000–2007
Source: Authors' calculation and estimates derived from data provided by Australian Bureau of Agricultural and Research Economics; CEIC; China Statistical Yearbooks; Deutsche Bank; Dragonomics; *Interfax China Energy Weekly*; International Energy Agency; Mysteel; National Development and Reform Commission, China; *The Standard*, January 21, 2006; Steelonthenet.

Table 3.1. ENERGY SUBSIDIES TO CHINESE STEEL, 2000–2007 (US$)

Period	Coking coal	Thermal coal	Electricity	Natural gas	Total
2000	551,246,600	-151,500,000	1,638,432		401,385,032
2001	855,538,270	796,180,000	1,778,568	-12,635,220	1,640,861,618
2002	1,147,718,590	-604,240,000	2,024,079	-31,604,300	513,898,369
2003	963,957,200	-991,200,000	2,415,480	-984,520	-25,811,840
2004	1,358,887,600	3,423,090,000	3,021,990	9,794,480	4,794,794,070
2005	3,932,915,270	1,772,030,000	304,193,760	91,783,920	6,100,922,950
2006	4,702,413,750	731,250,000	385,436,992	25,271,520	5,844,372,262
2007 (midyear)	1,774,456,060	5,878,100,000	215,875,881	-27,510,200	7,840,921,741
Total	15,287,133,340	10,853,710,000	916,385,182	54,115,680	**27,111,344,202 Grand total**

Source: Authors' calculation and estimates derived from data provided by Australian Bureau of Agricultural and Research Economics; CEIC; China Statistical Yearbooks; Deutsche Bank; Dragonomics; *Interfax China Energy Weekly*; International Energy Agency; Mysteel; National Development and Reform Commission, China; *The Standard* (January 21, 2006); Steelonthenet.

Note: The premiums (negative subsidy) paid for thermal coal and natural gas are included in the total subsidy calculations for steel because the amounts were significant and potentially affected overall subsidy amounts to steel. The premiums that industry paid reduced the subsidy amounts for steel in our calculations.

industry, which supplies about 80 percent of its products to the domestic steel sector, has traditionally suffered from fragmentation and overcapacity. At the end of 2005, China had 1,480 coke producers and a total production capacity of 300 million tons. Demand stood at 220 million tons in 2005, and capacity exceeded demand by as much as 100 million tons. Yet new coke facilities capable of producing 30 million tons were being planned across the country. The overcapacity led in 2007 to decreases in coke prices.[20] In the first half of 2007, recorded subsides to coke fell to $1.8 billion, substantially down from the same time last year.

Using the methodology outlined in chapter 2, this study determined that subsidies for coking coal to the Chinese steel industry from 2000 to midyear 2007 reached $15.29 billion. Subsidies to coking coal in 2006 reached an all-time high of $4.70 billion and from January through midyear 2007 fell to $1.77 billion. Coking-coal subsidies to Chinese steel from 2002 (immediately following China's WTO entry) through midyear 2007 approximated $13.88 billion.

Subsidies to electricity. Like the coal used to generate it, industry consumes the majority of the country's electricity, with 10 percent going to iron and steel production. Households account for 11 percent of demand, down slightly from a high of 12.5 percent in 2001.[21]

Statistics show that some energy-intensive industries have recorded rapid surges in production and profits. Specifically, the steel industry logged year-on-year profit surges of 360 percent in the first two months of 2007, with crude-steel production up 23.1 percent. In the same period, electricity-generation capacity went up 16.6 percent, 5.4 percentage points faster than growth in 2006.

Using the variables and methods covered in chapter 2, this study determined that total subsidies for electricity to the Chinese steel industry from 2000 to midyear 2007 reached $916.39 million. Subsidies to electricity in 2006 reached an all-time high of $385.44 million and from January through midyear 2007 were about $215.88 million. Electricity subsidies to Chinese steel from 2002 (immediately following China's WTO entry) through midyear 2007 approximated $912.97 million. The coal-price subsidies (to compensate for the increased price of coal) that started in 2005 dwarfed the recorded provincial subsidies. Because of the circumstances surrounding electricity generation described in chapter 2, most of the subsidies to electricity have probably not been uncovered.

Subsidies to natural gas. Despite the low usage of natural gas in the Chinese steel industry's cost structure, the industry benefited in 2005 from the artificially low prices. However, as natural-gas prices have risen 8 percent per annum, many of these gains appear to have eroded. Also, a tight gas market created an incentive for CNPC and Sinopec to supply residential customers at the expense of industry. Several companies had difficulty ensuring reliable supply at the government-stipulated price. Using the data and methods outlined in chapter 2, this study determined that subsidies for natural gas to the Chinese steel industry from 2000 to midyear 2007 reached $54.12 million, but four of these years saw losses of subsidies. Subsidies to natural gas in 2005 reached a record high of $91.78 million and from January through midyear 2007, because of the supply problems, the loss of subsidies amounted to approximately $27.51 million. Natural-gas subsidies to Chinese steel from 2002 (immediately following China's WTO entry) through midyear 2007 approximated $66.75 million.

CONCLUSIONS

The research revealed that subsidies to Chinese steel generally declined after 2000, but then shot up sharply in 2004 and later, synchronizing with the buildup in steel capacity in China and the rise in steel exports from China. Preliminary regression analysis outlined in table 3.2 shows that

Table 3.2. RELATIONSHIPS BETWEEN CHINESE ENERGY SUBSIDIES, CHINESE STEEL EXPORTS WORLDWIDE, AND US IMPORTS OF CHINESE STEEL

	Pearson Correlation Coefficient	Significance (1-tailed)	*N*
Chinese Steel Exports Worldwide with *Chinese Energy Subsidies to Steel*	.959	.000	8
US Imports of Chinese Steel with *Chinese Energy Subsidies to Steel*	.883	.002	8

Source: Haley and Haley 2007.

Chinese Energy Subsidies to Steel had a very strong correlation[22] with both *Chinese Steel Exports Worldwide* and *US Imports of Chinese Steel*.[23]

The Chinese central government's policies appear to be aimed at consolidating the steel industry and curbing excess capacity. However, the policies have failed to reduce energy subsidies to steel and are unlikely to do so, as pronouncements from the steel companies' senior executives indicated. For example, on October 26, 2007, Chairman Li Xiawei of Hunan Valin Iron and Steel Group said China would keep exporting steel despite governmental efforts to rein in exports of low-end products (*Shanghai Securities News* 2007). Hunan Valin planned to export between 2.2 million and 2.3 million tons of steel products in 2007, a rise of at least 24 percent from the previous year, Chairman Li said. Valin Group, China's tenth largest producer, planned to raise its output by 9 percent to 10.8 million tons in 2007, and the company expected revenue to rise 12 percent to about RMB 45.5 billion, Li said. "This year a few dozen million tons were supposed to be shut; if they haven't it creates more pressure for next year. So far, I haven't seen the policies have much effect," he said (*Shanghai Securities News* 2007).

What one hand takes away the other hand gives, and vice versa. As previously stated, the center and provinces differ on policies and goals toward steel.[24] The central government's removal of subsidies has often resulted in the provincial government's increasing them. For example, at a State Council conference held on April 27, 2007, the NDRC's director, Ma Kai, revealed that 10 provinces and municipalities, that is, Beijing, Hebei, Shanxi, Liaoning, Jiangsu, Zhejiang, Jiangxi, Shandong, Henan, and Xinjiang, had signed a first round of written commitments to shut down and to eliminate outdated iron-making capacity and obsolete steelmaking capacity of 39.86 and 41.67 million tons respectively in the next five years; 22.55 and 24.23 million tons were to be closed down by the end of 2007. Five out of the above-mentioned steelmaking provinces, Hebei,

Shanxi, Henan, Jiangsu and Shandong, were responsible for 70 percent of the nation's outdated iron-making capacity and 50 percent of obsolete steelmaking capacity. However, according to the NDRC, some enterprises reconstructed those would-be eliminated facilities and expanded production scale to ward off the elimination; some only suspended production with the intention of resuming operation at a more favorable time; some sold outdated equipment to other regions; and some switched iron-making blast furnaces to the production of ductile iron pipes and ferroalloy, which were already severely oversupplied, thereby thwarting the agreements (*Shanghai Securities News* 2007). To bolster employment in the current economic slowdown, provincial subsidies to steel have continued, even increased, obfuscating true market demand for coking coal, thermal coal, and electricity. As Goldman Sachs noted in July 2012, local governments in Hebei and Shanxi Provinces had increased subsidies to steel mills and coal producers to support manufacturing through weak demand and bulging inventories, contributing to even greater excess capacity (Grant 2012).

In conclusion, substantial energy subsidies pervade China's steel production and have done so since China entered the WTO. These subsidies have contributed directly to the ballooning of Chinese steel exports and have affected the global and US steel industries. The Chinese central government's policies on consolidating the Chinese steel industry appear to have had limited or no effect on the provinces' subsidies. Future policy initiatives from both the United States and China regarding China's steel exports and compliance with WTO standards may need to accommodate these provincial realities to enhance effectiveness.

NOTES

1. The research for this study was funded by a grant from the Alliance for American Manufacturing, Washington, DC. As indicated in this study, we sometimes include estimated data on supply, demand, and growth in the Chinese steel industry calculated in 2007 for subsequent years. With hindsight, these estimates have proven reasonable. Gaps in Chinese sources limit our abilities to replace these estimates with consistent, reported data.
2. U.S. Department of Commerce, ISI Analytics.
3. Growth in China's global steel exports is derived from data from the Iron and Steel Statistics Bureau, Mysteel, and Mathur (2007); growth in China's steel production is derived from data from Citigroup Global Markets (2005) and Mysteel.
4. Outline of the Eleventh Five-Year Plan for National Economic and Social Development, available at http://en.ndrc.gov.cn/hot/W020060531535878205383.jpg.

5. Beijing has chosen Baosteel, Beijing Shougang, Tangshan Iron and Steel, Anben Steel, and Wugang as a focus for industry consolidation activities, with limited success.
6. ISI Analytics.
7. BNP Paribas.
8. World Steel Dynamics Inc.
9. BNP Paribas.
10. Interfax—*China Metals Weekly*, 2006.
11. The China Iron and Steel Association measured Chinese steel supply in 2007 at 489.2 million tons and demand at 434.4 million tons.
12. Other estimates have indicated that Chinese costs are about 30 percent lower than European costs. See Taube and in der Heiden (2009).
13. RNCOS Industry Research Solutions.
14. BNP Paribas.
15. Mysteel; BNP Paribas; CEIC database; US Department of Commerce.
16. US Department of Commerce; Bureau of Census.
17. See remarks of Cheng Siwei, vice chairman of National People's Congress, and Xu Jian, director of the Central Bank, quoted in Lovasz and White (2007); and analysis by Credit Suisse (2007).
18. The International Energy Agency (2007) estimated that in 2006, total energy consumption subsidies in China (net of taxes) amounted to $11 billion with coal as the most heavily subsidized product. Our research synchronizes with those general results.
19. International Energy Agency (2006).
20. RNCOS Industry Research Solutions; National Bureau of Statistics.
21. CEIC database.
22. In this analysis, the Pearson correlation coefficient measures the strength of the linear relationship between the variable *Chinese Energy Subsidies to Steel* and the two variables, *Chinese Steel Exports Worldwide* and *U.S. Imports of Chinese Steel*. The coefficients in the analysis are very close to 1, and highly significant, indicating an almost perfect relation between the variables.
23. Haley and Haley (2007).
24. See Haley, Haley and Tan (2004) for an elaboration of the historical and strategic divergence between the Chinese central and provincial governments' goals and strategies.

CHAPTER 4
Through the Looking Glass: Subsidies to China's Glass Industry

This chapter documents the explosive growth of China's glass and glass products industry and the government subsidies that bolstered this growth from 2004 to 2008.[1] In 2009, China was the largest producer of glass and glass products globally, had the greatest number of glass-producing companies and had the largest number of float-glass production lines in the world. Since 2003, glass production in China had more than doubled. Concurrently, production capacity in China had also doubled since 2003 and increased more than threefold since 2000.

The glass and glass products industry in China consists of five sectors: flat glass, glass fiber, container glass, glass tableware, and specialty glass. From 1987 to 2007, China's total glass output rose, on average, by 18 percent year on year. Table 4.1 shows some of this output and growth for the industry and the flat-glass sector. Through May 2008, output of all glass products (except laminated glass) displayed double-digit year-on-year growth: for example, flat glass in total grew by 12.22 percent, glass fiber by 43.45 percent, sealed insulating glass by 35.91 percent, tempered glass by 17.77 percent, laminated glass by 9.78 percent, household-glass products by 12.79 percent, and heat-preserving glass receptacles by 19.01 percent (China Economic Information Network). Sales of glass and glass products jumped 30.98 percent from the previous year to $16.48 billion through May 2008, while gross industrial output value reached $17.07 billion, up 31.27 percent (China Economic Information Network).

Along with increasing production, as table 4.2 shows, the industry experienced a sevenfold increase in exports from 2000 to 2007. China had become the largest exporter of flat glass and glass fiber in the world.

Table 4.1. OUTPUT AND GROWTH OF CHINESE GLASS, 2003–2007

Year	Glass and glass products industry		Flat-glass sector	
	Industrial output (billions of yuan)	Year-on-year growth (%)	Industrial output (billions of yuan)	Year-on-year growth (%)
2003	82.4		20.3	
2004	123.4	49.8	28.6	40.9
2005	150.8	22.2	31.9	11.5
2006	190.4	26.3	36.1	13.2
2007	258.4	35.7	45.7	26.6

Source: National Bureau of Statistics, China; authors' estimates.

Flat glass comprises a core sector of the glass and glass products industry in China. In 2007, official statistics indicate that China produced a total of 497 million weight boxes[2] of flat glass (National Bureau of Statistics, China); however, some private sources have estimated that Chinese flat-glass production may have reached 600 million weight boxes in that year.[3] Globally, nearly two-thirds of flat-glass production flows into the construction industry, and about a quarter flows into the transportation industry for the making of auto safety glass. The production of mirrors accounts for less than 9 percent of flat-glass production. In China too, the construction industry absorbed the bulk of Chinese flat glass, followed by automobiles.

China's strong economic growth, together with the introduction of float-glass technology, had contributed to some of the increased glass output since

Table 4.2. EXPORTS OF CHINA'S GLASS AND GLASS PRODUCTS INDUSTRY, 2000–2007

Year	Export value (US$100 million)	Year-on-year growth (%)
2000	11.5	
2001	14.0	21.7
2002	18.0	28.6
2003	23.5	30.6
2004	32.5	38.3
2005	44.5	36.9
2006	56.5	27.0
2007	71.0	25.7

Source: National Bureau of Statistics, China; General Administration of Customs, China

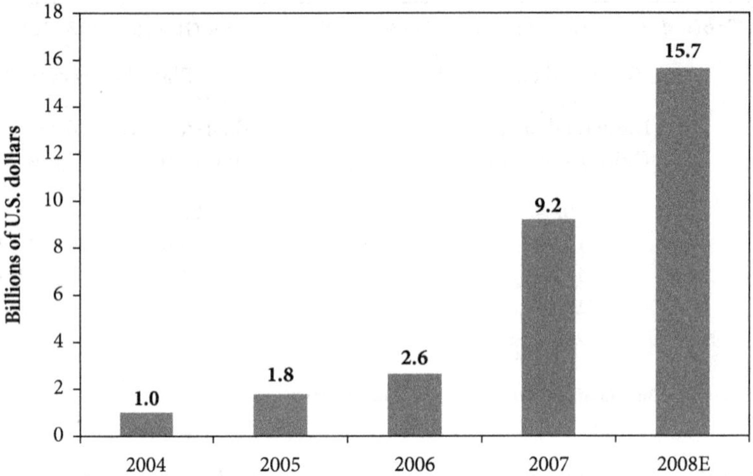

Figure 4.1
Subsidies to China's Glass and Glass Products Industry, 2004–2008
Source: Authors' calculations and estimates based on *Asia Pulse*, October 11, 2007; China Economic Information Network; CEIC; glass.cn; *Interfax—China Metals Weekly*, October 26, 2007; International Energy Agency; *KeyBanc Capital Markets*; National Bureau of Statistics, China; *The Standard* (Hong Kong), January 21, 2006; steelonthenet.com; US Geological Survey.

the late 1980s. However, industry characteristics and government policies show that generous government subsidies bolstered growth as well. Data and calculations in this study reveal that China's glass industry received total subsidies approximating at least $30.29 billion from 2004 to 2008. Figure 4.1 traces these subsidies to the glass and glass products industry, which include subsidies to heavy oil, coal, electricity, and soda ash.

INDUSTRY CHARACTERISTICS AND STRUCTURE

By the end of November 2007, 3,430 enterprises, the most in the world, engaged in all aspects of China's glass and glass products industry (National Bureau of Statistics, China). China's glass industry appeared to enjoy no economies of scale. Despite the central government's stated policy and ostensible efforts to eliminate inefficient glass production,[4] the concentration ratio of China's glass industry remained comparatively low. In November 2007, the sales-revenue concentration ratio of China's top 10 glass and glass-product enterprises was 7.92 percent, or 1.38 percentage points lower than in the same period in the previous year; the profit-concentration ratio of the top 10 enterprises was 13.97 percent. Table 4.3 shows the performance of China's glass and glass products industry by size

Table 4.3. PERFORMANCE OF CHINA'S GLASS AND GLASS PRODUCTS INDUSTRY BY SIZE OF ENTERPRISE, 2007

Enterprises	Sales			Profits	
	Actual Value (Billions of Yuan)	Year-on-Year Growth (Percent)	Change in Growth over Prior Year (Percentage Points)	Actual Value (Billions of Yuan)	Year-on-Year Growth (Percent)
Glass & Glass Product	220	32.8	2.5	15.6	7.4
Large Size	24	17.7	-7.5	2.5	1.5
Medium Size	88	31.1	8.1	7.3	3.9
Small Size	108	38.4	-0.5	5.8	2.1

Source: China Economic Information Network

in 2007. The industry's sales and profits were dominated by medium-sized and small enterprises, which were also the fastest growing in both sales and profits. Table 4.4 indicates the ownership of the industry. Private, other/unknown, and foreign-invested enterprises (FIEs) appeared the most profitable.

Table 4.4. OWNERSHIP OF THE GLASS AND GLASS PRODUCTS INDUSTRY, 2008

	Sales			Profits	
	Actual Value (Billions of Yuan)	Year-on-Year Growth (Percent)	Change in Growth over Prior Year (Percentage Points)	Actual Value (Millions of Yuan)	Year-on-Year Growth (Millions of Yuan)
Entire Industry	114.6	30.5	-2.3	7,040	1,576
State Business	3.0	11.3	-3.8	43	-14
Regional Owned	2.6	19.4	-25.4	150	-3
Co-operative Entity	1.1	7.7	-20.5	49	-16
Shareholding	7.9	16.6	-24.1	659	148
Private Enterprise	44.5	40.1	0.8	2,780	890
Foreign Funded	33.1	24.7	-2.0	2,353	237
Other	22.4	32.9	1.2	1,005	334

Source: China Economic Information Network

The industry was geographically fragmented as well. As table 4.5 indicates, flat-glass production occurred throughout China, with enterprises operating in 29 of its 32 provinces, autonomous regions, and municipalities. Hebei, Guangdong, Jiangsu, Shandong, and Zhejiang produced the most glass, with the first three provinces contributing over 40 percent of China's total flat-glass output. The industry appeared to enjoy no distributional advantages and spanned North, East, and South Central China, with fewer enterprises in Northeast, Southwest, and Northwest China. In 2007, East China produced 37 percent of all flat-glass output, North China 21 percent, South Central China 28 percent, Northeast China 6 percent, Southwest China 4 percent, and Northwest China another 4 percent.

Table 4.5. REGIONAL FLAT-GLASS PRODUCTION IN CHINA, 2007

Region	Gross industrial output (millions of yuan)	Industrial value-added (millions of yuan)	Number of employees
National	45,591	12,761	120,203
Beijing	161	28	406
Tianjin	463	105	1,168
Hebei	5,867	1,559	21,758
Shanxi	300	69	1,060
Inner Mongolia	1,166	413	3,140
Liaoning	1,415	384	4,306
Jilin	822	295	1,327
Heilongjiang	296	92	1,478
Shanghai	901	196	2,913
Jiangsu	6,988	1,648	12,920
Zhejiang	1,293	297	3,887
Anhui	609	106	2,123
Fujian	2,335	1,052	2,980
Jiangxi	47	19	170
Shandong	5,615	1,173	13,090
Henan	4,874	1,387	17,501
Hubei	1,945	589	5,060
Hunan	1,022	331	2,967
Guangdong	6,295	1,911	8,905
Guangxi	407	88	1,126
Hainan	118	40	500
Chongqing	164	46	1,210
Sichuan	1,333	565	4,241
Yunnan	232	24	1,179

Table 4.5. (*Continued*)

Region	Gross industrial output (millions of yuan)	Industrial value-added (millions of yuan)	Number of employees
Shaanxi	544	189	2,338
Gansu	370	112	1,598
Qinghai	49	23	318
Ningxia	32	9	294
Xinjiang	30	9	240

Source: National Bureau of Statistics, China.

In 2008, China had 268 flat-glass manufacturers (China Economic Information Network), more than any other country in the world. Yet, just as in the industry as a whole, 96 percent of China's flat-glass manufacturers operated small and medium-sized facilities, as table 4.6 indicates. These facilities also appeared the most vibrant. Indeed, small enterprises experienced 65 percent year-on-year growth in sales revenues, as opposed to large ones, mostly joint ventures (JVs) or foreign-invested enterprises (FIEs), which experienced about 9 percent growth. Most of China's glass producers also ran much smaller float-glass production lines than those operated by the big five global glass giants (Asahi Glass, Pilkington, PPG,

Table 4.6. PERFORMANCE OF CHINA'S FLAT-GLASS ENTERPRISES BY SIZE, 2007

		Sales		Profits	
	Number of Enterprises	100 million Chinese Yuan	Year-on-Year Growth (%)	100 million Chinese Yuan	Year-on-Year Growth 100 million Chinese Yuan
Large-sized Enterprises	10	103.79	8.6	5.50	–5.63
Medium-sized Enterprises	73	219.60	33.1	16.44	–5.40
Small-sized Enterprises	185	88.46	65.0	4.21	0.05
Total	268	411.85	31.1	26.15	-10.99

Source: China Economic Information Network

Saint Gobain, and Guardian Industries). Only 23 percent of China's production lines had daily output of more than 500 metric tons, compared with the big five's production lines of more than 700–800 metric tons per day.[5] In 2009, 64 percent of China's glass manufacturers had production runs of between 300 and 400 metric tons a day, and 13 percent had runs of less than 300 metric tons per day.[6] The majority of glass producers in China operated at the low to medium end.

Since 2001, China had also become the largest flat-glass producer in the world. The flat-glass sector exhibited the same ownership breakdown as the industry. In 2007, most of China's flat-glass manufacturers (about 117) were privately owned. The flat-glass sector also had small numbers of SOEs (8), collectives (8), equity JVs (2), shareholding companies (20), companies with unknown ownership (59), and FIEs (54). Yet FIEs extracted 33 percent, or the bulk, of revenues, and those of unknown ownership another 32 percent. Private enterprises had 15 percent of revenues. Collectives and SOEs appeared to have lower revenues than their competitors, with 4 percent and 7 percent respectively. Equity JVs and shareholding companies that had state ownership had 1 percent and 8 percent of revenues respectively.

ANALYSIS OF GLASS SUPPLY

This section looks at the growth of Chinese glass production and the building of excess capacity. It also traces the effects of Chinese glass production on Chinese exports and US imports.

Production Capacity

In 2008, China's glass industry contributed over 31 percent of global glass production. The country had the greatest number of float-glass production lines and the largest production capacity for float glass in the world. Figure 4.2 outlines the total number of float-glass production lines and production capacity in China from 2000 to 2007. Production capacity of glass in China had more than doubled since 2003 and increased threefold since 2000. China produced 497 million weight boxes of flat glass in 2007, an increase of 13 percent from the previous year. China's output of flat glass also more than doubled from 2003 to 2008. The growth rate of glass production showed no sign of abating, increasing the demand for raw materials. Indeed, the production of pure alkali (a key input into

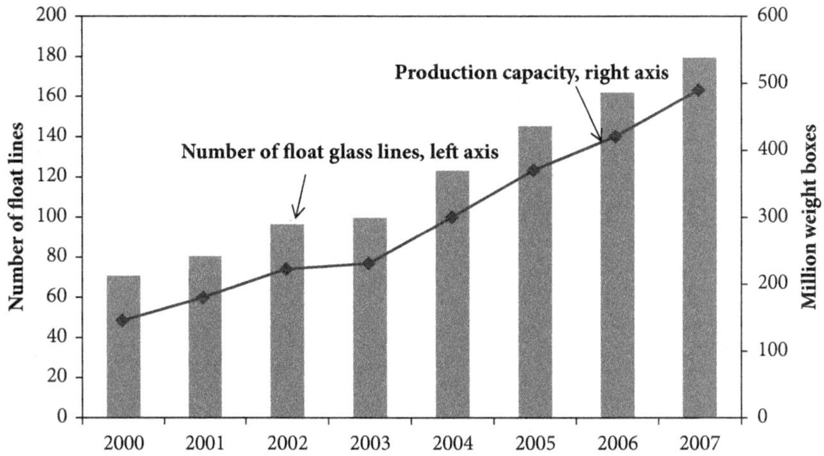

Figure 4.2
Float-Glass Production Lines and Production Capacity in China, 2000–2007
Source: National Bureau of Statistics, China; ResearchinChina.

glass production) increased by 11 percent from January to October 2007, while production of glass increased by more than 18 percent, significantly more than upstream industrial production increased (China Economic Information Network).

Figure 4.3 shows that despite competitive pressures, more production capacity was added annually to China's glass industry, at least quadrupling annually the production capacity added in 2003. Indeed in 2007, 19 float-glass production lines were added, which brought 62.6 million weight boxes of new production capacity. Over 40 production lines were under construction or planned for construction in 2008 and 2009, contributing to more increased capacity and even fiercer price competition. As the next section elaborates, the supply of medium and low-grade float glass greatly exceeded demand in China, while the supply of high-grade float glass sometimes fell short of demand. With the central government's encouragement, the number of production lines with larger capacity and higher quality increased, including CSG's two lines of high-grade float glass with daily melting capacity of six million and seven million tons respectively; Shanghai Yaohua Pilkington Glass Company's line for Changshu ultra-clear and rolling glass; and Xinyi Group's line for Dongguan high-grade float glass with daily melting capacity of nine million tons. Despite these efforts, the great bulk of new lines continued to emphasize the production of lower-grade float glass.

Overcapacity and overheated growth constituted major forces exerting downward price pressures on China's glass-manufacturing industry.

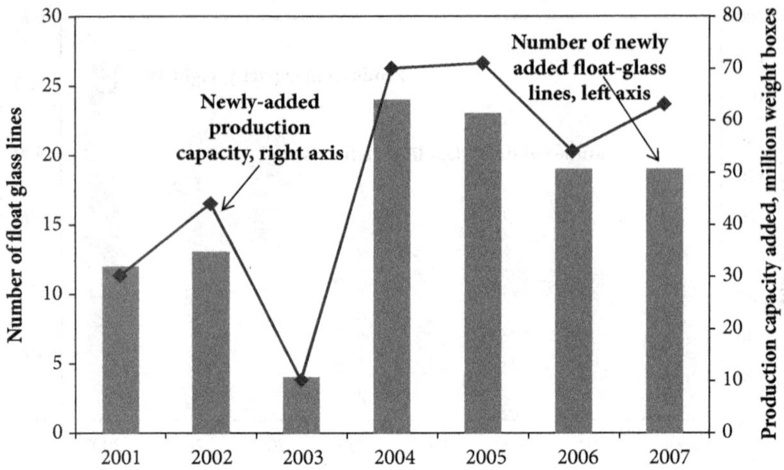

Figure 4.3
Newly Added Float-Glass Capacity in China, 2000–2007 (100 million weight boxes)
Source: National Bureau of Statistics, China.

Without the ability to extract significant economies of scale and with oversupply, margins were squeezed. Operating data from key enterprises in China's glass industry from January to April 2008 showed that cumulative total profits declined 7 percent year on year, with profit margins falling to 15 percent from 42 percent. A significant proportion of these enterprises experienced on-the-book losses, although the proportion of losses started to decline. For example, by the end of November 2007, 554 of the total 3,430 enterprises engaged in China's glass industry, making up 16 percent of the total, suffered economic losses, lower than in the corresponding 2006 period of the previous year, 18 percent. The economic losses for the 554 companies in 2007 amounted to RMB 1.7 billion, down 40 percent from the corresponding period of the previous year. Government subsidies and transfers contributed to bolstering profits and to increasing sales (China Economic Information Network). In May 2008, glass prices continued to decline, while the price of the major inputs into glass, pure alkali and heavy oil, continued to rise.

Exports and Imports

China's increased glass production transformed it into an export juggernaut. In the first six months of 2008, exports of Chinese glass and glass products exceeded four billion dollars, paralleling the growth rate of the

Table 4.7. CHINA'S EXPORTS AND IMPORTS OF FLAT GLASS, 2003–2008 (10,000 M^2)

	2003	2004	2005	2006	2007	2008 (Jan–June)
Imports	3,153	4,291	2,719	2,786	2,870	1,074
Exports	12,441	14,466	19,937	24,459.4	28,695.9	13,001

Source: National Bureau of Statistics, China; BMI.com.

industry (China Economic Information Network).[7] The results held across sectors. For example, Chinese exports of flat glass far outstripped its imports, as table 4.7 shows. In 2007, China exported about 16 percent of its total flat-glass production. Because of existing and planned production capacity, glass exports from China were expected to continue to increase at least until 2011, outpacing projected increases in demand and increasing its trade surplus.

Figure 4.4 shows US exports and imports of glass and glass products from China from 2000 to 2008; both increased threefold in that period. However, US exports of glass and glass products to China remained at a comparatively low level. Consequently, as figure 4.4 also shows, the US trade imbalance with China in glass and glass products increased dramatically from 2000 to 2008 with repercussions for strategic trade policy as discussed in the last chapter.

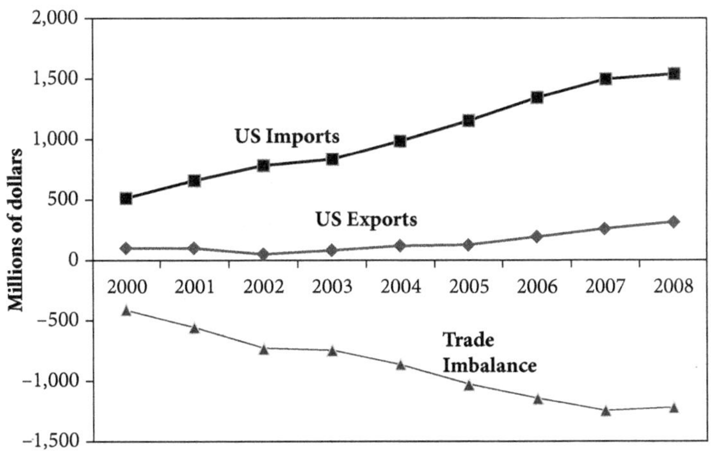

Figure 4.4
US-China Trade in Glass and Glass Products, 2000–2008
Source: International Trade Administration.

Starting from July 1, 2007, China adjusted tax rebates for the exports of glass and glass products down to 5 percent from 13 percent. The drop in export-tax rebates forced some enterprises to raise the prices of exports, to some extent weakening their competitive positions as low-cost suppliers. However, China's automobile-glass exports seemed unaffected in 2007. For instance, Fuyao Glass's revenues from auto glass reached RMB 3.554 billion in 2007, up 23 percent from the previous year. Forty-one percent of Fuyao's revenues came through exports. Its exports increased by 26 percent year on year, and the company's original equipment manufacturer (OEM) market grew 130 percent. Meanwhile, as figure 4.4 shows, the US trade imbalance with China in glass and glass products remained relatively flat from 2007 to 2008.

ANALYSIS OF GLASS DEMAND

China is the largest consumer of glass in the world, accounting for over 33 percent of global demand. Fabricated flat glass encompasses insulating glass, tempered glass, laminated glass, mirrors, and other specialty products and accounted for over 20 percent of overall Chinese flat-glass demand in volume in 2007.[8] Though total product demand had risen nearly threefold over the previous decade, intense competition existed in the flat-glass sector. Table 4.3 shows that most Chinese manufacturers were small and medium-sized enterprises that could not extract economies of scale and scope. Consequently, many flat-glass products constituted commodities, with price the most critical selection factor. The existence of relatively few markets further heightened competitive pressures, as many products competed for use in a limited number of applications. In addition, numerous new flat-glass manufacturers had begun operations, making product differentiation more difficult. The construction and automobile industries serve as the largest consumers of Chinese flat glass, and sectoral analysis of each follows. The section concludes with a brief survey of the rapid growth of the Chinese glass-fiber sector.

Construction. The architectural market had historically constituted the largest outlet for flat glass in China, accounting for 86 percent of total demand by area in 2006 and 80 percent in 2007. Demand for flat glass used in residential-building applications totaled 900 million square meters in 2006, making up over 70 percent of the total architectural market. Over the past decade, residential demand had increased 8.7 percent per year, rising in line with residential-building-construction expenditures. Slow growth in new building construction[9] restrained market gains during the period under study. The residential market encompassed both new construction and improvements and repairs of single-family homes and apartment buildings. However, moderated growth in the overall population and in households was estimated to act as a counterbalance restraining residential flat-glass market gains through 2012. New-construction applications accounted for just over 75 percent of residential flat-glass demand in China in 2006: the long-lasting properties of flat glass resulted in a low level of replacement demand. In addition, Chinese consumers were much less likely to replace still-functional window glass for style, energy, or safety considerations.

However, in 2008, like much of the world, China suffered a real-estate decline that has continued to 2012. From July 2007 to July 2008, national statistics showed single-digit growth in the average price of commercial and residential real estate. In contrast, real-estate brokers indicated that prices fell from peaks reached earlier in 2008, while the number of transactions plunged. Volumes first dropped precipitously in southeastern China, and the decline spread across the country. With few buyers, sellers cut prices for residential and commercial real estate. In some cities, prices dropped by 10 percent to 40 percent. In other parts of the country, transactions fell, but prices have only started to follow. For instance, the number of home sales plunged by two-thirds in Harbin in the northeast, though prices fell as little as 4 percent from the same period in the previous year. A wealth effect also occurred as the share prices of real-estate developers plunged. For example, Vanke, the country's biggest publicly-traded developer, was down by 35 percent in August 2008 from a year earlier. Several analysts we spoke to believed that the real-estate downturn created a matching downturn in the construction sector and contributed to enormous excess inventory in Chinese glass.

Automobiles. Float glass constituted the major raw material for automobile-glass production, and this sector was the second-largest consumer for Chinese flat glass. China has over 130 automakers, and they served as customers of automobile-glass makers. The average automobile uses over 4.2 square meters of glass. The automobile-glass-consumer market consisted of the matching OEM market and the fittings-repair aftermarket. Chinese enterprises competed domestically on the matching market and globally on the international fittings-repair market.

After falling off in 2005, China's automobile market grew steadily for a couple of years: market demand for automobiles exceeded eight million units in 2007, about 18 percent higher than in 2006. However, in

2008, the Chinese automobile market saw fierce competition and price cutting, despite rapidly rising raw material prices. The China Association of Automobile Manufacturers (CAAM) reported that in 2008, the Chinese automobile market had its worst year in a decade, with annual passenger-car sales rising only 7.3 percent. In January 2009, year-on-year sales of cars and light commercial vehicles fell by 7.7 percent. The Chinese government acted with success to stimulate car purchases in January 2009 through tax cuts and cash incentives (Waldmeir 2009a). Chinese car sales rose 90 percent year-on-year in August 2009 amid signs that tax cuts and subsidies from Beijing could propel China to record vehicle sales of 12 million that year (Waldmeir 2009b).

China's automobile glass industry is highly consolidated; for the period under study, three companies accounted for more than 80 percent of total market share in China. Chinese automobile glassmakers' expansions had been on the upstream raw-material side with most having plans to build float-glass lines to improve raw material supply. On end-product lines, capacity expansion had been relatively modest. In 2008, China had over 200 automobile-glass manufacturers. Only a small proportion of these automobile-glass manufacturers engaged in large-scale production; most were small and also had poor product quality. Chinese glass producers passed only ISO9002 Authentication; yet the more rigorous QS9000 Authentication and VDA Authentication constituted the ISO9000 quality-system standards for the global auto-manufacturing industry.[10]

In 2005, China exported about 650,000 square meters of automobile glass to the United States with an average selling price of $31.80/m^2. Export volume rose to 5.4 million square meters in 2007, but the average selling price dropped to $18.50/m^2 (China Association of Automobile Manufacturers). Overcapacity in the auto industry resulted in further downward pressure on vehicle-component prices, including automotive glass.

Glass fiber. Starting from a fairly low base, in 2007 China became the largest exporter of glass fiber in the world and exported most of its production. In 2007, China exported 1.1 million tons of glass fiber, or 68 percent of its gross production, and cornered 29 percent of global glass-fiber exports. China produced about 1.6 million tons of glass fiber in 2007, up 38 percent year on year. From January to April 2008, the production of glass fiber accelerated to 476,000 tons, up 42 percent year on year; and exports increased by 62 percent compared to the same period in 2007.

MANUFACTURING COSTS OF CHINESE GLASS

Manufacturers have used the float-glass process since the 1980s, and it constitutes the dominant glass-manufacturing method in use today. Heavy oil, soda ash, and silica sand form the primary raw materials for the production of glass. Drawing on case studies, competitor analysis, and independent research, figure 4.5 indicates the cost structure of China's glass and glass products industry. Heavy oil and soda ash contributed to 65 percent of the costs of manufacturing Chinese glass and glass products. Utilities and coal contributed another 12 percent to the cost. Labor contributed only 2 percent of the costs of manufacturing glass in China.

Heavy oil and soda ash. A Cost of Goods Sold (COGS) Sensitivity analysis was done for Xinyi Glass, one of the largest exporters of automobile glass in China, and the most profitable glass enterprise in China. Despite its value-added products, prices of raw materials remained one of the major uncertainties for Xinyi's earnings outlook. Its vertical integration into upstream float-glass production would not shelter it from upstream costs such as heavy oil, soda ash, and silica sand. A major investment

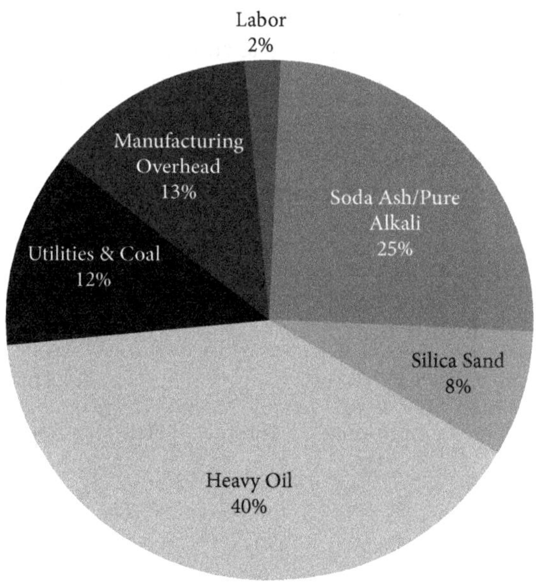

Figure 4.5
Cost Structure of China's Glass and Glass Products Industry
Source: BNP Paribas; ResearchinChina; authors' estimates.

Table 4.8. COGS: HEAVY-OIL SENSITIVITY ANALYSIS FOR XINYI GLASS

Growth in heavy oil prices	0%	1%	5%	10%	15%	20%
Margins (percent):						
Gross	34.5%	34.3%	33.3%	32.0%	30.8%	29.5%
Net	20.5%	20.2%	19.3%	18.1%	16.9%	15.7%
Margin changes (percentage points):						
Gross		−0.2	−1.0	−1.2	−1.2	−1.2
Net		−0.3	−0.9	−1.2	−1.2	−1.2

Source: Xinyi Glass; BNP Paribas.

company estimated that a 1 percent increase in the heavy-oil price could lead to a 0.2 and 0.3 percentage point decrease in gross margin and net margin, respectively, for Xinyi Glass (see table 4.8). The cost of heavy oil shot up sharply from 2005.

China has low-grade soda ash and relies primarily on synthetic soda ash. Chinese soda-ash consumption was approximately seven million tons in 2008, and the glass and glass-product industry was the major consumer of this product. About 30 percent of soda ash went into container glass, and another 15 percent went into flat glass. A large disconnect existed between the price of Chinese synthetic soda ash and the export price of North American soda ash. In fact, the price of North American soda ash sold into North and South Asia in December 2008 was below the average cash cost of the Chinese synthetic product (see table 4.9). China had more than 60 soda-ash manufacturers, mainly located along the eastern

Table 4.9. COST DISADVANTAGE OF CHINESE VERSUS US SODA-ASH PRODUCERS (US DOLLARS/SHORT TON)

	To North Asia			To South Asia		
	FOB[a]	Additional CIF[b]	Total	FOB[a]	Additional CIF[b]	Total
US	65–70	90–95	155–65	65–70	90–95	155–60
China	175–90	55–60	230–50	175–90	70–75	245–65

Source: Gabelli & Co.

[a] Free on board.

[b] Cost, insurance, freight.

coastal regions. The top five manufacturers accounted for more than 40 percent of domestic production, and the top 10 manufacturers for more than 50 percent. Only one soda-ash producer was added between 2005 and 2008 (Qinghai Soda Ash, with annual production capacity of 900,000 metric tons). Though the soda-ash price remained relatively stable during 2006, increasing demand in downstream industries such as the production of float glass pushed the price up from 2007. In 2008, 1.3 million tons of Chinese synthetic soda-ash capacity was mothballed, and projects accounting for over three million tons of new Chinese synthetic capacity were deferred or canceled, adding to an already-tight supply/demand balance.[11]

Following up on the previous COGS sensitivity analysis for heavy oil, a major investment company estimated that a 1 percent increase in the price of soda ash could lead to a 0.2 percentage point decrease in both gross margin and net margin, respectively, for Xinyi Glass (see table 4.10).

Raw-material prices rose steeply in early 2008. Data from the Pearl River delta regions show that the soda-ash price rose by 50 percent to RMB 2,400 per metric ton and the heavy-oil price rose by 30 percent to RMB 4,500 per metric ton. These price increases, combined with increases in silica-sand prices and transportation costs, pushed the glass-manufacturing cost for each weight box up by 20 to 30 percent in the first quarter of 2008. Despite the sharp increases in raw material prices, the price of float glass did not increase appreciably in China between 2001 and 2008, hovering between RMB 25 and RMB 30 per square meter, indicating the presence of both price competition and manufacturing subsidies.

Table 4.10. COGS: SODA-ASH SENSITIVITY ANALYSIS FOR XINYI GLASS

Growth in soda ash prices	0%	1%	5%	10%	15%	20%
Margins (percent):						
Gross	34.5%	34.3%	34.0%	33.2%	32.0%	30.4%
Net	20.5%	20.3%	19.9%	19.2%	18.1%	16.6%
Margin Changes (percentage points):						
Gross		−0.2	−0.4	−0.8	−1.2	−1.6
Net		−0.2	−0.4	−0.7	−1.1	−1.5

Source: Xinyi Glass; BNP Paribas.

SUBSIDIES TO CHINA'S GLASS AND GLASS PRODUCTS INDUSTRY

Using the methodology and variables indicated in chapter 2, this section calculates the subsidies to China's flat-glass sector for heavy oil, coal, electricity, and soda ash. An analysis extends the results to the glass and glass products industry in China. Table 4.11 lists the subsidies.

Subsidies to flat-glass sector. Discernible total subsidies for all inputs to the flat-glass sector in China between 2004 and the third quarter of 2008 reached $4.8 billion. The increase was steepest after 2006, when the price of both heavy oil and coal rose sharply and a subsidy payment appeared for soda ash. Because the calculations included only those subsidies that could be traced, confirmed, and recorded, the total subsidies in this study constitute very conservative estimates for the Chinese flat-glass sector. The trend of rising subsidies explains to some extent why, despite no significant increase in prices of flat glass during this period and a great increase in those of raw materials, so many small companies remained profitable. Labor only accounted for 2 percent of the costs of producing flat glass, and the lack of economies of scale and scope strongly suggest that the inefficient and polluting Chinese glass industry had been getting support, probably from provincial governments. Figure 4.6 traces subsidies to the flat-glass sector over the last five years.

Subsidies for heavy oil to the flat-glass sector in China between 2004 and the third quarter of 2008 reached $3.5 billion. The increase

Table 4.11. SUBSIDIES TO THE CHINESE FLAT-GLASS SECTOR, 2004–2008 (US$)

Year	Heavy oil	Coal	Electricity	Soda ash	Total
2004	119,611,789	95,719,595	20,910,133	0	236,241,517
2005	277,322,091	43,653,135	51,785,811	0	372,761,037
2006	234,169,336	159,744,414	62,422,541	44,188,442	500,524,733
2007	1,309,451,286	240,015,384	78,530,248	0	1,627,996,918
2008 (3rd quarter)	1,540,020,237	471,870,217	76,233,208	0	2,088,123,662
Total	3,480,574,739	1,011,002,745	289,881,941	44,188,442	**4,825,647,867 Grand Total**

Source: Authors' calculations and estimates based on *Asia Pulse*, October 11, 2007; China Economic Information Network; CEIC; glass.cn; *Interfax—China Metals Weekly*, October 26, 2007; International Energy Agency; *KeyBanc Capital Markets*; National Bureau of Statistics, China; *The Standard* (Hong Kong), January 21, 2006; steelonthenet.com; US Geological Survey.

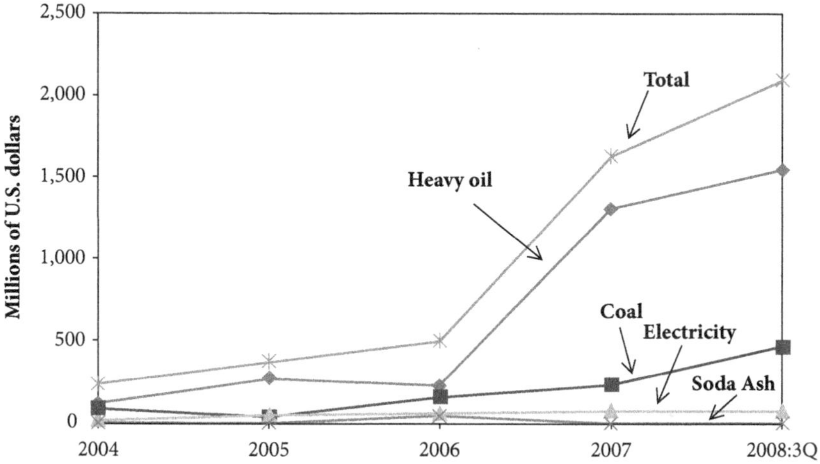

Figure 4.6
Rising Subsidies to Flat Glass in China, 2004–2008
Source: Authors' calculations and estimates based on *Asia Pulse*, October 11, 2007; China Economic Information Network; glass.cn; *Interfax—China Metals Weekly*, October 26, 2007; International Energy Agency; *KeyBanc Capital Markets*; National Bureau of Statistics, China; *The Standard* (Hong Kong), January 21, 2006; steelonthenet.com; US Geological Survey.

was steepest in 2007 and 2008, when the price of heavy oil skyrocketed. As mentioned in chapter 2, the oil companies recorded subsidies from the central government as revenues spread out over years. Consequently, the total subsidies to heavy oil would be very difficult to discern.

Subsidies for coal to the flat-glass sector in China between 2004 and the third quarter of 2008 reached $1.01 billion. The increase was steepest in 2008, when the price of coal soared.

Subsidies for electricity to the flat-glass sector in China between 2004 and the third quarter of 2008 reached $290 million. Chapter 2 defined the breakdowns of coal-price and provincial subsidies. The total for provincial subsidies approximated $164 million; the total for coal-price-increase subsidies reached $126 million.

Discernible subsidies to soda ash in the flat-glass sector could only be gauged for the year 2006, because of murky data. In 2006, subsidies to soda ash approximated $44 million. As shown in figure 4.5, soda ash constitutes a key cost for Chinese glass manufacturers, almost all of whom use Chinese soda ash, which is considerably more expensive than the US version. Additionally, the price of soda ash climbed after 2005, putting a strain on companies' operating margins. Yet the poor-quality data on prices did not reveal this. The price paid for soda ash was gathered from

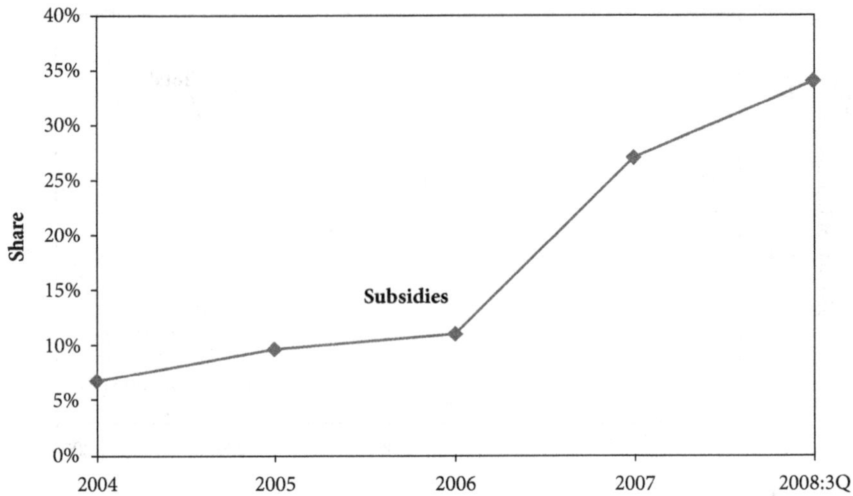

Figure 4.7
Subsidies as Share of Gross Industrial Output Value of Chinese Flat Glass, 2004–2008
Source: National Bureau of Statistics, China; authors' estimates.

industrial surveys and could have indicated the list price rather than the actual price.

Subsidies to the glass industry. As figure 4.7 shows, subsidies to China's flat-glass industry rose steadily as a share of the gross value of flat-glass output from about 7 percent in 2004 to 34 percent in 2008. As we demonstrated earlier, drawing on industry characteristics, discussion with glass-industry experts, and academic practice, the flat-glass sector seemed to reflect overall trends in the glass and glass products industry of China. Several reasons support our assumption that the subsidies identified in this study provided similar benefits to the remainder of the glass and glass products industry. Consequently, this report used subsidy rates in flat glass to estimate total subsidies in the entire industry. Structural factors and precedent that support this assumption include, (*a*) as shown in this study, the industry characteristics of fragmentation, enterprise size, excess capacity, stage of technology, and increases in production of the flat-glass sector paralleled those of the entire glass and glass products industry, (*b*) roughly the same cost structure spanned all sectors of the industry, (*c*) interviews with analysts, managers, and glass industry experts confirmed that subsidies were not unique to the flat-glass sector and that other sectors within the glass and glass products industry also received similar subsidies, and (*d*) in situations where industry-wide data are limited or nonexistent, extrapolating from a sample of companies to the industry constitutes accepted academic practice. Indeed, many industrial associations in China extrapolate from nonrandom samples when conducting industrial surveys.

The Chinese flat-glass sector was responsible for approximately 21 percent of the output of the glass and glass products industry between 2004 and the third quarter of 2008. This share has been relatively constant, though declining slightly, throughout the period under study. Assuming that inputs to glass and glass products were subsidized at rates similar to those found for the flat-glass sector, this report estimates that total subsidies to the glass and glass products industry between 2004 and the third quarter of 2008 were at least $30.29 billion and have been increasing annually.

CONCLUSIONS

In 2008, six Chinese governmental departments released a document with guidelines on improving the structure of the flat-glass sector specifically and for the glass and glass products industry generally (China Economic Information Network). Concerns included the following:

a. Unbalanced and uncontrolled production capacity, which pervaded the industry and was geared toward low-end production. As the document emphasized, only 25 percent of Chinese flat glass underwent further processing, well below the world average of 55 percent (with industrialized countries having averages of between 65 and 85 percent). Chinese glass processing added value of less than 250 percent, yet the average for the industrialized countries approximated 500 percent. Float glass had 52 Chinese manufacturers with an average capacity of just 6.83 million weight boxes. This contrasted sharply with scale economies possessed by the industry's top four international companies, which produced 41 percent of sheet glass in the world and 50 percent of processed glass.
b. Some Chinese manufacturers were cutting corners by labeling nonstandard products as standard, thereby increasing fears about product safety.

Beijing's goals included the following (China Economic Information Network):

a. Limiting flat glass's total production capacity to 550 million weight boxes, with float glass taking more than 90 percent of the total.

b. Emphasizing quality float glass and special glass, which would comprise 40 percent of total float glass.
c. Stressing that 40 percent of all glass and glass products would go through further processing.
d. Encouraging the largest 10 enterprises to generate 70 percent of sales and individual enterprises to reach annual production of 30 million weight boxes or more through mergers and acquisitions and investing abroad to acquire expertise and brand recognition.
e. Limiting capacity by insisting that new float-glass projects require approval from provincial governments, instituting more checks and controls on the glass industry in the east, but encouraging growth of the industry in the west, and requiring the central government's review of all new projects approved since 2006.
f. Encouraging Luoyang float-glass technology, developed in China, as the industry standard, thereby supporting a subsidy based on brand equity.[12]
g. Encouraging business associations to collect and to publish supply/demand analysis and data on this spottily covered industry, as well as to make suggestions on governmental policy.

The central government's goals and exhortations appear to have had little support from provincial governments and no effect on glass production. Anecdotal evidence suggests that subsidies to Chinese glass have been increasing since 2009. Besides the subsidies highlighted in this report, Beijing's stimulus package during the global recession included elimination of export taxes, devaluation of the currency, and an infusion of loans into the manufacturing sector to boost exports. For example, in 2009 the Wuxi municipal government offered up to $146,000 to each local business that increased exports in the last three months of that year, including glass manufacturers (Bradsher 2009).

NOTES

1. The research for this study was funded by a grant from the Economic Policy Institute, Washington, DC.
2. One weight box contains approximately 50 kilograms of glass.
3. Authors' interviews.
4. See last section for governmental policy in China toward glass.
5. Authors' estimates.
6. Authors' estimates.

7. Figures from 2008 are estimated from partial year data; these figures were compiled from various sources that could not provide data for the full year.
8. Authors' interviews.
9. New building construction is measured in floor space.
10. Authors' interviews.
11. Authors' interviews.
12. G. T. Haley (2009) identified a new subsidy used by the Chinese government that was based on developing domestic brand equity.

CHAPTER 5

No Paper Tiger: Subsidies to China's Paper Industry

In 2008, China overtook the United States to become the world's largest producer of paper and paper products.[1] In 2008, China had been poised to become a net exporter of paper and paper products, but the fall in global demand led to greater than expected inventories for Chinese producers. In November 2008, China's National Bureau of Statistics reported that the industry's output had increased to 83.9 million tonnes, up 9.6 percent from the previous year. In 2009, China produced over 17 percent of the world's total output in the paper industry; with exports of $7.6 billion in paper and paperboard, China consolidated its position as a lead exporter in the industry (CEIC database). As figure 5.1 shows, since 2000, China has increased production of paper threefold to assume a leading role in the global paper industry. Yet China has no competitive advantage in this capital-intensive industry and lacks the natural resources to fuel it. With saturated domestic markets, proportionately much smaller per capita than in developed countries, exports have served, and are expected to continue to serve, as the primary engine of growth for China's paper industry, adversely affecting the US and global economies.

In 2010, China had by far the fastest-growing paper industry in the world. Yet, China also had among the smallest forestry resources in the world to support this industry's expansion. Consequently, it imported the bulk of its raw materials at world prices—yet paper in China generally sold at prices much lower than in the United States or EU. Globally, and in China, labor constitutes a very small part of the costs of the paper industry—high capital investments play a major role. In China, government subsidies and loans have provided strong support for the paper industry's

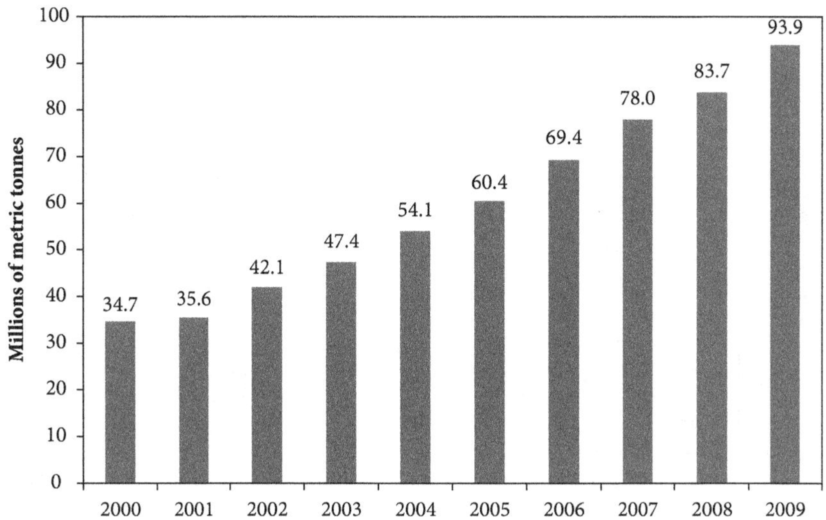

Figure 5.1
China's Production of Paper and Paperboard, 2000–2009
Source: FAO and China Paper Online.

expansion. Combined with saturated domestic product markets, the expansion has led to enormous overcapacity in China and a meteoric increase in China's paper exports.

This chapter tracks the remarkable transformation of the Chinese paper industry from 2002 to the present through focused government policy, massive capacity expansion, export-led development, and over $33.1 billion in government subsidies. Figure 5.2 summarizes some subsidies to the Chinese paper industry from 2002 to 2009, covering electricity, coal, pulp, recycled paper, subsidies reported in companies' annual reports, and interest-free loans. As described later, because of extensive missing data, subsidies to pulp could only be calculated from 2004 to 2009, and subsidies to recycled paper from 2004 to 2008. Subsidies for some inputs fell dramatically in 2009 as reported below: world commodity prices plummeted in the recession; price differentials between Chinese and world prices fell, resulting in a decline in the corresponding subsidies.

CHARACTERISTICS OF CHINA'S PAPER INDUSTRY

Since 2002, the number of paper companies in China has steadily increased. In 2007, China had 8,376 companies manufacturing paper and paper products. By November 2008, the number of companies in this industry

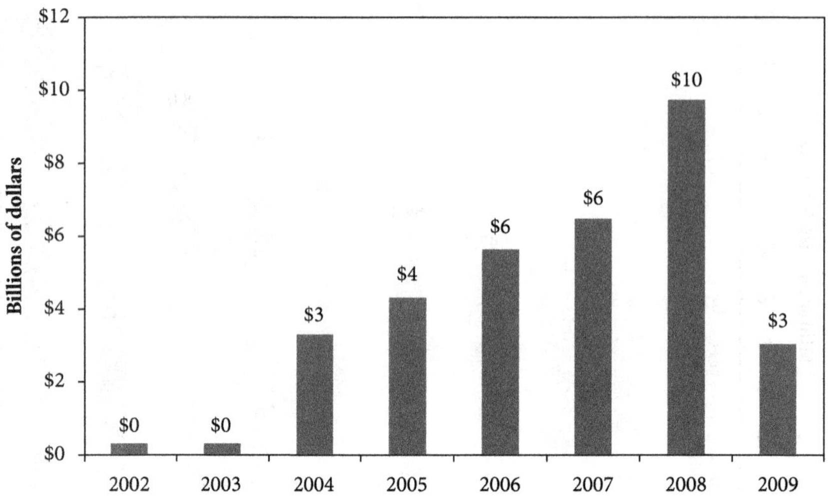

Figure 5.2
Total Subsidies to China's Paper Industry, 2002–2009
Source: Authors' calculations and estimates based on data from American Forest and Pulp Association; Australian Bureau of Agricultural and Research Economics; *China Market Pulp Report*; *China Recovered Paper Report*; CEIC; China National Development and Reform Commission; companies' annual reports; Deutsche Bank; Food and Agricultural Organization; Interfax; International Energy Agency; Macquarie Research; Morgan Stanley; National Bureau of Statistics, China; Steelonthenet.

had grown to 8,731 (National Bureau of Statistics, China). On average, the extremely fragmented Chinese paper industry showed no economies of scope or scale,[2] has shown poor profitability, and has no technological advantages. However, as we later elaborate, the central government has proposed and implemented various policies, with varying degrees of success, to consolidate the paper industry in China. These policies have aimed to fuse the interlinked forest-pulp-paper sectors, siphon huge investments into new, large, state-of-the-art paper mills, and shut down old, inefficient and small mills.

Sectors. The Chinese paper industry displayed no economies of scope through distributional or marketing efficiencies or strategies such as product bundling. Companies manufactured and sold a range of seemingly unrelated products spanning various sectors including machine-made paper and paperboard, paper and paper containers, converted paper, pulp, handmade paper, and other paper products.

Most of the companies focused on manufacturing low-quality products. In 2008, machine-made paper and paperboard accounted for 56 percent of industrial output and had 56 percent of the companies. Paper and paper containers had 39 percent of the companies with 25 percent of output. The other sectors had many fewer companies and generated far less output: converted paper (5 percent of companies and 3 percent of output), pulp (1 percent of companies, 2 percent of output), handmade paper (0.3 percent of companies and 0.2 percent of output), and other paper products (19 percent and 13 percent respectively). This sector has also served as a focus for more efficient production in the industry. Unchanged from 2007, companies manufacturing machine-made paper and paperboard had the highest-valued assets in this industry of RMB 450 billion[3] ($65.6 billion), or 64 percent of the entire industry. Paper containers comprised 26.3 percent of the industry's asset value, pulp 6.5 percent, while handmade paper and converted paper comprised 2.8 percent each. However, new capital investments had been flowing into paper and paper containers and other paper products, which in 2008 experienced growth rates of 4 percent and 13.8 percent respectively.

Fragmentation. China's paper industry generally enjoyed no scale economies and the industry was highly fragmented. Globally, the top 15 companies in paper had about one-third of the world market of 400 million tonnes. Conversely, the Chinese paper industry had very few large companies and thousands of smaller companies operating nationwide. About 88 percent of all companies in China's paper industry were small, while 12 percent were medium sized. The top 10 companies in China controlled about 20 percent of the total domestic market with the balance spread across a range of small, inefficient companies.

Since 1996, Beijing had been increasing its investments in "New China" paper mills of greater than 50,000 tons per year, with large, fast, and efficient machines that used mostly imported pulp and paper (see Flynn 2006). The largest Chinese paper company of this ilk, Nine Dragons, had not yet emerged as a top 15 global player in 2010. However, in 2007, Nine Dragons announced that it planned to double its production capacity of 5.4 million tons with a one-billion-dollar investment over two years. If this announced capacity expansion has taken place, Nine Dragons will have become one of the five largest paper companies in the world by 2012. However, as with other companies in this industry, and as covered in chapter 2, data on Nine Dragons' strategic plans and funding remained hard to decipher for S&P, Citibank, and the authors.

The Chinese paper industry displays geographic fragmentation as well. As table 5.1 shows, paper companies operated in 30 of China's 31 provinces. Shandong, Zhejiang, Guangdong, Jiangsu, and Henan produced between 8 percent and 20 percent of China's paper and paper products. Fujian, Hebei, Shanghai, Hunan, and Sichuan produced about 2 percent to 5 percent each, and every other Chinese province produced less than 2 percent of China's paper output.

Table 5.1. PAPER MANUFACTURERS IN CHINA BY REGION, 2007

Region	Number of enterprises	Gross industrial output value (RMBmn)	Number of employees (thousands)	Share
National	*8,376*	*632,545.1*	*1,383.0*	*100.0%*
Beijing	120	6,503.8	11.4	1.0%
Tianjin	174	5,149.5	14.9	0.8%
Hebei	284	22,121.2	56.6	3.5%
Shanxi	26	1,073.3	6.1	0.2%
Inner Mongolia	32	2,956.7	10.3	0.5%
Liaoning	293	11,292.6	32.8	1.8%
Jilin	63	4,146.3	12.7	0.7%
Heilongjiang	67	3,976.5	19.2	0.6%
Shanghai	335	18,762.4	36.9	3.0%
Jiangsu	637	75,677.9	105.4	12.0%
Zhejiang	1,390	71,894.2	151.0	11.4%
Anhui	167	7,735.1	24.0	1.2%
Fujian	558	29,141.0	80.1	4.6%
Jiangxi	127	8,214.9	17.9	1.3%
Shandong	886	134,541.6	211.6	21.3%
Henan	387	53,405.6	96.6	8.4%
Hubei	214	11,470.9	29.9	1.8%
Hunan	307	19,277.2	49.4	3.0%
Guangdong	1,468	99,860.0	249.6	15.8%
Guangxi	161	8,380.6	32.4	1.3%
Hainan	14	6,479.2	4.5	1.0%
Chongqing	90	3,203.0	9.9	0.5%
Sichuan	306	14,429.3	51.1	2.3%
Guizhou	34	610.0	2.9	0.1%
Yunnan	81	3,735.8	14.5	0.6%
Shaanxi	75	3,720.3	23.0	0.6%
Gansu	27	862.5	6.4	0.1%
Qinghai	3	7.2	0.1	0.0%
Ningxia	16	2,376.0	14.8	0.4%
Xinjiang	34	1,540.6	7.2	0.2%

Source: National Bureau of Statistics, China.

Performance. In November 2007, 635 paper companies (7.6 percent of the total) in China reported losing money, with total losses of RMB 2.2 billion ($295 million). In November 2008, the number of companies reporting losses increased to 1,577 (18.1 percent of the total), with total losses of RMB 3.7 billion ($542 million). Table 5.2 shows that losses seeped through all

Table 5.2. LOSSES OF CHINA'S PAPER MANUFACTURERS, 2008

Industry	Number of companies	Number of loss-making companies	Losses (RMB 100 million)
Total paper and paper products	8,731	1,577	37.0
Pulp	116	28	4.4
Machine-made paper & paperboard	3,006	581	18.0
Handmade paper	29	8	3.8
Converted paper	467	91	1.9
Paper and paper container	3,432	584	6.8
Other	1,681	285	5.5

Source: CBI China.

Note: Data are for January–November.

sectors of China's paper industry. A handful of backward-integrated companies had some pricing power in this industry and displayed less vulnerability to margin squeezes by controlling raw-material supplies. For example, Meili owned its plantations, grew its trees, and could pace pulp production. However, Chinese containerboard producers, including the very large Nine Dragons and Lee & Man, did not have integrated raw-material supplies and had more exposure to falling prices for their products.

China's paper industry also had liabilities/assets ratios of about 60 percent nationally, indicating possible difficulties in collecting accounts receivable. However, the average paper company in China's top paper-producing provinces (with Hainan having the lowest liability/asset ratio of 30 percent) had higher ability to pay debt than the national average for the industry (National Bureau of Statistics, China). In November 2008, the paper industry's liabilities had mounted to RMB 413.9 billion ($60.6 billion), up by 15.9 percent year on year. However, the liabilities/assets ratio of the industry remained at 59.3 percent, flat from 2007.

Technology. Despite the New China paper mills that employ state-of-the-art technology and new machines, China's paper industry generally used outdated, obsolete, and polluting machinery and technology. Consequently, it has evolved into a major source of China's industrial pollution. Papermaking using straw pulp currently contributes most heavily to industrial pollution. In straw-pulp paper production, alkali is recovered from less than 30 percent of output. Between 60 percent and 80 percent of total pollution load (chemical oxygen demand) comes from black liquor, a straw-pulp discharge and major water pollutant.[4]

Smokestack manufacturing facilities in the paper industry also consume large amounts of water, coal, electricity, and raw materials per ton of paper produced. For example, an average paper mill in the United States or Europe consumed 0.9–1.2 tons of coal per ton of pulp, and about 35–50 tons of water. Conversely, in China, the average mill consumed 1.4 tons of coal per ton of pulp, and about 103 tons of water. Only a few companies reach advanced industrial standards.

NATURAL RESOURCES, DEMAND, AND EXCESS CAPACITY

In 2010, China had the fastest-growing paper industry in the world. But China also had among the smallest forestry resources in the world per capita to support this industry's expansion—lower even than India, which has also experienced excessive deforestation. Consequently, China imported the bulk of its raw materials for paper production. Domestic demand only captured a very small part of the Chinese paper industry's expansion. Yet the Chinese paper industry continued to expand, contributing to global excess capacity.

Supply of natural resources. China enjoys no competitive advantages in the manufacturing of paper and paper products. With 175 million hectares, China ranks fifth in the world in terms of total forest reserves. In contrast, the United States, with almost twice the total forest reserves of China, ranks fourth.[5] Additionally, on both forests per capita and forest coverage as a percentage of land, China falls 40 percent below the global average (18 percent vs. 30.3 percent). Furthermore, surging domestic as well as international demand for wood products has made China the largest forest-product importer in the world (as opposed to the seventh largest 10 years ago).

Of China's forest area, plantations comprise about 30 percent, or 50 million hectares. Of those plantations, 10 percent (or 3 percent of total forests) include fast-growing forests for pulp and paper. Five provinces—Tibet, Heilongjiang, Sichuan, Yunnan, and Mongolia—together account for 62 percent of China's total forests. Since most of these provinces are located deep inland, transportation becomes a key cost. For some companies, transportation costs loom twice as high as log costs.[6] The government has announced plans to have 60 million hectares of plantations by 2010. These plantations cover coastal and inland areas in China, with plantations of more than one billion cubic meters lying inland to the north and south. The government also provides greater subsidies for reforestation of the desert lands found to the north and south.

Table 5.3. PER CAPITA CONSUMPTION OF PAPER AND PAPERBOARD BY COUNTRY, 2000–2006 (KGS PER CAPITA)

	Country			
Year	China	US	Japan	Taiwan
2000	29.0	331.7	249.9	229.4
2001	29.0	324.0	242.8	201.3
2002	33.7	314.2	241.1	205.6
2003	37.0	300.8	241.9	220.3
2004	42.0	312.0	246.6	226.6
2005	45.0	300.6	246.8	215.1
2006	50.0	300.6	247.4	208.3

Source: ChinaPaperOnline.

Demand for paper and paper products. RISI Inc. projects that China's overall paper demand will grow from approximately 60 million tons in 2005 to 143 million tons in 2021, overtaking the United States and Europe in 2013. However, the Chinese domestic market per capita for paper and products is very small compared to any industrialized country. As table 5.3 shows, per capita consumption of paper and paper products in China is about one-sixth that of the United States. The Chinese domestic market has experienced substantial growth for some products: for example, in 2007, the year-on-year growth in demand for coated, white paperboard was approximately 20 percent. Yet domestic demand tends to be concentrated in lower-grade materials and products. Additionally, several segmented Chinese markets are suffering from saturated or excess supply. Domestic consumption of paper and paper products has increased by about 40 percent over the last decade. However, the bulk of the growth in domestic demand has occurred downstream and in industrial markets also associated with China's other exports.

Paper for industrial use explains about 60 percent of domestic demand for paper and paper products. As manufacturing in China grew, so did the demand for paper and paper products. In 2008, domestic downstream demand for Chinese paper spanned several industries including food (17 percent of demand), drinks (14 percent), shoes (12 percent), electronic and electrical appliances (11 percent), garments (8 percent), daily chemicals (7 percent), medicine and hygiene (6 percent), machinery (5 percent), toys (2 percent), cigarettes (2 percent), and others (16 percent) (Papease). Light industry constituted the largest consumer for industrial use.

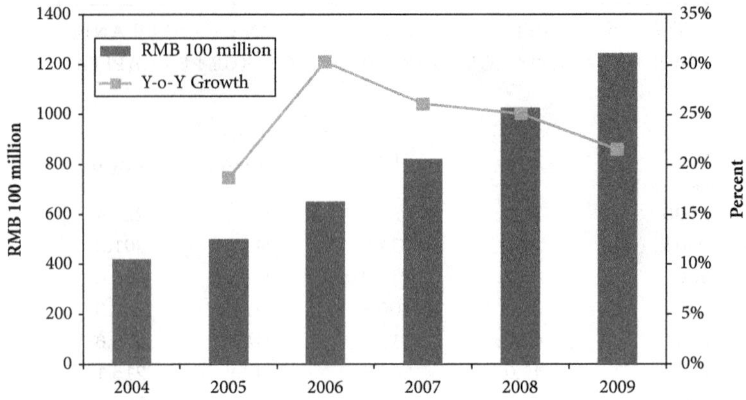

Figure 5.3
Fixed-Asset Investment in China's Paper Industry, 2004–2009
Source: China International Capital Corporation; Papease; China Economic Information Service.

Consequently, light industry complemented the development of paper for industrial use and also impacted the structure of China's paper industry.

Excess capacity. The global market for paper and paper products is being oversupplied. The majority of this oversupply has been to European and US markets, with Asia following closely.[7] From 14 percent in 2002, excess capacity in the global paper industry remained relatively flat from 2004 to 2010 at about 10 percent but is projected to grow sharply in the future, compounded by the global recession.[8]

Capacity expansion in the US and European paper industries has been falling. Yet China is currently adding capacity at a faster rate than global demand is increasing. China's paper industry has added on average 26 percent of new capacity every year from 2004. In 2008, the Chinese government once again reported massive additional capacity in China's paper industry, mostly concentrated in East China, especially Shandong. Some capacity expansion also occurred in south, central, and western China. Figure 5.3 shows annual fixed-asset investment in China's paper industry from 2004 to 2009. In 2009 and 2010, investment increased sharply in new projects of more than 200,000 tons, again concentrated in Shandong. The China Economic Information Service indicated that in 2009, year-on-year fixed-asset investment in China's paper and paper products industry grew 21.5 percent, despite some elimination of inefficient backward capacity and rapidly falling paper demand.

Consistent with the global paper and packaging market, China's domestic market is experiencing oversupply. Oversupply exists for nearly all products to some extent but most notably in printing and writing paper

Table 5.4. MAJOR PAPER PROJECTS UNDER CONSTRUCTION IN CHINA, 2009–2010

Company	Designed capacity (1,000 mt)	Products	Operational
Huai'an Yangguang Paper	100	Fine paper	
Hebi Ruizhou Paper	300	Fine paper	2011
Yueyang Paper	400	Munken paper[a]	2009
Fujian Nanping Paper	200	Copy paper	2010
MCC Paper Yinhe	200	Fine paper	2009
Nantong Oji Paper	800	Art paper	2010
Huatai Paper	800	Art paper	2010
Yibin Xingsheng Paper	15	Recycled paper	
Bohui Paper	350	Ivory card	2010
APP Hainan	1,400	Art paper	2010
APP Qinzhou	600	Ivory card	2010

Source: China National Light Industry Information Center, Papease.

[a] Munken paper is a branded, high-quality, bulky book paper made by Arctic Paper in Sweden; the company created the brand in the early twentieth century. Arctic's international headquarters has assured the authors that Arctic has never produced and has no plans to produce Munken paper in China. Arctic's managers referred to Yueyang's product as "so-called" Munken paper.

and containerboards. Supply of containerboards has spiked because the two largest Chinese companies, Nine Dragons and Lee & Man, have been aggressively adding capacity. Collectively, the two companies went from capacity of 8 million tons in 2007 to 15 million tons in 2009. Other companies are also building massive capacity. Table 5.4 shows some large scale-projects under construction in 2009–2010 and their expected tonnage.

IMPORTS AND EXPORTS OF CHINESE PAPER

Until 2007, China had been a net importer of paper and paper products. In 2009, with exports of $7.6 billion, China became a leading exporter of paper and paperboard in the world (CEIC). Figure 5.4 shows China's increasing exports and falling imports from 2003 to 2009. Given rapid growth in Chinese paper-production capacity, the country is likely to become a big net exporter when global paper demand recovers.

China is the world's largest importer of primary pulp and wastepaper. According to data from China Customs, in 2005 China's imports of pulp accounted for 16 percent of total commercial-pulp output in the world.[9] Concurrently, China's imports of recycled paper comprised 61 percent of global exports of recycled paper. In 2006, China imported 8 million tonnes

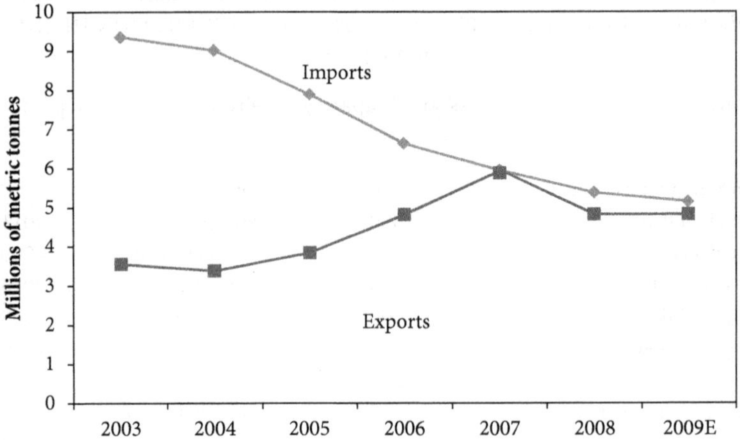

Figure 5.4
China's Imports and Exports of Paper and Products, 2003–2009
Source: FAO; ChinaPaperOnline; authors' estimates.

of pulp and 20 million tonnes of recycled paper, mostly from industrialized countries such as the United States and Japan. Domestically produced pulp only covered a tiny proportion of the Chinese paper industry's consumption. In 2008, pulp, mostly from Canada, the United States, and other forest-rich countries, again comprised the greatest part of imports for China's paper industry. As paper manufacturing increased, pulp imports rose to 9.5 million tonnes, accounting for 72 percent of total imports. Imports of other paper and paper products were 3.6 million tonnes and 125,000 tonnes respectively. Exports of paper and paper products were 4.1 million tonnes in 2008, explaining 75 percent of the total exports. The export levels of paper products and pulp were 1.3 million tonnes and 72,000 tonnes respectively.

In 2008, machine-made paper comprised 50 percent of Chinese exports in the paper and paper-products industry (RMB 22.9 billion, or $3.3 billion), with paper and paper containers comprising 27 percent (RMB 12.4 billion, or $1.8 billion), converted paper 5 percent, and other paper products 18 percent (RMB 8.4 billion, or $1.2 billion). As previously explained, Chinese exports of pulp and handmade paper are insignificant at about 0.1 percent and 0.2 percent respectively (National Bureau of Statistics, China). Although exports have led the growth of China's paper industry, analysts have difficulty deciphering final destinations for Chinese exports of paper products. For example, Asia's high demand for Chinese cardboard boxes appears to supply products for US and European end markets. As figure 5.4 shows, from 2002, Chinese imports of paper have been falling as exports have been rising.

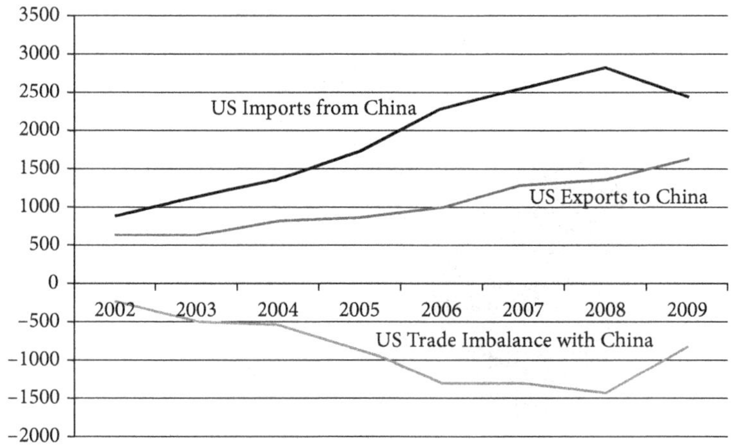

Figure 5.5
US Exports and Imports of Paper to and from China, 2002–2009
Source: US International Trade Commission.

In 2001, China joined the WTO and correspondingly increased both exports to the United States and imports from the United States. In February 2010, the value of Chinese imports into the United States was growing at an annualized rate of 21.9 percent. Figure 5.5 shows that though both US exports of paper to China and imports from China were growing, exports were growing from a much lower base and more slowly. Chinese penetration of the US market continued to grow despite the economic recession of 2008 and 2009. Indeed, US imports of Chinese paper were rising faster than those from any other country. In 2009, China ranked second in volume (behind Canada and overtaking Germany) as the source of paper imports into the United States (US International Trade Commission 2010). In the first quarter of 2010, China continued to hold this rank (US International Trade Commission 2010). The exponential growth of paper imports from China has caused a persistent and growing trade imbalance from 2002, as captured in figure 5.5. The trade imbalance shrunk in 2009 as US demand fell in the economic recession.

COST STRUCTURE AND PRICES

Figure 5.6 displays the cost structure of China's paper industry. Recycled paper (mostly old corrugated containers, or OCC) accounted for over half the costs of Chinese paper in this capital-intensive, resource-poor industry. On the other hand, labor provided about 4 percent to the average costs

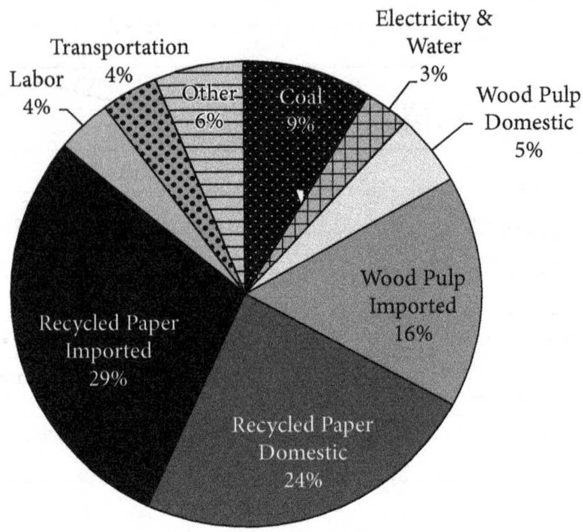

Figure 5.6
Cost Structure of China's Paper Industry
Source: Deutsche Bank; Lee & Man Paper Manufacturing Ltd; Shandong Chenming Paper Holdings; authors' calculations.

of Chinese paper production, across all companies. China enjoys no labor-cost advantage for the manufacture of paper. Indeed, labor costs have risen to about 6 percent of total costs in the handful of large Chinese companies that employ more-professionalized staff, making their labor costs comparable to US paper companies' at about 8 percent. In 2010, several provinces also instituted mandatory wage increases, making Chinese labor costs more in line with those in the United States: these included 13 percent increases in Jiangsu and 21 percent in Guangdong (*Economist Intelligence Unit* 2010), among the provinces that produced the most Chinese paper. As discussed in the previous section, imported raw materials contributed to about 45 percent of the total costs. China's paper-production lines mainly produce mechanical pulp and bleached hardwood kraft pulp (BHKP) for domestic consumption. Chinese imports have been relatively evenly split between softwood and hardwood pulp.

Raw-material prices have been increasing much faster than paper prices. Indeed, paper prices have performed poorly over the past decade, with real prices down, while prices of component materials have shown double- and triple-digit increases. As figure 5.7 shows, the price of recycled paper, the major component of Chinese costs, increased 150 percent between 2000 and 2008. Similarly, pulp increased about 30 percent. Energy prices too have been rising at a rapid rate since 2006. Both coal and oil prices have increased substantially with effects on the paper and paper-products

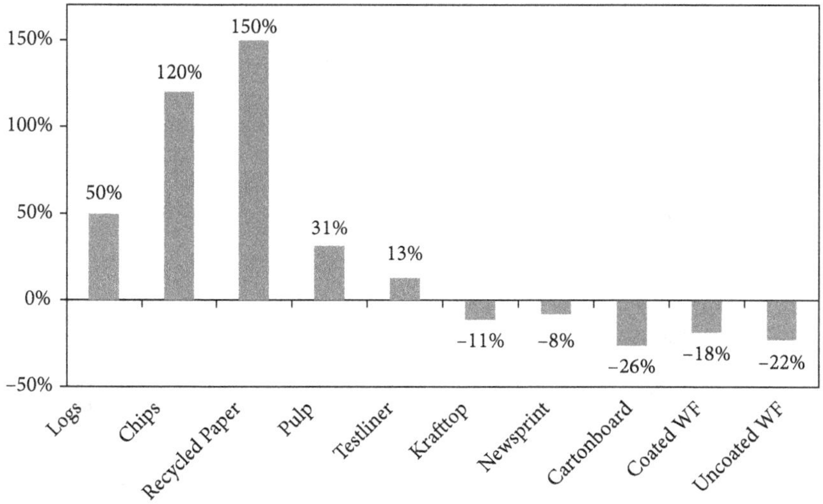

Figure 5.7
Changes in Values of Raw Materials and Paper Products between 2000 and 2008
Source: Datastream; Macquarie Research.

industry. Higher coal and oil prices affect operating costs such as electricity as well as transportation costs. Because of global oversupply, paper prices have not risen appreciably in the last decade.

Table 5.5 shows that Chinese paper prices have been consistently lower than those of the United States or Europe across a range of products. After controlling for the poor quality of domestically sourced raw materials, the price differentials are difficult to explain without subsidies. Nearly all Chinese paper producers have some form of pulping capacity, but generally, imported pulp heavily supports paper production. Relatively few producers of pulp exist in China, and in most cases they are integrated companies. Integrated paper companies, such as Yueyang, enjoy huge cost advantages, as they can control for pulp costs through transfer pricing. However, few integrated paper companies exist in China. Also, a plantation should reach at least 20,000 hectares to enjoy economies of scale.[10] The great bulk of Chinese companies in this industry are small and medium-sized. Only Yueyang and Meili have plantations large enough to achieve economies of scale.

ROLE OF GOVERNMENT POLICY

The Chinese government's policies on forestry assume high importance for the paper industry, as the government allocates resources for plantation development and trade. The policies have systematically aimed to reduce

Table 5.5. PRICES OF SOME PAPER PRODUCTS BY REGION, 2008 (US DOLLARS/TON)

Product	Country/Region		
	US	China	Europe
Kraftliner	820	590	780
Testliner	700	500	750
Newsprint	800	600	690
LWC	1025	820	1025
Printing paper	1375	925	1375

Source: Datastream; Macquarie Research July 2008.

China's dependence on imported raw materials by developing domestic wood fiber and subsidizing the paper industry's restructuring. Central and local governments have provided subsidies to develop fast-growing, high-yield plantations; reduced taxes and fees on plantations to stimulate investment; reduced tariffs on imports of processing machinery; promoted exports of wood and paper products through value-added tax rebates; provided loans and loan-interest subsidies for technology renovation; promoted foreign investment in SOEs; and, protected debt-ridden SOEs and small local companies with excess production capacity through local governments' soft loans, subsidies, and loan forgiveness. This section sketches the paper industry's ownership and regulatory structure, the role of local governments, and key legislation and policies.

Regulatory and Ownership Structure

All forests in China belong to the state unless the law stipulates that they belong to the collectives (a form of indirect state ownership). The state also prices all land, including for paper plantations. Collectives and private companies can lease land for forest production. Leases typically run for 40 years. Relatively opaque, local, state-owned asset supervision and administration commissions, or SASACs, manage state and collective farms. The state directly manages about 40 percent of mostly natural forests, collectives manage about 58 percent, and private companies manage less than 2 percent (Zhu, Taylor, and Feng 2004; authors' calculations).

As figure 5.8 shows, the State Forestry Administration (SFA) and State Council provide broad directional policy for the paper industry. Operationally, local forestry administrators and provincial administrators exert enormous power as they oversee and negotiate forest usage and logging concessions as well as interpret the central government's laws. To expedite projects, Beijing's development policies have relegated approval of new investments to local governments. For example, for projects involving SOEs, local governments, rather than the SOEs' managers, have final approval. Local governments determine which land companies may use and at what price. In some cases, local governments have leased land to companies at no charge (American Forest and Paper Association 2004). Local governments also provide subsidies for water and electricity and decide tax rates, tax holidays, and fee waivers. In practice, local governments have exceeded the central government's directives for development aid, including tax, financing, and trade measures, to shore up investment in their regions. Local governments have also strongly supported local companies in applying to the central government for preferential subsidies (e.g., the central government's loan-interest subsidies for paper companies investing in plantations). Interviews show that governmental decentralization has enhanced paper companies' needs for *guanxi*[11] with local governments. From securing logging concessions, to negotiating lease terms, to certifying new tree species, local governments can greatly impact companies' bottom lines.

The power of local governments manifests especially in the following ways:

- Logging quotas: The State Council, along with the SFA, sets five-year logging quotas, allocated to local governments to distribute among forests. The SFA's key principles include preserving natural forest and capping total logging to below total new plantations. But local governments allow special logging quotas in certain cases. For example, managers of commercial plantations above a "certain size" (determined by local governments) can develop their own quotas. Plantation managers can also determine the harvesting age of plantation-grown timber for industrial raw material.
- Loan-interest subsidies/financing support: All paper companies with plantations can apply for the Ministry of Finance's interest subsidies. Should local governments and the ministry deem the project good for forestry development, companies can receive up to 6 percent interest subsidy for three years. Furthermore, the People's Bank of China has also set aside billions of renminbi as a credit line for companies in forestry. According to the SFA, it lent RMB 4.7 billion ($562 million) in 2005 alone.

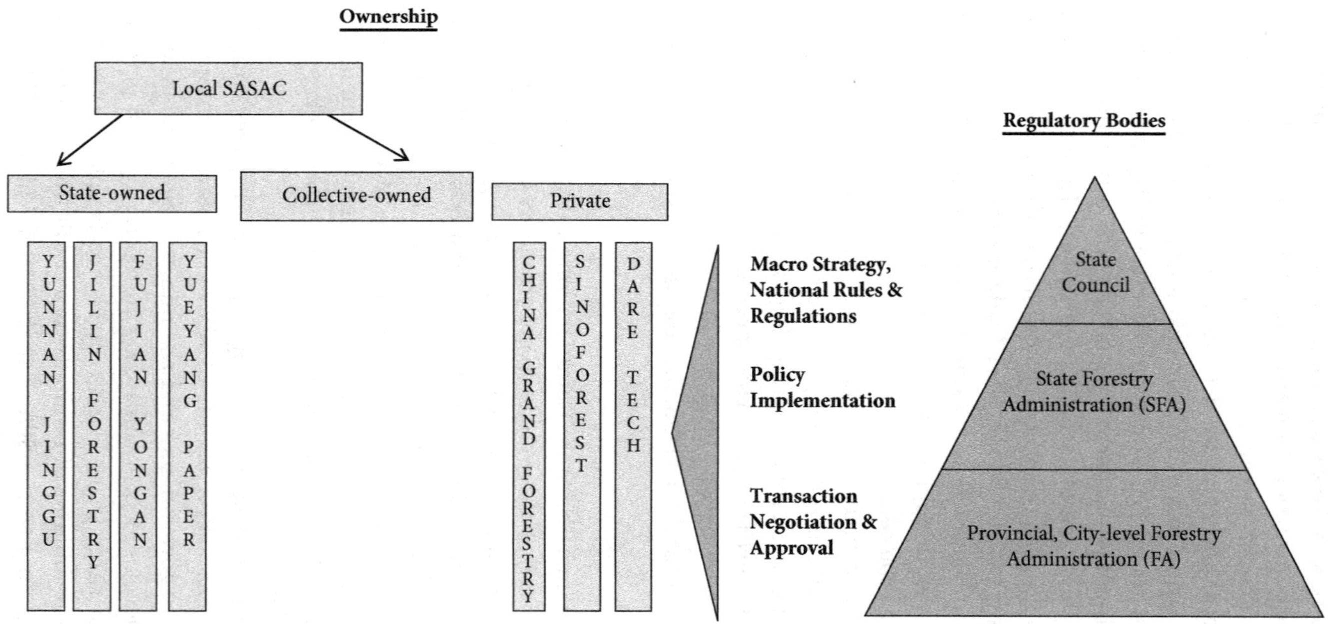

Figure 5.8
Regulatory and Ownership Structures of China's Forests
Source: Deutsche Bank.

- Preferential levy/tax treatments: Interviews with the SFA revealed that the government has started to remove gradually the Forestry Resources Levy (FRL). The FRL accounts for 25 percent of a plantation's revenue, a huge boost to the companies' profits. According to the SFA, Guangdong and Hunan Provinces have eliminated the FRL completely. In addition, the central government gives full value-added tax exemption. Companies with plantations can also enjoy income-tax exemptions or reduced income-tax rates on case-by-case bases. Local governments' support can prove the deciding factor.

SOEs' engaging in public-land management and product processing and marketing, along with opacity over public forests' objectives and ownership, have hindered sustainable forestry in China (Turnbull 2007). From the mid-1980s, through financing from the World Bank and its affiliate the International Development Association, Beijing spawned several projects to enhance forest productivity, improve resource-use efficiency, and build institutional capacities for sustainable forestry management, including the Forest Development Project for state-owned farms in Heilongjiang, Sichuan, and Guangdong from 1985 to 1990; the Da Xing An Ling Forest Fire Rehabilitation Project in 1988; the National Afforestation Project in 1990; and the Forest Resource Development and Protection Project in 1996. In 1998, the State Council implemented the Natural Forest Protection Program (NFPP) and logging ban, soon after several devastating floods. Industrial round-wood production from state-owned forests slowed down after the NFPP, and the government started relying on plantations to supply timber. In practice, provincial governments and individual companies bear the brunt of enforcing and making operational sustainability standards. IKEA found that only 7 percent of its Chinese wood suppliers complied with its sustainability standards, encompassing emissions, chemical management, and human rights; about one-fifth of the company's global purchases of wood comes from China (IKEA 2009). Sino-Forest, Stora Enso, and CERC have also developed strategies for sustainable management of their Chinese plantations (Turnbull 2007). No external audits have been conducted on the effectiveness of companies' sustainability strategies in China.

Legislative Framework

In 2002, the central government first announced its eight-year master plan for the forestry, pulp, and paper industries. The plan created major corporations with integrated operations in the three interlinking businesses of forest-pulp-paper. The government also outlined five major production areas for integrated paper production and encouraged the planting of industrial forests in flat areas with more than 400 millimeters of rainfall. Since 2002, integrated paper companies have benefited from favorable policies including (1) highly independent tree-planting and harvesting operations, (2) governmental rebates of forest-usage charges, (3) lower tax rates, and (4) local governments' favorable policies and subsidies.

Subsequent plans and policies reinforced the original state directives. In 2003, the "State Council's No. 9 Policy" set the legal framework for private companies to obtain forestry subsidies and concessions. Private companies could qualify for policy benefits such as tax exemptions and loan-interest subsidies. Forestry constitutes an agriculture activity, and in 2006, the rural policies of the Eleventh Five-Year Plan by the National People's Congress granted forestry businesses, including paper, special taxation status from 2006 to 2010.

Simultaneously, the Chinese government started promoting investment in the paper industry. In the 2005 edition of the Investment Guidance Catalogue for Domestic Investors, the government placed China's paper and paper-products industry on the "encouraged" list. By December 2009, the listing had not yet been revoked, and China's paper industry continued on the "encouraged list," despite the excess capacity discussed earlier (China Economic Information Service 2009).

In August 2007, seven central-government ministries and commissions jointly issued the "Main Points of Forest Industry Policy." The policy outlined the subsidies and other support that the government was offering listed paper companies owning forests, such as Yueyang Paper, Huatai Stock, and Chenming Paper. Government subsidies included (1) using preferential tax policies to exempt forest-project income from total corporate income, (2) expanding loans to forestry through policy-oriented banks such as China Development Bank, (3) extending the life of existing loans from 12 to 20 years for construction projects to plant timber and to expand forests for industrial raw materials, (4) actively transferring forest rights to companies for industrial production, and, (5) increasing discounted loans and loan-interest subsidies to the forestry industry and backward-integrated paper companies. On October 31, 2007, the National Development and Reform Commission (NDRC) also promulgated the advisory "Industrial Policy of China's Papermaking Industry" to accelerate the movement of paper production from the north to the area south of the Yangtze River, and to increase forest-pulp-paper integration. The policy addressed industrial development and layout, energy usage, environmental protection, and market entry.

In December 2009, five governmental agencies, the SFA, the NDRC, the Ministry of Finance, the Ministry of Commerce, and the State Taxation Administration, released a plan for the forestry sector's revitalization from 2010 to 2012 (LesProm 2009). The plan provides for governmental support and subsidies to 100 national leading enterprises and 10 large wood-industry clusters. The agencies aim to raise the sector's output value from RMB 1.4 trillion ($209.9 billion) in 2008 to RMB 2.3 trillion ($329.4 billion)[12] in 2012, as well as to maintain growth of around 12 percent annually. The agencies expect annual trade in wood products to exceed $90 billion, including over $50 billion in exports.

SUBSIDIES TO CHINA'S PAPER INDUSTRY

This section presents calculated subsidies to China's paper and paper-products industry for electricity, coal, pulp, recycled paper, as cash grants to some companies, and through interest-free loans to some paper projects. Descriptions of the data and methodology as well as the mathematical equations to calculate the subsidies can be found in chapter 2.

As figure 5.2 shows, discernible subsidies to China's paper industry from 2002 to 2009 reached at least $33.1 billion. Chinese government subsidies have increased steadily over the last decade, but rose most sharply after 2004, with implementation of the State Council's No. 9 Policy in which private companies could obtain forestry subsidies and concessions. Subsidies fell sharply in 2009 as world prices and corresponding Chinese prices (on which calculations of subsidies are based) fell as well. Table 5.6 details the subsidies to China's paper industry in each year of the period under study.

Because the calculations included only those subsidies that could be traced, confirmed, and recorded, the total subsidies to the Chinese paper industry in this chapter constitute very conservative estimates. The trend of rising subsidies explains to some extent why so many small and medium-sized companies remained profitable during this period despite an apparent squeeze between falling prices of paper products and very rapidly increasing raw-material prices. As discussed earlier, labor accounts for only 4 percent of the costs of producing paper. Additionally, the lack of economies of scale and scope strongly suggests that the inefficient and polluting Chinese paper industry received substantial and growing support through most of the study period, probably from provincial governments that wield decision-making power.

Table 5.6. SUBSIDIES TO CHINESE PAPER, 2002–2009 (MILLIONS OF DOLLARS)

Period	Thermal coal	Coking coal	Electric	Pulp	Recycled paper	Reported grants and subsidies	Total
2002		0.24	40.91			3.46	44.61
2003		0.18	44.73			10.25	55.16
2004	367.19	0.70	51.58	2,601.23		17.96	3038.66
2005	169.26	0.93	108.02	3,577.92	163.33	30.57	4,050.03
2006	64.99	1.08	118.02	5,039.47	70.25	73.39	5,367.20
2007	568.22	1.77	128.48	5,450.35		54.51	6,203.33
2008	1,484.37	7.75	138.17	6,285.28	1,459.58	101.07	9,476.22
2009	398.95		147.87	2,071.40		150.99	2,769.21
Total	3,052.98	12.65	777.78	25,025.65	1,693.16	442.20	31,004.42
Loan-interest subsidies							2,130.00
Grand total							**$33,134.42**

Source: Authors' calculations and estimates based on data from American Forest and Pulp Association; Australian Bureau of Agricultural and Research Economics; *China Market Pulp Report*; *China Recovered Paper Report*; CEIC; China National Development and Reform Commission; companies' annual reports; Deutsche Bank; Food and Agricultural Organization; Interfax; International Energy Agency; Macquarie Research; Morgan Stanley; National Bureau of Statistics, China; Steelonthenet.

Subsidies for electricity. Subsidies for electricity used by China's paper industry reached $777.8 million between 2002 and 2009. The total for provincial subsidies approximated $483.1 million; the total for coal-price-increase subsidies, which took effect in 2005, reached $294.6 million. Because this book relies solely on published prices and the NDRC's disclosures on provinces that had subsidized their paper industries, the provincial subsidies to electricity are probably underrepresented.

Subsidies for coal. Subsidies for coal consumed by China's paper industry reached $3.1 billion between 2002 and 2009. The total for thermal-coal subsidies approximated $3.1 billion; the paper industry is a small user of coking coal, and the total for these subsidies reached $12.7 million. Subsidies for coal increased most steeply in 2008, when the price of thermal and coking coal soared. Chinese subsidies for thermal coal have generally corresponded to world prices, rising and falling in tandem. As a major producer of thermal coal, China has also directly influenced domestic prices by ramping-up domestic supply in response to rising world prices. Subsidies for thermal coal used by China's paper industry (whose calculations depend on market prices) may show the delays that transpire between producing demanded coal and getting it to market. Interviews with industry analysts indicate that until 2004, China's paper industry was paying a premium for thermal coal. Similarly, the Chinese paper industry was paying a premium for coking coal in 2009. In 2009, world coking-coal prices plummeted by 57 percent, while Chinese coking-coal prices fell by only 22 percent.

Subsidies for pulp. Subsidies for pulp used by China's paper industry reached $25 billion between 2004 and 2009, when data were available. Table 5.6 indicates the presence of some subsidies to pulp (all grades) in each year of the period shown. Subsidies for pulp fell sharply in 2009 when the world price of pulp plummeted during the recession. The corresponding Chinese subsidy (calculated as a differential between Chinese and world prices) decreased in tandem with the world price.

The study greatly underestimates subsidies to pulp, as it uses pulp prices paid by most private companies for paper production. Yet, as discussed before, large, backward-integrated companies and SOEs get highly discounted pulp through transfer-pricing mechanisms for which data are publicly unavailable (Xie and Chen 2009). Costs of land take up between 30 percent and 60 percent of fast-growing forest costs, which in turn take up about 50 percent of the costs of domestic pulp. But the Chinese government subsidizes land for integrated producers and those acquiring land in desert areas, reducing the costs of pulp for these companies. For example, Chenming has been acquiring rental land in the Zhanjiang region to establish its own timber supplies. Significant cost advantages accrue to Chenming when using its own timber. On average, the cost per cubic meter of Chenming-owned trees hovers around RMB 200 ($29.20) compared with locally acquired timber costing about RMB 300–400 (about $43.90–$58.50). On the other hand, Meili's land rental is zero because it is using this plantation land for desert forestation.

Subsidies for recycled paper. Subsidies for recycled paper consumed by China's paper industry reached $1.7 billion between 2004 and 2008, when data were available. OCC comprises the largest component of recycled paper because of domestic-box recovery. Table 5.6 indicates the presence of some subsidies for recycled paper in each year of the period shown. The spike in subsidies in 2008 pertains to the largest Chinese companies; it shows the sharp increase in the world price, which was not reflected in the Chinese price for recycled paper. Because of incomplete data on recycled paper, no subsidies could be calculated for 2004, 2007, and 2009. Indeed, the Chinese paper industry appeared to have paid a premium for recycled paper in 2004 and 2007.

While the United States and Europe have sophisticated collection networks, China has numerous, inefficient, small paper-recycling operations; nationwide, China's collection rates hover around 30 percent, among the lowest in the world.[13] The average collection rate in the world approximates 50 percent, with the United States having a collection rate of about 52 percent, the UK 61 percent, and South Korea 85 percent.[14] The process of collecting recycled paper is expensive and can be capital intensive. Consequently, only a few of the very largest companies, such as Nine Dragons and Lee & Man, have backward-integrated recycling operations. Small and medium-sized paper companies generally directly bear the costs of purchasing low-quality, domestically recycled paper, and few data exist for these transactions. These small and medium-sized companies also use substantial amounts of imported, recycled paper that they purchase at global, market prices and sometimes at a premium. Data in 2008 came from the largest, integrated companies and before the global market softened for recycled paper.

Subsidies reported by companies. Subsidies reported in the annual reports of China's paper companies reached $442.2 million between 2002 and 2009. The 212 largest companies in this industry, primarily medium-sized and large, reported these as "Subsidy Income" in their annual reports. The great majority of these companies had no legal needs to disclose cash grants or subsidies from the government, and many of their managers probably misunderstood reporting requirements (see Yu 2009), so the reporting is sporadic with much missing data. Table 5.6 indicates the presence of some reported subsidies in each year of the period shown. The subsidies shot up in 2008 and 2009, when Lee & Man and Nine Dragons received large cash grants that they reported.

Loan-interest subsidies. In 2001, the State Development and Planning Commission (now the NDRC) identified 43 projects in China's paper industry that would receive loan-interest subsidies from 2002 to 2010. Of these 43 projects, the NDRC specifically provided $2.1 billion in loan-interest subsidies to 13 projects that focused on integrating paper-processing facilities with fast-growth, high-yield plantations (American Forest and Paper Association 2004). Table 5.7 lists the 43 projects that the NDRC chose and the 13 that received specified subsidies. The projects cover China's southern coast, Yangtze River delta, Huang-Huai plains, Northeast China, and Southwest China. The analysis assumes that the identified subsidies were equally distributed across the years of study.

The estimate of $2.1 billion dollars for loan-interest subsidies understates the amount of such subsidies from 2002 to 2009. Public information could not be gathered on how much money the government granted to the other 30 paper projects identified in 2001, or to those the government chose later for these subsidies. Interviews revealed that the Ministry of Finance could provide about 20 percent of the amount of a loan for plantations and technology renovations in the form of loan-interest subsidies, state-owned policy

Table 5.7. NATIONAL DEVELOPMENT AND REFORM COMMISSION'S 43 PROJECTS PLANNED FOR IMPLEMENTATION, 2002–2010

Province	Project funded by loan-interest subsidies
	Northwest
Xinjiang	*Xinjiang Zhunger Biology Engineering Co. Ltd.*
	Yili Forest and Paper Co. Ltd. Wood Base
Ningxia	*Ningxia Meili Paper Company Wood Base*[a]
	Inner Mongolia Pangu Group[a]
	Inner Mongolia Dongda Group Liner Board Project integrated with Shaliu Plantation
	Gansu Zhangye Forest and Paper Cooperative Project
	Southwest
Sichuan	*Yibing Paper Co. Ltd. Wood Base*
	Changjiang Paper Co. Ltd. Wood Base
	Leshan Paper Mill Wood Base
	Zhongzu Paper Company Wood Base
Guizhou	*Qianbei Bamboo Pulp and Forest Paper Project*
	Yun Nan Yunjing Forest and Paper Company[a]
	Southern coast
Guangdong	*Guangzhou Paper Co. Ltd.*[a]
	Zhanjiang Pulp Mill
	Guangning Paper Mill
Guangxi	*Nanning Phoenix Paper Co. Ltd.*
	Liu Jiang Paper Mill
	He Zhi Co. Ltd.
Fujian	*Nan Zhi Holding Co. Ltd.*[a]
	Qingshan Holding Co. Ltd.[a]
	Longyan Paper Industrial Co. Ltd.
	Yuexiu Shaowu Pulp and Paper Co.
Hainan Island	*Hainan 600,000 ton pulp mill*
	Yangtze River delta
Jiangxi	*Jiangxi Paper Co. Ltd.*
Hunan	*Yueyang Paper Group Co. Ltd.*[a]
Anhui	*Anhui Forest and Paper Co. Ltd.*
	Northeast
Heilongjiang	*Jiamusi Paper Group Wood Base*
	Heilongjiang Sida Paper Co. Ltd. Wood Base
	Qiqihaer Paper Company Wood Base[a]
	Mudanjiang Forest and Paper Wood Base
Jilin	*Yanbian Paper Company Wood Base*
	Fulun Paper Co. Wood Base
Liaoning	*Liaoning Paper Making Wood Base*
	Liaoxi Paper Making Wood Base

Continued

Table 5.7. *(Continued)*

Province	Project funded by loan-interest subsidies
	Huang-Huai Plains
Henan	*Henan Jiaozuo Forest and Paper Group C. Ltd.*
	Puyang Paper Mill[a]
Shanxi	*Shanxi Xiangfen Paper Group*[a]
Shandong	*Shandong Tralin Paper Co.*[a]
	Shandong Sun Paper
	Rizhao Pulp Company Material Base JV[a]
	Huatai Group Material Base[a]
	Fenglingdu Paper Industrial Group
	Chengwu Hongda Paper Co. Ltd. Material Base

Source: Derived from American Forest and Paper Association 2004; Stewart 2007.

[a] NDRC identified amounts of loans to these projects.

banks (such as the China Development Bank) could provide 70 percent of the capital in the form of loans that companies may never repay, and provincial and municipal governments could provide 3 percent (as well as other incentives, depending on municipal budgets) with companies and other sources raising the remaining balance. Companies may have used some of the money earmarked for technology renovations for inefficient capacity expansion (see Xie and Chen 2009 for inefficient uses of forestry subsidies).

IMPLICATIONS FOR US INDUSTRY

A decade ago, China compared with India in national competitive advantages for the support of a paper industry. In 2010, while India ranked twenty-fourth in exports of paper to the United States, China had rapidly become the largest producer and exporter of paper in the world and the second-largest exporter (behind Canada) to the United States (US International Trade Commission 2010). This chapter has argued that Chinese government subsidies and loans have fueled the enormous growth, excess capacity, and low prices that characterize China's paper industry. As discussed earlier, in December 2009 the Chinese government announced new policies for continued support of its paper industry. Data show that the Chinese paper industry will continue to expand at least through 2014 based on current policies and planned expenditures. Indeed, in 2009, Chinese paper-production capacity grew 21.5 percent over the previous year, despite the global economic slump.

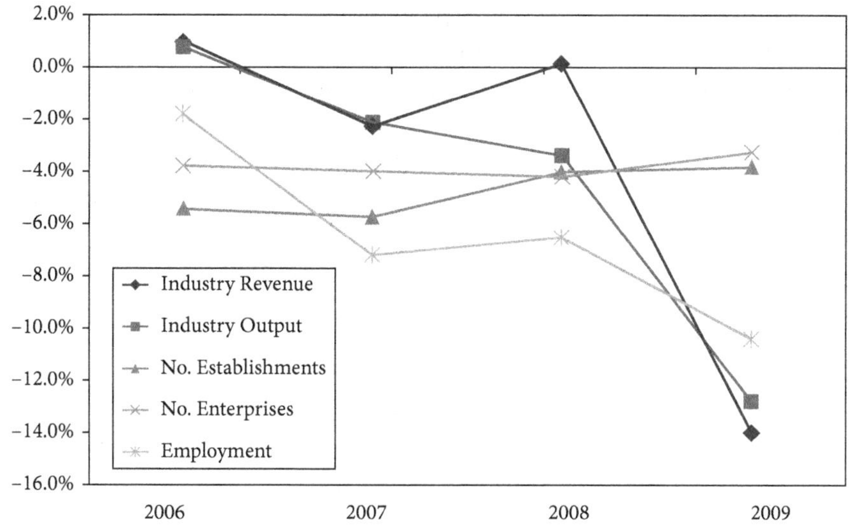

Figure 5.9
Real Growth of US Paper Mills, 2006–2009
Source: Authors' calculations; IBISWorld; Federal Reserve Board.

The saturated Chinese market for paper cannot absorb present or planned output of Chinese paper. Consequently, one can reasonably assume that exports have driven the growth of China's paper industry. Chinese policies on foreign investment also continue to emphasize production to fuel and to produce exports at least through 2014. For example, China's "Catalogue Guiding Foreign Investment in Industry"[15] strongly supports foreign investment of chemical wood-pulp projects above 300,000 tons; chemical mechanical-pulp projects above 100,000 tons; investments in plantations to integrate forest-wood-pulp; and investments in high-quality paper and paperboard production (except newsprint paper). The policies favor joint ventures with domestic partners over wholly owned enterprises and target higher-value-added sectors. Attracted by favorable Chinese governmental policy, some US companies, such as Kimberly-Clark, have announced that they will expand their manufacturing facilities in China (HKTDC 2010).

Cheap, subsidized Chinese paper exports have affected the US paper industry.[16] Despite comparable cost structures, high efficiencies, and plentiful natural resources, US paper companies have failed to compete globally or nationally on price against much-cheaper Chinese imports. In 2010, the United States remained a net importer of paper and paper products. Imports from China were rising faster than those from any other country for this industry, with the value of US imports from China growing at an annualized rate of 22 percent. Figure 5.9 shows how US paper mills have shrunk with drops in output, employment, revenues, and number of companies, corresponding to the rise in Chinese imports. As the appendix to this book indicates, US government policymakers have incorporated research from this book to forge a regulatory environment that reverses the trend. Without strategic trade policy (further discussed in chapter 7), the United States may well become the supplier of raw materials for Chinese production of paper, until Chinese plantations reach their planned potential, with continued erosion of profitability and manufacturing jobs in the US paper industry.

NOTES

1. The research for this study was funded by a grant from the Economic Policy Institute, Washington, DC.
2. Economies of scale primarily refer to operational efficiencies through supply-side changes, such as increasing production for single product types; reductions in unit costs can occur as the scale of facilities or production increases. Economies of scope primarily refer to efficiencies through demand-side changes, such as increasing the scope of marketing or distribution for different types of products; synergies can reduce costs in families of products through bundling and other marketing strategies.
3. For RMB to US$ conversions, the authors used the official exchange rate in the month or day of the statistical release, or in midyear if the month and day were not specified.
4. Authors' interviews.
5. Canada, with 9.8 hectares per capita, ranks number one in forest resources per capita, as compared to China's 0.2 hectares per capita.
6. Authors' interviews.
7. Excess capacity refers to a situation in which actual production is less than what is achievable or optimal for firms. For the paper industry, excess capacity indicates that the market demand for paper falls below what companies could potentially supply to the market. Oversupply indicates an excess of supply to markets. In the paper industry, oversupply in some sectors has resulted in depressed prices and/or unsold products as supply has exceeded existing demand.
8. RISI data; Macquarie Research.
9. Authors' interviews.
10. Authors' interviews.
11. No literal translation to English exists from the Mandarin, but *guanxi* generally captures concepts of trust and relationship building.
12. 2008 exchange rates.
13. Among major paper producers, only India has a lower collection rate than China of about 28 percent.
14. RISI data and Macquarie Research.
15. Last revised in November 2007.
16. See Scott (2010) for a general discussion of trade with China and US job losses.

CHAPTER 6
Pedal to the Metal: Subsidies to China's Auto-Parts Industry

This chapter analyses subsides to Chinese auto parts from 2001 to 2011 and the government policies that have transformed this Chinese industry.[1] Auto-parts consumption is directly linked to the demand for new vehicles. In January 2009, for the first time, China overtook the United States to become the largest car market in the world by volume (*Bloomberg*, 2009). As Chinese government subsidies and other policies spurred demand, auto companies sold 13.8 million vehicles in China, an increase of 48 percent year on year (International Trade Administration 2010), compared with 10.4 million cars and light trucks sold in the United States, the lowest level in 27 years. Feverish predictions commenced about China's domination of the automobile industry. In 2010, estimates had China producing around one-seventh of the world's vehicles, ranking second after Japan in passenger-car production, and second after the United States in commercial-vehicle production.[2] *China Automotive Review* projected that vehicle sales in China could reach 18 million units in 2010, cementing its place as the world's biggest market. Meanwhile, J.D. Power estimated that vehicle sales in the United States could reach nearly 11.6 million units (Cable 2010). In December 2010, General Motors (GM) announced that Shanghai GM, one of its two joint ventures (JVs) in China with state-owned enterprise (SOE) Shanghai Automotive Industry Corporation (SAIC), succeeded in becoming China's largest car manufacturer. GM became China's first passenger-car manufacturer to achieve annual sales of 1 million vehicles (Cable 2010).

As auto sales in the rest of the world slumped during the 2008 recession, the Chinese central government cut sales taxes on smaller,

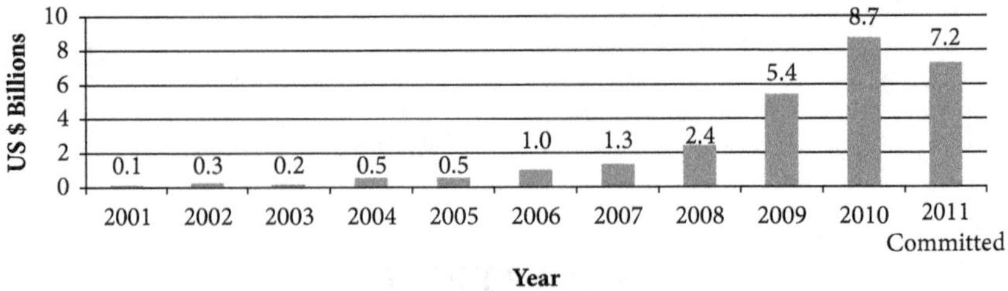

Figure 6.1
Total Identified Subsidies to China's Auto-Parts Industry, 2001–2011
Source: Authors' analysis and estimates based on data from Australian Bureau of Agricultural and Resource Economics and Sciences; Beijing Waterwood Technologies Corporation; Bloomberg; China.org.cn; China Association of Automobile Manufacturers; China Data Online; companies' annual reports; CEIC; Credit Suisse / First Boston; Fathom China; Interfax; International Energy Agency; ISI Emerging Markets; MEPS International; *Mining Exploration News*; National Bureau of Statistics, China; Netscribes; SteelontheNet; SWS Research; Sun (2010); Ward's Automotive Group.

fuel-efficient cars and spent $730 million on subsidies for buyers of larger cars, pickup trucks, and minivans. Stimulus spending on building highways and other public works also helped to boost sales of vehicles. While subsidies stimulated demand, the Chinese central and provincial governments continued to subsidize the production of auto parts. However, the growth of China's auto-parts industry also reflects multinational corporations', notably US corporations', global strategies and manufacturing and distribution decisions (see Haley and Haley 2008). This chapter covers some of the subsidies that the Chinese government has provided for auto-parts manufacturing in China and some ramifications of Chinese policymakers' and foreign companies' strategic decisions on the US and global economies. As figure 6.1 shows, discernible subsidies to China's auto-parts industry from 2001 to 2011 reached at least $27.5 billion, growing by 90 percent. The Chinese central government has committed an additional $10.5 billion in subsidies for 2012 to 2020.

CHARACTERISTICS OF CHINA'S AUTO-PARTS INDUSTRY

China's auto-parts industry has expanded very rapidly in the new century, on the back of the growth in the country's vehicle industry. The industry grew by 150 percent from 2004 to 2008, recording total sales of $136.5 billion in 2008. The number of auto-parts companies registered with the Chinese government rose from 4,205 in 2002 to 10,331 in 2008, employing about 1.9 million people. About 15,000 nonregistered automotive-component manufacturers also appeared to exist in

China (KPMG Huazhen). These nonregistered companies included captive operations of diversified groups whose main products were not auto parts, or were small aftermarket-equipment manufacturers, or small companies supplying parts for the commercial vehicle, agricultural, and off-highway sectors.

Partial-year statistics from January to August 2009 from the China Association of Automobile Manufacturers (CAAM) show that the total output by value of 10,761 Chinese auto-parts companies topped $110 billion and was expected to reach $176 billion in 2010 (*Xinhua News Agency* 2010). For 2010, analysts predicted industry revenue of $195.31 billion, up 10.2 percent from 2009, and with annualized growth of 23.2 percent since 2005 (using constant 2010 dollars), slower than previous years because of the global financial crisis and slightly weaker downstream demand (IBISWorld). Table 6.1 shows the growth of the auto-parts industry in China from 2003 to 2008. Although fixed assets have been rising, output value has been rising just as fast if not faster—demonstrating the Chinese auto industry's transition into higher value-added manufacturing and the success of government policies regarding technology development and creation of world-class competitors.

Despite the very rapid growth of China's automotive sector over the last decade, its auto-parts industry remained relatively small but has been expanding at a rapid pace. By value, China's auto-parts industry equals just one-fifth of the United States' total, and one-twentieth of the world's total. This small share reflects the low position that so many of China's auto-parts manufacturers occupy on the value chain. Over the last decade, the Chinese government has increased various subsidies for international auto-parts makers to relocate higher-value-added

Table 6.1. GROWTH OF THE AUTO-PARTS INDUSTRY IN CHINA, 2003–2008

Year	Fixed assets (millions of yuan)	Year-on-year growth (%)	Gross industrial output (millions of yuan)	Year-on-year growth (%)
2003	112,306		257,418	
2004	157,941	40.63	354,548	37.73
2005	191,178	21.04	415,988	17.33
2006	226,902	18.69	550,118	32.24
2007	276,954	22.06	763,659	38.82
2008	369,007	33.24	987,038	29.25

Source: National Bureau of Statistics, China.

production to China. For example, in the second half of 2008, Honda increased the local content of its Jazz, produced in Guangzhou for export, from 60 percent to 90 percent. Some analysts expected the industry to reach about $350 billion in value by 2015 from $136.5 billion in 2009 (KPMG Huazhen).

Figure 6.2 describes the value chain in China's auto-parts industry. Auto parts include those used by original equipment manufacturers (OEMs) and aftermarket parts. Original-equipment parts go into the assembly of new motor vehicles (automobile, light truck, or truck), or OEMs purchase these auto parts for their service networks. Suppliers of OEM parts fall into three levels. Tier 1 suppliers sell finished components directly to OEMs. Tier 2 suppliers sell parts and materials for the finished components to Tier 1 suppliers. Tier 3 suppliers (not in the figure) provide raw materials such as steel to any of the above suppliers or directly to vehicle assemblers. Much overlap exists between the tiers, with many OEMs having captive, in-house auto-parts manufacturers. Most OEMs focus on their core skills in assembling and source noncore auto parts through their networks of global suppliers. Generally, the largest Chinese auto-parts manufacturers, with scale economies and strong R&D, directly supply system modules to OEMs, while the smaller companies focus on the aftermarket segments.

Chinese government policy has successfully upgraded some aspects of the auto-parts value chain (Rodman & Renshaw Equity Research). First, in the last five years, many automakers have transferred design functions to their Tier 1 suppliers.[3] To meet OEMs' specific needs, the Tier 1 suppliers have also started customizing their products. Many Tier 1 suppliers that used to work with the OEMs' designs have started proposing their own. Second, as automakers started implementing "just in time" and "quality at source" methods for cost savings and quality assurance, they began to rely on Tier 1 suppliers to achieve the same. Consequently, foreign automakers became more involved in specifications of their Chinese Tier 1 suppliers' quality systems and started cultivating long-term relationships with these suppliers. Correspondingly, many automakers have required that their Tier 1 suppliers operate in close proximity to them. Finally, US and other global automakers have started allowing their Chinese Tier 1 suppliers into their global-purchase systems. Leading auto companies have established global-purchasing and sourcing systems to approve their Tier 1 suppliers' production and quality-control systems. Once a Chinese auto-parts company enters such a global-purchasing system, it can bid worldwide for supply contracts with any automaker operating under its OEM's standards.

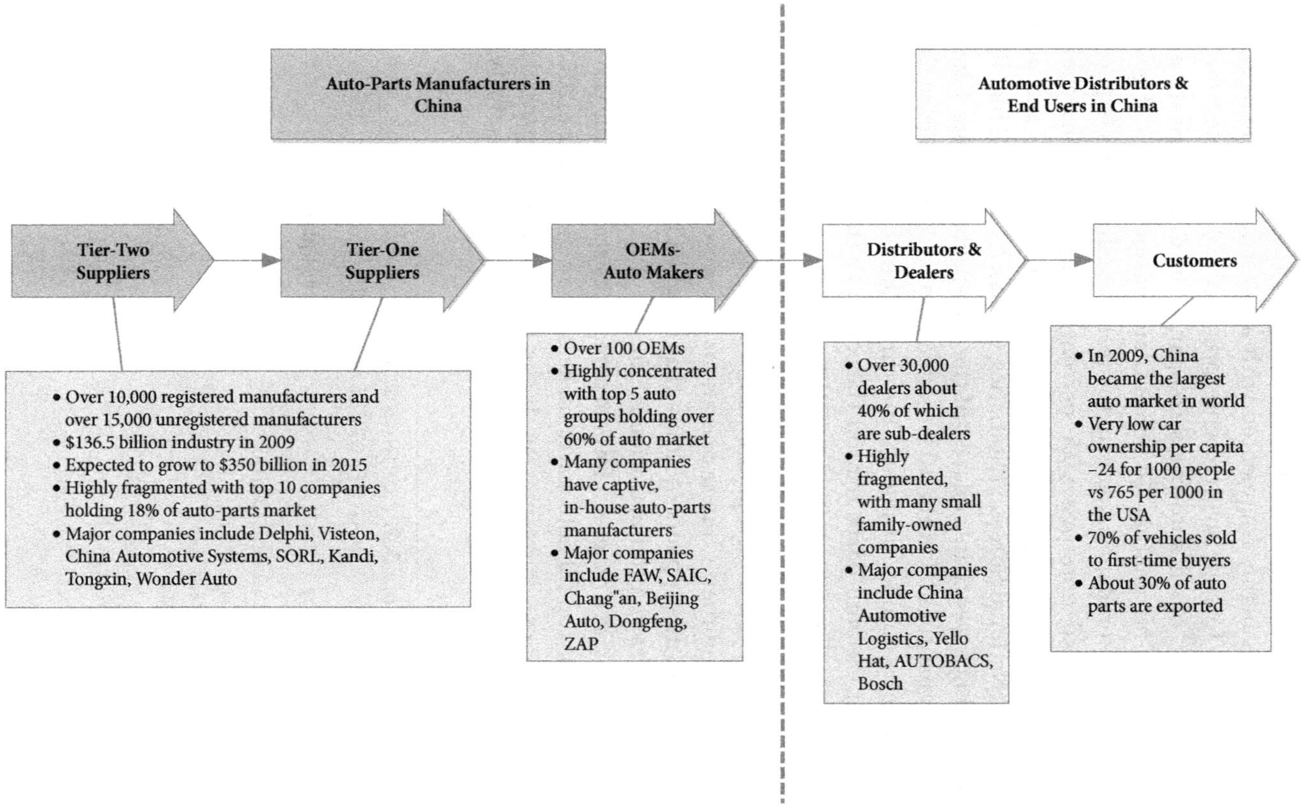

Figure 6.2
The Automotive Value Chain in China
Source: Compiled from authors' interviews with industry analysts and experts; Rodman &Renshaw

Industry Fragmentation and Foreign Companies

Despite governmental efforts at consolidation, the Chinese auto-parts industry remains highly fragmented with at least 20,000 smaller companies. In 2008, foreign-invested enterprises (FIEs) accounted for only about 23 percent of all auto-parts companies in China. Private enterprises accounted for another 44 percent, and various modes of government-controlled companies made up the rest, including SOEs (4 percent), collectively owned enterprises (5 percent), cooperative shareholding enterprises (3 percent), joint-stock enterprises (3 percent), and others (18 percent) (National Bureau of Statistics, China). As table 6.2 highlights, despite owning fewer than a quarter of the auto-parts companies, foreign companies constituted 7 of the 10 largest auto-parts companies in China, as measured by number of plants. The three Chinese companies on the list represent the auto-parts arms of the country's three leading vehicles makers—SAIC, First Auto Works (FAW) Group, and Dongfeng Motor (Dongfeng). In 2009, more than 70 of the top 100 global auto-parts companies had manufacturing operations in China, and many continued to open or to expand their Chinese operations. For example, GM reported it had more than 198 suppliers in China that supplied its global operations (International Trade Administration 2009).

The proportion of Chinese to foreign companies stays roughly the same across the list of top 50 auto-parts makers. The top 50 in the 2008 list featured 13 Chinese companies, with the balance from Japan (also 13 companies), Europe (12), North America (10), and South Korea (2). Within

Table 6.2. CHINA'S TOP AUTO-PARTS MANUFACTURERS, 2008

Company	Number of plants
Hyundai Mobis (S. Korea)	6
Yazaki (Japan)	6
Bosch (Germany)	9
Delphi (US)	13
Johnson Controls (US)	14
Denso (Japan)	20
Dongfeng Parts (China)	23
Visteon (US)	29
Fawer (China)	35
SAIC (China)	40

Source: Compiled from data from KPMG and JD Power.

the ranks of the top 50, their principal customers dictate companies' business models. The large SOEs have run vertically integrated conglomerates. A handful of Chinese groups, such as Wanxiang, have been establishing themselves as independent auto-parts companies. Chinese car companies, such as Chery and Geely, have been sourcing their components largely at the lowest possible cost, but also to raise technological standards and strengthen export potential.

Strict regulations do not permit wholly foreign-owned enterprises in auto assembly. In 2009, JVs had a 73 percent share of passenger-car production in China, compared to only 5 percent in commercial-vehicle production (Rodman & Renshaw Equity Research). Over 25 foreign JVs make passenger cars in China. SAIC, Dongfeng, and FAW constitute the dominant SOEs in the automotive sector. FAW has JVs with Volkswagen and Toyota, Dongfeng with Citroen and Nissan. Local governments also play major roles in the Chinese auto-parts industry, such as the Shanghai government with SAIC, a JV partner of GM and Volkswagen. Similarly, the Anhui provincial government owns Chery, the Liaoning provincial government owns Brilliance Automotive, and the Beijing municipal government owns Beijing Automotive Industry Company and currently has a JV with Daimler, its latest in a long line; Beijing Jeep, China's first JV, was established in 1984 with American Motors. Tianjin Automotive Industry Corporation and Guangzhou Automotive Industry Corporation also fall under their municipal governments' control. Many of China's automakers, especially those owned by local governments, appear to benefit from preferential financing as well. Employment and potential tax revenues from automotive ventures drive local governments' interest and support.

Since 2004, the government has allowed 100 percent foreign ownership of auto-parts companies.[4] Yet direct and indirect Chinese government ownership or influence has remained prevalent. Many of the large auto-parts companies have affiliations with the large vehicle-assembly groups that local governments partly own. Other unaffiliated auto-parts companies benefit from government ownership directly. For example, the Xiaoshan municipal government partially owns the Wanxiang Group. Most foreign auto-parts companies have entered China through JVs with local and regional governments, thereby securing access to government equity capital, as well as near-guaranteed access to preferential bank loans.

According to AT Kearney, in 2009, the top 10 auto-parts companies accounted for 18 percent of the total auto-parts market. Our analysis of revenue breakdowns in the auto parts industry by ownership showed that in 2009, foreign companies (generally large) and private companies (generally small and family-owned) had the greatest share of revenues, 46 percent and 28 percent respectively; conversely, SOEs, collectively owned enterprises, joint-equity cooperatives, and shareholding enterprises, all government-controlled in some fashion, had 4 percent, 2 percent, 1 percent, and 5 percent of the revenues, with other enterprises having 14 percent.[5] In 2009, only 38 auto-parts companies had annual revenues greater than $146.4 million. Foreign companies dominated in terms of value and also operated higher up in the value chain. Fiducia (China) estimated that foreign companies manufactured over 90 percent of the key functional auto parts: China had been levying high import taxes (of 25 percent, later reduced to 10 percent) for auto-parts imports, which forced foreign companies to set up their own auto-parts manufacturing plants and to invest heavily in R&D. Since no foreign-ownership cap existed for setting up auto-parts companies, most preferred to operate as wholly foreign-owned enterprises with limited technology transfer to domestic Chinese firms, unless constrained to do so.[6]

Geographic Spread and Clustering

Table 6.3 details the wide geographic dispersion of China's auto-parts industry, with major vehicle and auto-parts manufacturers in every major industrial region, across coastal provinces from north to south, as well as several inland provinces along the Yangtze River. However, 55 percent of the companies cluster around the relatively well-developed East China region and 22 percent in the middle South China region, with higher per capita incomes, larger populations, and therefore higher usage of automobiles. Twenty-three percent of the other auto-parts companies are scattered across the rest of China, with only about 1 percent in Northwest China.[7] In 2010, the provinces of Zhejiang, Jiangsu, Shanghai, Shandong, Guangdong, and Hubei accounted for about 57.5 percent of total industry revenue.

In addition to these major centers, new vehicle makers—especially carmakers—continue to set up in locations with no previous automotive history. Chery, based in Anhui, and Geely, based in Zhejiang, constitute the two leading examples; but more than 100 other companies are spread across the country, most of them producing fewer than 50,000 vehicles a year.

To date, investment in vehicle-assembly plants has more than doubled that in auto-parts. The general policymaking and company strategy involves first establishing vehicle-assembly facilities, and then bringing in the auto-parts manufacturers to supply to them. For example, in 1997,

Table 6.3. AUTO-PARTS SECTOR IN CHINA BY PROVINCE, 2008

Region	Number of enterprises (units)	Number of loss-making enterprises (units)	Gross industrial output (thousands of yuan)	Number of employees
National	10,331	1,664	987,038,310	1,927,723
Beijing	229	52	31,454,100	35,409
Tianjin	272	72	49,094,201	59,918
Hebei	296	38	25,062,159	61,809
Shanxi	30	12	2,756,572	13,794
Inner Mongolia	13	5	715,653	2,002
Liaoning	393	78	35,215,973	71,654
Jilin	380	92	55,095,161	96,296
Heilongjiang	77	17	3,806,371	12,644
Shanghai	651	122	99,470,035	146,242
Jiangsu	1,333	189	113,744,478	219,606
Zhejiang	1,964	208	134,968,694	275,704
Anhui	417	100	23,580,326	58,688
Fujian	331	44	24,645,095	68,339
Jiangxi	138	7	8,135,877	20,375
Shandong	790	77	80,214,597	141,696
Henan	367	32	39,293,863	61,361
Hubei	770	175	56,872,204	136,885
Hunan	172	15	14,585,652	38,819
Guangdong	545	111	92,561,791	159,316
Guangxi	255	73	22,471,108	44,791
Hainan	28	4	1,654,727	3,860
Chongqing	506	81	34,028,811	102,069
Sichuan	290	37	24,437,056	59,885
Guizhou	29	11	2,142,091	11,545
Yunnan	18	4	1,042,135	4,719
Shaanxi	35	7	9,868,846	20,112
Gansu	0	1	17,513	30
Xinjiang	0	0	103,221	155

Source: China Data Online.

Guangzhou had no auto-parts industry. Since then, it has transformed itself into one of China's leading automotive centers by persuading Honda, Toyota, and Nissan to open plants first and subsequently bring in their auto-parts networks.

Globally, auto-parts production requires thrice as much capital investment as final vehicle assembly in fully developed vehicle-supply chains.

However in China the ratio of capital investments in auto-parts production to vehicle-assembly approximates 0.3 (*Xinhua News Agency* 2010); consequently, the Chinese auto-parts industry has room for expansion. Auto-parts investment will likely grow much more rapidly than vehicle assembly in the next several years: the assembly sector has already invested heavily in production capacity, and very strong central and local governmental support exists for more technically advanced and specialized auto-parts production in China. In addition to the central government, 24 provinces individually consider auto parts (along with autos) as a pillar, strategic industry, key for provincial and national security (G. T. Haley 2007, 2009).

Impending Overcapacity

Despite China's rank as the world's largest auto market, China's car-ownership rate remains very low compared to developed countries. China has 24 passenger cars per 1,000 people, while the global average stands at 120. The United States has the highest car ownership with 765 per 1,000 people (Rodman & Renshaw Equity Research). With China's booming economy and rising income levels, many foreign companies expect an increase in passenger-car penetration over the coming years, and they have factored this into their strategic-expansion plans. In addition, these companies expect that favorable government policies (such as preferential sales-tax rates) will stimulate consumer spending on durable goods like passenger cars.[8] However, Chinese cities prefer to subsidize their own auto and auto-parts companies. For example, in July 2012, as China's auto sales started slowing, two Chinese cities, Chongqing in the southwest and Changchun in the northeast, started giving subsidies of between RMB 3000–7000 for purchases of local state-owned autos so that the companies could continue to expand (Yang 2012). Chongqing's subsidy is only for Chongqing Changan Automobile Co and Changchun's only for FAW.

According to CSM Worldwide, in 2008, North American and European countries had excess auto-production capacity of 44 percent and 23 percent, respectively. From 2009 to 2011, the global automobile industry had average excess production capacity of 30.5 million units, exacerbated in part by the global recession. However, automotive companies in China are expanding production capacity to tap expected growth in domestic demand and also to maintain local aspirations.

In November 2009, the National Development and Reform Commission (NDRC) announced that China's auto industry is likely to have overcapacity given present market growth of 10 percent (*Asia Pulse* 2009). Given the market's current level of investment and companies' production-expansion plans, the industry's capacity-utilization rate will fall below 70 percent in the following years, according to the survey the NDRC conducted (*Asia Pulse* 2009). Indeed, since 2010, the Chinese auto-parts industry has been operating at around 65 percent of capacity —far below the 80 percent firms need for profitability. Yet new production facilities continue to rise. According to the NDRC, at this rate, China's auto-manufacturing capacity will increase again in the next three years by an amount equal to all the auto factories in Japan, or nearly all the auto factories in the United States (Bradsher 2012).

Concurrently, industrial parks for auto parts and accessories have been established rapidly and widely around China, even in some regions with relatively weak automotive industries, such as those surrounding the cities of Yinchuan, Jiangmen, Huizhou, and Neijiang. In 2009, Tianjin's Great Wall Motor invested $1.24 billion to produce 500,000 vehicles within three years. In 2010, China had more than 30 similar bases at design stages for the production of auto parts and accessories around the country.

The new energy vehicle (NEV) sector, to which the Chinese government gives particular attention in strategic plans, also attracted large amounts of investment. In 2009, Beijing planned for NEV production capacity of 500,000 completed vehicles by upgrading the existing production capacity by 2011, and encouraging the production of electric vehicles, plug-in hybrid-electric vehicles, and ordinary hybrid-power vehicles. However, by the end of 2009, production capacity at the design stage had already surpassed the target of 500,000 completed vehicles. The country had at least 19 companies investing more than $15 million in founding large-scale power-cell production bases. In November 2009, Tianjin Lishen Battery had invested $110 million to expand the production of lithium cells and planned to invest a further $220,000 in the next couple of months. Hunan Shenzhou Science and Technology had invested $44 million in a Tianjin base and would put in an additional $205 million. Forever Battery planned to invest $193 million to set up a cell plant with an annual output of 365 million ampere-hours (Ah). In addition, China's BYD and CITIC Guoan Mengguli had similar plans. Chen Bin, head of NDRC's Department of Industry, said that the industry's supply might be much heavier than the market demand after 2010 in light of companies' expansion plans (*Asia Pulse* 2009).

IMPORTS AND EXPORTS OF CHINESE AUTO PARTS

Figure 6.3 sketches Chinese imports and exports of auto parts from 1996 to 2010. In 2005, for the first time, China achieved a net surplus in auto-parts trade. In 2008, China became the fourth-largest exporter of auto parts in the world after Germany, the United States, and Japan (International Trade Administration 2009, 2010). Data from CAAM showed that Chinese auto-parts exports hit $32.67 billion in the first 10 months of 2010, up 44.4 percent year on year (Just-Auto 2010). According to CAAM, during the first nine months of 2010, China's imports totaled $18.42 billion (Sinofile Information Services 2010).

For China, most auto-parts imports consist of higher-end systems and components to incorporate into Sino-foreign vehicle makers' autos. Figure 6.4 shows Chinese imports and exports by country. Japan accounts for more than one-third of total imports and Germany more than one-quarter, reflecting the roles of Volkswagen in the mass market, and BMW and Mercedes-Benz in the luxury. The three companies have great reliance on imported components. In contrast, China imports very little from the United States, reflecting the presence of American companies at the top end of China's auto-parts industry. JVs serve as the greatest importers of auto parts into China, with 64 percent of the imports. However, unlike the Japanese and German, US automotive JVs have made decisions to source parts from Chinese auto-part manufacturers, thereby contributing to the bilateral trade imbalance. The United States has also been by far the leading export destination for Chinese auto parts, indicating the

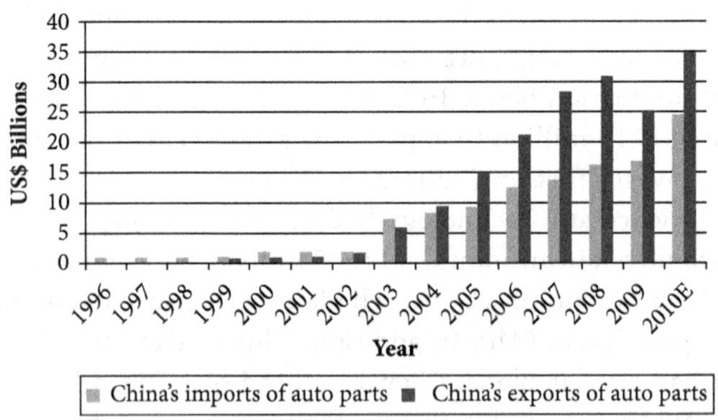

Figure 6.3
China's Trade in Auto Parts, 1996–2010
Source: China Automotive Information Net; ResearchinChina; China Association of Automotive Manufacturers.

extensive integration of US auto-parts companies in the Chinese export machinery.

In auto parts, China runs trade deficits with every other major auto producer, including Japan, South Korea, Germany, Canada, and France. However, China's trade surpluses on auto parts with the United States constitute a notable exception. As other foreign auto companies operating in China have linked to auto-parts suppliers back home, US auto companies have increasingly cut ties with US suppliers or encouraged them to manufacture in China. In 2006, Ford announced that to cut costs, the company planned to double the value of the auto parts that it sourced from China to about $3 billion from about $1.6 billion in 2005 (Dyer 2006). In 2008 GM, which bought 20 million parts a month from 190 Chinese suppliers, announced that it intended to buy more and increasingly sophisticated car components in China for worldwide assembly.[9] The company stated that it would increase its procurement spending in China by 25 percent per year in the period 2005–2010 (Zubko 2008). US global auto strategy has progressively centered around manufacturing in China and exporting back home. Consequently, China's exports of auto parts to the United States are thrice those of China's next highest trading destination, Japan.

China's auto-parts exports are expected to grow even more dramatically in the future, driven primarily by two factors: (*a*) exports to overseas automakers and (*b*) exports to overseas Tier 1 suppliers.[10] Foreign, primarily US, automakers' captive centers in China will probably supply most of their home bases directly. GM and Ford have already officially indicated

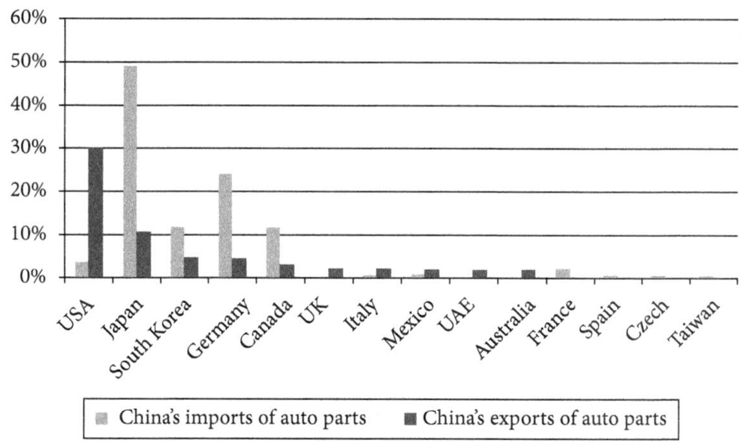

Figure 6.4
China's Trade in Auto Parts by Country, 2009
Source: China Customs.

their intentions in this regard with escalating purchases of more advanced parts from their sourcing centers in China.

In 2008, China overtook Germany to become the fourth-largest source of imports for US auto parts (after NAFTA partners Canada and Mexico, and Japan), and in 2011 was among the fastest growing source of US imports (along with Korea and Mexico). As figure 6.5 shows, from 2000 to 2010, imports of Chinese auto parts into the United States increased about eightfold and are expected to continue to increase. During the same period, the US trade deficit with China on auto parts increased ninefold.

In 2009, the NDRC, China's central economic-planning agency, released "Directives on Promoting the Healthy and Sustainable Growth of Domestically-Made Auto Products" to increase auto-parts exports. According to the directives, the government will facilitate auto and auto-parts manufacturers' efforts to get loans from domestic banks to fund their exports. The government has also pledged the services of the state-owned export-credit insurer, China Export and Credit Insurance, to manage credit risks in overseas markets for auto-parts companies that export (China Automotive Technology & Research Center 2009).

The Chinese government has additionally pledged to help domestic auto and auto-parts companies to build overseas R&D centers and to acquire foreign peers to improve their technology and product-development capabilities. With its support, the government envisions domestic automakers expanding their exports from mainly commercial vehicles, to passenger

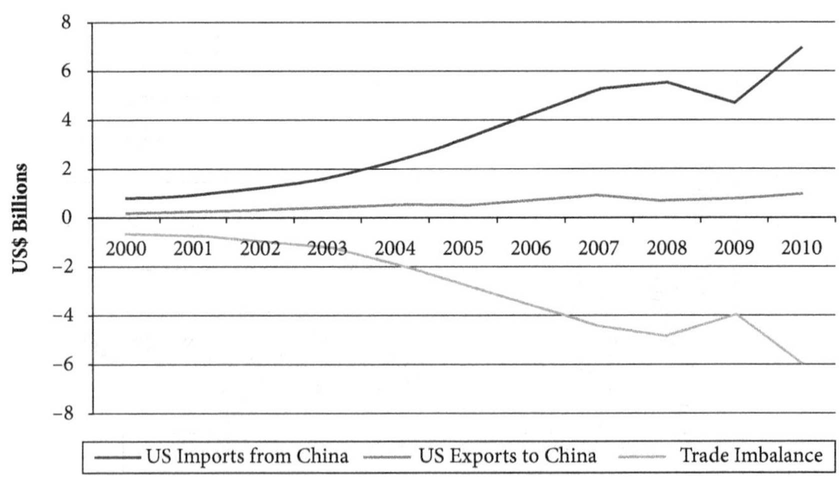

Figure 6.5.
US Trade with China in Auto Parts, 2000–2010
Source: US International Trade Commission.

vehicles, compact cars, and small and medium-sized buses, according to the directives. The government also expects domestic parts suppliers to shift their export focus from mechanical products to machinery and electrical and electronic products. With these support measures, the NDRC stated that in 2009 it expected to see the export value of automobiles and auto parts made by domestic companies to grow 10 percent annually and to reach $85 billion by 2015 (China Automotive Technology & Research Center 2009).

COST STRUCTURE OF CHINA'S AUTO-PARTS INDUSTRY

The costs of auto parts constitute about 70 percent of the total production cost of the entire automobile.[11] Table 6.4 outlines some of the major raw materials and subcomponents used in this highly complex industry spanning auto glass / float glass, car tires, car wheels, engine-oil radiators, and intercoolers as well as car batteries. The great majority of the companies focus on particular parts or markets, and most concentrate on single products. Only some larger companies can manufacture a wide variety of auto parts. Typically, Chinese auto parts sell for around 30 percent to 50 percent less than comparable auto parts made in Europe, North America, or Japan. Estimating costs in the Chinese auto-parts industry becomes especially difficult because of subsidies to Tier 3 suppliers, including steel and glass manufacturers, and government-controlled pricing of energy, as we have described in previous chapters.

Table 6.4. RAW MATERIALS AND SUBCOMPONENTS IN CHINESE AUTO PARTS

Auto parts	Major companies	Main raw materials and subcomponents
Glass / float glass	Fuyao Glass	Soda ash / pure alkali, heavy oil, silica sand
Tires	AEOLUS Tyre, GuizhouTyre, Yellow Sea Rubber	Caoutchouc, synthetic rubber, carbon black, steel tire cord
Wheels	Wanfeng Auto	Aluminum
Engine-oil radiators and intercoolers	Yinlun Machinery	Stainless Steel, cold-rolled steel, aluminum alloy, brass, aluminum materials
Batteries	Fengfan	Lead

Source: Compiled from authors' interviews with industry analysts; Haley 2009.

In 2010, mechanical parts and accessories, including bearings, filters, covers, brakes, and clutches comprised the largest segment of this industry, accounting for 56 percent of total revenues. Mechanical parts formed the majority of automobile components, and their prices have increased in the past few years because of rising raw-material prices. Electric motors, including starting motors, alternators, control units for electronic systems, and mechanical and electronic drivers comprised the second-largest industrial segment, accounting for 23 percent of total revenues. Electronic parts and accessories, including electronic-control systems for engines, antilock brakes, meters, GPS, transducers, entertainment systems, and items used for control, safety, communication, and entertainment comprised the third industrial segment in the industry, accounting for 21 percent of total revenues.

Figure 6.6 provides a cost breakdown for China's auto-parts industry.[12] Raw materials and subcomponent purchases, including iron, cold-rolled steel, glass, rubber, and machine parts contributed to 66 percent of the costs of manufacturing Chinese auto parts. Labor accounted for just 5 percent of costs, with another 2 percent for management costs.[13] Total industry wages increased significantly during the period under study, with an annualized growth rate of 22 percent. Total wages experienced fastest growth in 2008, when the employment level rose by 45 percent (IBISWorld). The average wage per employee steadily increased over the current performance period, and simultaneously, the share of wages in industry revenue decreased. This indicates technology changes, higher usage of machinery and equipment, and higher skill requirements in this

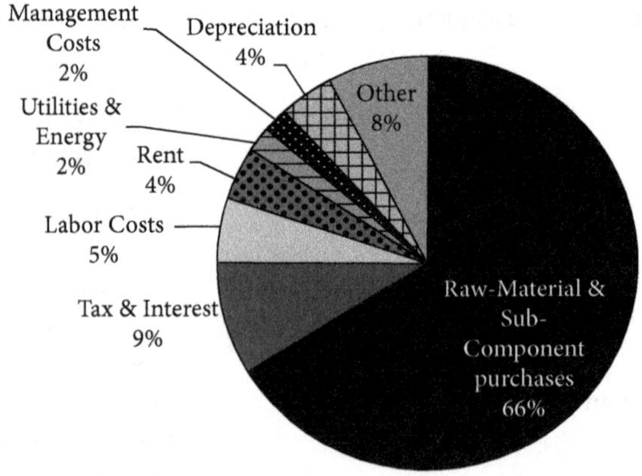

Figure 6.6
Cost Structure of China's Auto-Parts Industry
Source: Authors' interviews with industry analysts.

industry. Besides some raw materials and components, costs addressed in this study include utilities and energy (2 percent of total costs) and taxes and interest (9 percent of total costs). Other costs (8 percent) that depend on individual companies' operations, such as logistics and transportation, storage, maintenance, subcontractors, insurance, advertising, and other expenses that differ across companies, are not estimated in this chapter.

The Chinese auto-parts industry has high capital-intensity.[14] Foreign and SOE companies' large-scale production requires significant capital to install automated processes, equipment, and machinery. Upgrades of plant and equipment for process and product development also require significant investment. Many manufacturing processes involve repetitive activities that large and foreign companies have automated to increase production speeds and cost efficiencies. Small-scale domestic manufacturers generally have lower capital-investment levels than larger firms because of the high costs of acquiring new equipment and because of the basic auto parts they produce. In 2011, foreign capital accounted for over 36 percent of China's auto-parts market. Foreign companies monopolized Chinese production of some complex auto parts, such as high-end electronic controls, fuel-injection systems, transducers, brake systems, and steering systems.

ROLE OF GOVERNMENT POLICY IN CHINA'S AUTO-PARTS INDUSTRY

The automotive industry in China benefits immensely from government support. The government considers this industry as a pillar or strategically important industry for the economy and has adopted various policies and initiatives to spur strong growth and development (G. T. Haley 2009). As Zhang Ji, deputy director of import and export of machinery and electronic products at China's Ministry of Commerce (MOFCOM) stated in an interview: "Automobiles are in a way different from other merchandises. Automobile export adds to the dignity of a nation.... The auto industry represents a country's overall economic strength. The government should provide vigorous support" (*China Automotive Review* 2006). Governmental policy has aimed at increasing domestic auto and auto-parts manufacturing with foreign partners, enabling technology transfer and creating an auto-parts supply base for exports.[15] The government has offered market access to foreign auto companies in return for technology; both soft and hard technology acquisition, not capital acquisition, has motivated China's opening of its auto industry to FDI (Thun 2004). The central government's policy has also aimed at modernizing and restructuring SOEs to create principal actors or "national champions" in their industries and to displace imported products in China's domestic market. National champions in the automotive sector include the vertically integrated SAIC, FAW, and Dongfeng, which include captive auto-parts manufacturers.

Soviet aid helped to start the Chinese automotive sector in 1953 with the establishment of China's first car company, First Auto Works (FAW). In the late 1970s, China's auto industry continued to transform through its open-door policy. To modernize its industrial infrastructure, China needed foreign technology, management, and finance to supplement low domestic savings and nascent R&D capabilities. Import-substitution policies built on a protectionist framework helped the auto and auto-parts industry to evolve under shelter. In the 1970s, China's auto industry had very small production capacity focused on truck production. In 1978, the country had 56 auto-assembly plants that produced slightly fewer than 150,000 units based on Eastern European designs from the 1950s (Ministry of Machinery 1994). In 1984, Premier Zhao Ziyang announced that China planned to produce exportable sedans up to world standards, to increase production volumes, and to switch from an "all-under-one-roof mentality of small-scale development" to a "cooperative industrial complex system, centered around large-scale factories based on modern technology" (Iwagaki 1986, 11). Specific objectives included consolidating production in the industry into three large and three small producers with high local content, acquiring advanced technology, and achieving high volumes. JVs with foreign companies would serve as the primary vehicle of industrial upgrading (Thun 2004). In 1986, the central government designated the automotive industry as a pillar of the national economy. In 1987, the government began to encourage JVs with foreign auto companies, while its trade policy continued to nurture domestic auto-parts production. This new policy included compulsory licensing of imports and new production facilities. In the 1991 five-year plan, Beijing referred to the automotive industry as a "pillar industry" for China. In 1994, the State Planning Commission issued an industrial-policy statement formalizing the state's objectives for the auto industry, which it modeled on perceived Japanese and Korean experiences, except the reliance on JVs for industrial upgrading. Since then, 24 provincial governments have also designated the automotive industry as a pillar industry with local governmental support for restructuring, growth, and exports.

The Auto Industry Development Policy (AIP), issued by the NDRC with every five-year plan, serves as the blueprint for developing China's auto industry. The 2004 AIP encouraged local automakers to develop R&D

capabilities, to produce vehicles independently, and to increase exports to $35 billion to $40 billion by 2010, accounting for around 40 percent to 50 percent of output. The policy also aimed to have auto parts derive from a series of industry clusters, where domestic companies could establish their own brands and compete in international markets, with advanced technology and capital-intensive products accounting for around 60 percent of exports. The plan has fallen short of these targets.

China's 2004 AIP also formalized some technology-transfer requirements for foreign companies wanting to invest in China's automotive sector. Pursuant to article 47 of the 2004 AIP, foreign-investment projects in China's automotive industry require the establishment of R&D facilities with an investment of at least RMB 500 million. In Annex II of the 2004 AIP, foreign investors seeking approval of new automobile production plants must file technology-transfer agreements (Trade Lawyers Advisory Group 2007). In 2011, Beijing announced that foreign auto companies that want to expand in China must launch new brands with their Chinese partners. Earlier in 2011, Volkswagen AG received government permission to build a new assembly plant in South China only after it had agreed to create a new brand for its JV with FAW. The government-financed China Automotive Technology and Research Center concluded that "With this rule, the government hopes to force global automakers to contribute more technology to their joint ventures" (China Automotive Technology and Research Center 2011).

In the 2004 AIP, two significant laws restricted foreign ownership to 50 percent shares of any vehicle-manufacturing company in China and restricted foreign vehicle manufacturers to two local JV partners. Foreign OEMs have had to set up JVs for vehicle production, implicitly compelling them to cooperate on vehicle distribution with their local partners. The AIP also paved the way for China's auto-parts industry to become part of the global automotive-purchasing system and started to restructure the automotive industry into large groups capable of competing globally. In its 11th Five-Year Plan (2006–2010) for the automotive industry, the government eliminated the need for state approval for any new investment in auto-parts manufacturing. To create a strong R&D platform in auto parts and to boost technology transfer from foreign companies, Beijing had previously removed the 50 percent ownership restriction on JVs in auto-parts production. In 2010, auto-parts companies could have 100 percent foreign ownership and start production without state approval, while auto-assembly companies still could not.

Unlike the central government's deliberated policies, provinces often issue policies quite abruptly, taking markets by surprise. For example, in

1999, local governments in 13 cities banned the use of diesel vehicles with almost no warning or lead time. The governments have since retracted this policy. As with the subsidies mentioned before, local governments also often pass laws that favor their local economies and businesses rather than national interests (JD Power & Associates 2007). For example, some provinces set vehicle specifications for taxis to match those of locally manufactured autos. As governmental fleets have traditionally been the largest consumers of autos, these regulations have major repercussions on sales of autos and auto parts.

Provincial and local governments have also actively implemented the policy of "coordinative development" to attract investment by unifying the production chain within industrial clusters. Within industrial clusters, interconnected enterprises in a particular industry share related production inputs, specialized labor pools, distribution and communication channels, and network associations (Specialty Steel Industry of North America 2008).

To help China's automotive industry negotiate the global economic crisis, China's government quickly introduced two stimulus packages. The first, in January 2009, sought primarily to boost vehicle sales. Its range of policies included halving the purchase (sales) tax on cars with engines of less than 1.6 liters, providing large subsidies for rural residents to trade in old vehicles for new, and lowering retail fuel prices. The second package announced in March 2009 included initiatives aimed at restructuring and strengthening the industry. It announced the goal of making "new energy" cars reach 5 percent of passenger-vehicle sales and backed up this target by offering funds for research into alternative energy and vehicle safety. The government also encouraged auto-finance companies to loosen credit requirements and to lower interest rates. The package additionally reiterated the government's desire to consolidate the top 14 companies (including their in-house parts makers) into 10 major auto groups organized into two distinct tiers: Tier 1 companies with annual production capacity of two million units, and Tier 2 companies with annual production capacity of one million units. Since 2000, Beijing has released at least three plans to consolidate the automotive industry with no discernible effect, as these plans have clashed with provincial interests. For example, in 2000, Beijing released a plan to consolidate all of China's car manufacturers into the three biggest SOEs. Almost immediately, Anhui Province's Chery, founded in 1997, began selling a minicar. Rather than force Chery to shut down, Beijing required it to sell 20 percent of its shares to Shanghai-based SAIC. Three years later, Chery bought back its shares from SAIC. In 2009, Chery sold over 500,000 cars as China's largest stand-alone car manufacturer.

In addition, the 2009 stimulus provisions included incentives for domestic carmakers to export 20 percent of total production. The provisions also aimed to increase the market share of domestic branded passenger vehicles to 40 percent from 34 percent in 2008. Toward its efforts to increase the R&D capabilities of China's automotive industry, the government has mandated that newly approved auto projects commit $60 million toward R&D. As stated earlier in this chapter, the government planned to set up production capacity for 500,000 NEVs, and to increase market share of NEVs to 5 percent of total auto sales. The government was also continuing its financial and economic subsidies to its auto-parts industry.

In 2009, GM offered a glimpse of its R&D capabilities and cooperation with the Chinese government when it introduced the Chevrolet New Sail, which it developed entirely in China. The Pan-Asia Technical Automotive Center (PATAC) in Shanghai, a 13-year-old JV with GM's local partner SAIC, developed the product. GM has begun exporting the New Sail to Chile (*Automotive News China* 2011). In February 2011, the company announced plans to introduce 20 new and upgraded models in China over the next two years as it expanded into different segments. By the end of 2011, GM opened the doors of its $150 million GM China Advanced Technical Center (CATC) in Shanghai for R&D on auto parts and autos (*Automotive News China* 2011). "As an integral element of our global product development strategy, the [CATC] will create advanced technologies and lead GM's global research in targeted areas," said Kevin Wale, president and managing director of the GM China Group (GM Media 2010). "We expect it to become one of GM's most important and comprehensive technical and design facilities worldwide." The CATC will incorporate 62 test and nine research labs and hire over 300 engineers and scientists. Its labs will include (*a*) the China Science Lab for R&D on advanced-propulsion systems, manufacturing processes, megacity smart traffic, customer-driven advanced vehicles, battery-cell material and fabrication, and lightweight materials; (*b*) the Vehicle Engineering Lab for R&D on electric vehicles, alternative-energy vehicles, battery technology in conjunction with Chinese suppliers, and product development featuring advanced-technology and design solutions with GM's domestic JVs; and (*c*) the Advanced Powertrain Engineering Lab for R&D on advanced-propulsion systems, including electrification technology, alternatives to petroleum-based fuels in conventional powertrains, and unique conventional powertrains for the local market, as well as new materials for powertrain products. The facility aimed to complement GM's engineering and product-development partnerships in China, including PATAC and the China Automotive Energy Research Center (CAERC) in Beijing (GM Media 2010).

The Chinese central and provincial governments have implemented a raft of direct and indirect governmental subsidies to carry out its industrial policies. These governmental support measures include

- direct subsidies to companies including subsidized financing, cash grants, tax subsidies, export subsidies, interest-free loans and R&D grants.
- indirect subsidies to the industry including artificial, government-controlled prices to energy, raw materials and key inputs.

According to Zheng Xinli (2010), deputy director of the Economic Committee of the National Committee of the Chinese People's Consultative Conference, and former deputy director of the Policy Research Center of the CPC Central Committee, industrial upgrading, including in autos and auto parts, remained an investment priority for the Chinese government. The Twelfth Five-Year Plan would see the government increasing its input into R&D and encouraging international mergers and acquisitions (M&A) to acquire foreign technology. "Geely has outflanked FAW Group, DFAC [Dongfeng] and SAIC in middle-and-high-end automobile technology R&D through acquiring Volvo. Thus, we should make the most of international scientific and technological resources, and enhance our innovative capacity through M&A."

China's four largest state-owned banks, Industrial and Commercial Bank of China (ICBC), China Construction Bank, the People's Bank of China, and the Agricultural Bank of China, account for over 60 percent of all loans. In accordance with central or local governments' industrial policies, these banks have made loans based on political directives (or policy loans), rather than the borrowers' creditworthiness or other market-based factors. The Chinese government has instructed banks in China to provide loans to further its industrial policies on numerous occasions. In just one example, SAIC, China's largest automaker, received "huge amounts of bank credit for its market expansion" (*People's Daily Online* 2000). The Chinese government also has provided other companies in China's automotive sector with significant subsidies in the form of subsidized (or reduced-interest) loans for SOEs' strategic restructuring and technical transformation of key production technologies.

SUBSIDIES TO CHINA'S AUTO-PARTS INDUSTRY

This section presents calculated subsidies provided directly to companies in China's auto-parts industry as stated in their annual reports, and indirectly to the industry as subsidies for coal, electricity, natural gas, glass, and cold-rolled steel, and as revealed in policy statements. Chapter 2 has provided descriptions of the data and methodology, as well as the mathematical equations to calculate the subsidies. Chinese government subsidies to its auto-parts industry have increased steadily over the last decade, but rose most sharply after 2008, with a year-on-year increase of 125 percent from 2008 to 2009 alone; these increases synchronized with Chinese policy statements and announced support for R&D in auto parts. Table 6.5 provides a detailed breakdown of the subsidies.

Because the calculations reported here included only those subsidies that could be traced, confirmed, and recorded, the total subsidies to the Chinese auto-parts industry in this chapter are very conservative

Table 6.5. SUBSIDIES TO CHINESE AUTO PARTS, 2001–2010 (MILLIONS OF DOLLARS)

Year	Coking and thermal coal	Natural-gas	Electric	Glass	Cold-rolled steel	Reported grants and subsidies	Total
2001	29.06					46.94	76.00
2002	3.74		22.97			218.35	245.06
2003	3.05		24.98			105.02	133.05
2004	79.89	3.28	32.15	34.85	130.36	157.82	438.35
2005	41.34	32.30	52.65	55.83	159.64	168.40	510.16
2006	26.92	8.86	59.61	83.50	593.91	254.26	1,027.06
2007	109.44	15.16	67.09	311.92	479.09	319.72	1,302.42
2008	356.32	110.64	65.78	480.06	877.45	495.58	2,385.83
2009	80.17	46.54	96.01	267.43	301.38	6.54	798.07
2010 (est.)	313.61	94.52	174.32	326.34	714.69	548.69	2,172.17
Total	1,043.54	311.30	595.56	1,559.93	3,256.52	2,321.32	**9,088.17**
Industrial restructuring and technology-development subsidies							18,414.29
Grand total							**27,502.46**

Source: Authors' analysis and estimates based on data from Australian Bureau of Agricultural and Resource Economics and Sciences; Beijing Waterwood Technologies Corporation; Bloomberg; China.org.cn; China Association of Automobile Manufacturers; China Data Online; companies' annual reports; CEIC; Credit Suisse / First Boston; Fathom China; Interfax; International Energy Agency; ISI Emerging Markets; MEPS International; *Mining Exploration News*; National Bureau of Statistics, China; Netscribes; SteelontheNet; SWS Research; Sun, L. (2010); Ward's Automotive Group.

estimates. Missing data prevented calculation of subsidies across all years of the study and for the great majority of over 10,000 registered Chinese auto-parts companies and 24 provinces that independently list the automotive industry as a pillar industry. The trend of rising subsidies explains to some extent why Chinese auto-parts sell for around 30–50 percent less than comparable auto parts made in Europe, North America, or Japan despite very rapidly rising raw-material prices. As discussed earlier, labor accounts for only 5 percent of the costs of producing Chinese auto parts.

Subsidies reported by companies. Subsidies reported in the annual reports of China's auto-parts companies reached about $2.3 billion between 2001 and 2009. Only 73 companies, out of over 10,000 registered companies, reported the subsidies they received. The companies reported subsidies as "Subsidy Income" and "Government Grants" (without repayment terms), which amounted to $951 million; and as "Tax Refunds (Minus VAT Refunds)," which amounted to $1.36 billion. The great majority of these companies had no legal needs to disclose cash grants or subsidies from the government, and many of their managers probably misunderstood reporting requirements (see Yu 2009), so the reporting is sporadic with much missing data.

Over the period of study, auto-parts companies benefited from a variety of subsidy programs if they satisfied export-performance requirements or purchased Chinese-made accessories and equipment rather than imports. The subsidy programs included grants, policy-directed discounted loans, and other credit benefits from state-owned banks, income-tax benefits to foreign invested firms, tariff exemptions, and income-tax refunds (Haley 2007; Szamosszegi 2007). Generally, "Subsidy Income" in companies' annual reports included interest subsidies and investment subsidies that the companies received from central and provincial governments. Interest subsidies were the refunds by the Chinese governments of interest charged by banks to companies that were entitled to such subsidies. Investment subsidies were payments to encourage foreign investors to set up technologically advanced enterprises in China.

BYD, one of the world's largest manufacturers of rechargeable, lithium-ion batteries, and a company in which Warren Buffet invested $232 million in 2008 (Oliver 2008), demonstrates the effects of government subsidies on companies' operations. In 2008, BYD's released financial statements showed slim margins for all its products, including auto parts. Without the local government's reported subsidies, BYD's profits would have fallen by 26 percent. BYD used more than three-quarters of its subsidies and government grants for "automotive research and development," with the remainder paying interest on bank loans. The grant conditions did not specify any repayment terms. Most of BYD's grants and subsidies appeared to have come from its local Shenzhen city government, but the breakdown between Beijing's and Shenzhen's allocations remained unclear. State-run banks in Shenzhen had also lent generously to BYD without demanding collateral. BYD's unsecured bank loans stood at $1.3 billion by the end of 2008, with 77 percent of its loans as unsecured (GaveKal Dragonomics 2009).

Subsidies for coal. Subsidies for coal consumed by China's auto-parts industry reached about $1 billion between 2001 and 2010. The total for thermal-coal subsidies approximated $76.3 million; the auto-parts industry is a small user of coking coal, and the total for these subsidies reached $23 million. Subsidies for coal increased most steeply in 2008, when the price of thermal and coking coal soared.

Chinese subsidies for thermal coal have generally been used to offset shifts in world prices; the subsidies and prices rise and fall in tandem. As a major producer of thermal coal, China has also directly influenced domestic prices by ramping up domestic supply in response to rising world prices. Subsidies for thermal coal used by China's auto-parts industry (whose calculations depend on market prices) may show the delays that transpire between producing coal (when demand increases) and getting it to market. Interviews with industry analysts indicate that in 2002 and 2003, China's auto-parts industry was paying a premium for thermal coal. Similarly, the Chinese auto-parts industry was paying a premium for coking coal in 2009. In 2009, world coking-coal prices plummeted by 57 percent, while Chinese coking-coal prices fell by only 22 percent.

Subsidies for electricity. Subsidies for electricity used by China's auto-parts industry reached $596 million between 2002 and 2010. The total for provincial subsidies approximated $343 million; the total for coal-price-increase subsidies, which took effect in 2005, reached $253 million.

Subsidies for natural gas. Subsidies for natural gas to the auto-parts industry reached about $311 million between 2004 and 2010. In prior years, the auto-parts industry was paying a premium for natural gas. The auto-parts industry in China does not constitute a major user of natural gas.

Subsidies for key inputs: glass and steel. As table 6.4 outlines, the complex auto-parts industry is a major consumer for various upstream industries, including raw materials and subcomponents, each with their own cost structures and regulatory environments. Our calculations of subsidies to Chinese auto parts include two major inputs—automotive glass and cold-rolled steel sheets. For an in-depth analysis of the structure and subsidies received by China's flat-glass and steel sectors see chapters 2 and 3.

Subsidies for glass to the Chinese auto-parts industry approximated about $1.6 billion from 2004 to 2010. Fuyao Glass serves as China's largest automotive glassmaker with over 50 percent of the market. Subsidies for cold-rolled steel sheet reached about $3.2 billion from 2003 to 2010. The auto-parts industry paid a premium for cold-rolled steel sheets in 2003. Additionally, despite a generally steady growth in subsidies for both glass and steel for the period under study, subsidies to both inputs fell in 2009 as the global financial crisis hit auto-parts sales and production. However, as production picked up in 2010, subsidies for both glass and cold-rolled steel picked up as well.

Article 32 of the revised 2009 AIP central-government plan for China's auto-parts industry reiterates governmental subsidization of downstream industries by stating: "Key support will be given to developing the capabilities of iron and steel manufacturers to supply sheet steel for sedans. Support will be given to the establishment of professional mold design and manufacturing centers so as to improve automobile mold design and manufacturing capabilities. Support will be given to petrochemical enterprise technological progress and product upgrading so as to cause the quality of such oil products as processed oil and lubricating oil to attain [an] advanced international level and satisfy the development needs of the automotive industry" (Automotive Industry Development Policy 2009).

Technology development and industrial-restructuring subsidies. The Chinese central and seven local governments distributed about $18.4 billion in subsidies to the auto-parts industry through technology-development and industrial-restructuring policies from 2001 to 2011. Table 6.6 indicates the identified subsidies. In addition, the Chinese central government has already committed $10.9 billion for disbursement of technology-development and industrial-restructuring subsidies between 2012 and 2020.

In 2007, the automotive sector remained among the most R&D-intensive sectors in the world, with four auto companies, Toyota, Ford, DaimlerChrysler, and General Motors, among the top 10 investors in R&D in the world across all sectors. In 2008, notwithstanding the worldwide decline in auto sales, global auto investments in R&D accounted for 16 percent of total spending. Indeed, R&D spending in the industry increased, but only by 0.6 percent. Toyota, Ford, and General Motors continued among the top 10 investors (Jaruzelski and Dehoff 2007, 2009).

Understanding that investments in R&D underscore global competitiveness, the Chinese government's auto policies strongly encourage the development of cutting-edge and green-research capabilities in the local supplier industry such as pure-electric, plug-in, hybrid, and other new-energy vehicles, as we identified earlier. To establish global

Table 6.6. GOVERNMENTS' INDUSTRIAL-RESTRUCTURING AND TECHNOLOGY-DEVELOPMENT SUBSIDIES AFFECTING CHINA'S AUTO-PARTS INDUSTRY, 2001–2020

	2001–2011	US$
Central	Auto-industry revitalization plan (2009–2011)	1,457,560,000
	Industrial-technology upgrades plan (2009)	2,915,120,000
	Development and production of new energy vehicles (2010–2011)	3,828,000,000
	Advancement of manufacturing technologies (2009–2011)	1,443,960,000
	863 plan of electric vehicles (2001–2005)	96,647,200
	13 cities project (2009–2010)	4,905,164
Local	Jinan and Tangshan: E-auto battery subsidies (2010–2011)	7,908,606,666
	Shanghai: Power-station subsidies (2010–2011)	22,419,975
	Shanghai: E-auto subsidies (2011)	151,462,000
	Hangzhou: Alternative-energy-vehicle purchase subsidy (2009–2011)	127,385,451
	Hefei: Alternative-energy-vehicle purchase subsidy (2009–2011)	128,594,712
	Beijing: Vehicle-purchase subsidy (2009–2011)	303,583,800
	Chongqing: Road & bridge toll subsidy (2009–11)	6,693,708
	Kumming: Technology-enhancement subsidy (2009–2011)	19,348,194
	Total	**$18,414,286,870**
	2012–2020	
Central	Development and production of new energy vehicles (2012–2020)	**10,872,000,000**

Source: Netscribes; SWS Research; Fathom (China); Sun 2010; authors' interviews with industry analysts.

competitiveness, Chinese policies have attempted (1) to build capabilities through domestic R&D and (2) to attract foreign direct investment (FDI) (Zhao and Lv 2009). The government views technological development and industrial restructuring in the automotive sector as prime drivers for the entire Chinese economy, including several commodity and service-related sectors such as machinery, rubber, petrochemicals, electronics, glass, steel, textiles, auto financing, and auto-distribution channels.

Most local companies' R&D efforts, including industrial leaders such as BYD, fall short by global standards. For example, BYD's founder, Wang Chuanfu, stated that in the development of new products, BYD had learned 60 percent from public documents, 30 percent from finished products, and just 5 percent from BYD's own R&D. "Our creativity comes from picking out the patented parts of technology and putting together the parts that are not patented" (GaveKal Dragonomics 2009).

Consequently, the Chinese central and local governments see as their priority providing enormous support to local companies to improve industrial processes, circumvent patents, acquire technology, and copy competitors to catch up.

LOCAL CONTENT

Many subsidies to auto-parts manufacturers appear tied to local content; this chapter concludes by focusing on focusing on some of the policy implications.

The International Trade Administration (2009) has stated that the Chinese government's auto policies, including automotive-related R&D activities, strongly encourage the development of the local supplier industry. Yet, according to the Chinese government, since China's accession to the WTO, Chinese bureaucrats have worked hard to remove all WTO-forbidden local-content requirements from legislation. Officially, Chinese law contains no local-content requirements either regionally or nationally in any sector. The reality in the auto-parts industry, including ties to the disbursement of Chinese central and provincial subsidies, appears somewhat different.

In spring 2006, the United States, EU, and Canada requested WTO dispute settlement with China regarding regulations on imported auto parts. The countries argued that China's auto-parts-tariff classifications resulted in higher tariffs than China agreed to in its WTO accession agreement, and discouraged auto manufacturers in China from using imported auto parts. Chinese regulations imposed the same tariff rates as for vehicles on imported auto parts if they exceeded a fixed percentage of the final vehicle content or vehicle price, or when specific combinations of imported auto parts were used in the final vehicles. The tariff on automobiles is typically 25 percent, and on imported parts typically 10 percent. In 2008, China appealed the WTO's ruling that China must bring its import tariffs for foreign auto parts into compliance with international trade rules. However, in December 2008, the WTO rejected China's appeal. In September 2009, in response to the WTO's ruling, China eliminated the additional charges on imported auto parts (International Trade Administration 2009).

By 2012, Beijing had removed tariff barriers, yet nontariff barriers continued in the Chinese auto-parts industry. Specifically, local-content requirements continued unofficially and informally, especially in the provinces, as *Neibu*—undisclosed rules for the approval of foreign-investment projects. *Neibu* existed alongside *Gongkai*, or public regulations (OECD 2003). For autos and auto parts, project loans from Chinese policy banks and provincial governments have become contingent on foreign companies' willingness to commit to local content. Reports refer to a secret 60-percent rule under which foreign companies must have 60 percent local content to obtain state grants, bank loans, and even access to provincial markets.[16] In 2002, Beijing enacted the Government Procurement Law of the People's Republic of China, which continues to influence purchasing by SOEs, especially in projects that require government investment. In 2009, as China began to disburse $586 billion as economic stimulus, the NDRC and eight other ministries jointly released Circular 1361:[17] "Government investment projects should purchase domestic products, unless these domestic goods, construction, engineering or services are not available in China or cannot be acquired on reasonable commercial terms. Projects requiring imported products will need prior approval from relevant government authorities."

Although never officially recognizing the existence of local-content regulation, the Chinese government has used other regulation as well as inducements to enforce content agreements from foreign auto companies. A 2007 NDRC circular, *Suggestions Concerning Structural Readjustment of the Automotive Industry*, stated: "Sino-foreign joint ventures should be engaged in activities in accordance with the terms of the contracts signed by both parties and approved by the government. Those who fail to fulfill what is required in the contracts should correct their actions in a timely manner. If no correction is made, construction of any new plant will be temporarily halted and any application for the promotion of new products will also be suspended." Foreign auto assemblers have to fulfill product feasibility requirements, and Chinese government officials have classified foreign companies' new products as unfeasible for failing to honor any part of the local-content agreements they had signed. An official involved in drafting the rules on foreign companies' new-product-feasibility reports said: "In the feasibility report on a new product, localized production is a core requirement" (quoted in Liao 2007).

Foreign companies have responded to Chinese persuasion on local content. In 2006, Helmut Panke, BMW's CEO, went to Beijing twice for secret talks with Bo Xilai, China's minister of commerce. Soon after, Eberhard Schrempf, BMW-Brilliance's president and CEO, announced that BMW would expand local production in China, with local sourcing to increase from $111 million in 2005 to $384 million by 2006. The company also said that it would increase the number of local suppliers from 45 to 83 over the same period. In May 2006, Till Becker, DaimlerChrysler Northeast Asia's chairman and CEO, declared that Beijing Benz-DaimlerChrysler would increase local sourcing in China from $100 million to $840 million within two years in its locally produced cars. In response, in July of the same year, the General Administration of Customs of China announced that it would postpone the date to introduce the rules on completely-knocked-down (CKD) auto-parts imports, from July 1, 2006, to July 1, 2008 (Liao 2007).

NOTES

1. The research for this study was funded by a grant from the Economic Policy Institute, Washington, DC.
2. According to the European Automobile Manufacturers Association (2010), in 2009, of 47.5 million passenger cars produced worldwide, the European Union produced 29.5 percent, but China led among nations, producing 22 percent, followed by Japan with 14.5 percent. NAFTA (the United States, Canada, and Mexico combined) produced 8.5 percent of the world's passenger cars. Light trucks in the United States constitute a higher proportion of vehicle production than in other countries.
3. Technology transfer in the automotive sector has not always achieved success. See Haley, Haley, and Tan (2004) for interviews with Beijing Jeep's senior managers on their experiences.
4. State Development and Reform Commission of the People's Republic of China, Automobile Industry Development Policy No. 8 (June 28, 2004).
5. Authors' analysis of data from All China Marketing Research Co. and IBISWorld
6. See G. T. Haley (2007, 2009) for some of the constraints facing foreign auto and parts makers in China
7. Authors' analysis of data from IBISWorld, All China Marketing Research Co.
8. Authors' interviews.
9. Bo Andersson, group vice president in charge of GM's global purchasing and supplier chain said that 90 percent of the materials and parts in a Chinese-made GM cars were sourced locally, 60 percent from foreign companies, and 40 percent from local Chinese companies (Zubko 2008).
10. Authors' interviews.
11. Authors' interviews.
12. Authors' interviews; KPMG International; IBISWorld.
13. In contrast, research conducted by the authors indicates that managerial and labor wages comprise about 15 percent of auto-parts costs in the United States, not accounting for productivity differences between the United States and China, which remain substantial.
14. Using depreciation as a proxy for capital, and wages as a proxy for labor, the capital-to-labor intensity for auto-parts production in China approximated 1:2 in 2010: the average company in this industry required two units of labor for each input of capital.

15. See Haley, Haley, and Tan (2004) for how the policymaking process in China, and differences of interests between the center and provinces, affect subsidies.
16. Nancy Leigh, Baker & McKenzie, Hong Kong.
17. "Opinions on the Implementation of Decisions on Expanding Domestic Demand and Promoting Economic Growth and Further Strengthening Supervision of Tendering and Bidding Projects," Circular 1361, May 27, 2009.

CHAPTER 7
Subsidies, Business Strategy, and Trade Policy

Since Adam Smith and David Ricardo, theories of commercial policies have debated the advantages of free trade versus protectionist policies that restrict imports and promote exports. Following Rodrik's (1995) analysis of trade outcomes, we classify forces of supply and demand as shaping subsidies. The demand side incorporates business strategy and includes individuals' and interest groups' preferences. The supply side incorporates trade policy and includes policymakers' preferences and governments' institutional structures. This chapter first analyzes how subsidies to industry, specifically to Chinese industry, have affected and are affected by business strategy and trade policy. The Chinese subsidy practices we cover in this book have impact beyond the boundaries of the steel, glass, paper, auto parts, and solar industries on which we have focused. We next explore the implications of Chinese manufacturing subsidies for firms, for the global economy, and for future research.

BUSINESS STRATEGY

Some empirical research shows that Chinese manufacturing subsidies positively affect firms' exports and performance and therefore elicit strategic behaviors from firms. Girma and colleagues (2007, 2009) documented evidence that the effects of production subsidies vary by firms' characteristics. Using an unbalanced panel data set of more than 140,000 firms from 1999 to 2005, they found that Chinese production subsidies affected domestic exporters' performance and their volume of exports, not just through covering losses but through compensating for some strategic costs. They found that subsidies affected Chinese exporters' performance most strongly when they operated in capital-intensive industries located in noncoastal regions and were already profitable. They based their conclusions on economic theoretical modeling that departs from assuming fixed costs of exporting and allows instead for variable market-penetration costs. They argued that Chinese production subsidies help existing exporters afford the higher, market-penetration costs they incur when expanding sales in export markets.

Business strategies include not just lobbying for subsidies but advocating for protection from subsidized foreign competitors. A large theoretical and empirical literature exists on which domestic groups in industrialized countries seek protection (e.g., Krueger 1974; Lavergne 1983; Ray 1981). Most theories on the political economy of trade have focused on the elicited demand for protection rather than on the range of corporate trade responses. Many of the theorists have argued that a given set of uncompetitive industries prefers protectionist policies at home to other trade solutions. Some researchers have portrayed business efforts to lobby for protection as rent seeking.[1] For example, Lenway, Morck, and Yeung (1996) characterized the steel industry's lobbying strategies as political rent-seeking to secure future returns in trade protection. They presented empirical evidence from 1977 to 1988 to argue that trade protection returns private benefits to shareholders, senior workers, and lobby firms' CEOs, rewards less-innovative firms, and frustrates the Schumpeterian development of an industry. However, Lenway, Morck, and Yeung assumed free markets and perfect competition in the absence of government regulation to protect domestic markets—not situations where massive subsidies may distort markets prior to government regulation, as currently exists with Chinese trade.

Indeed, free trade may lead to suboptimal outcomes, and protectionism can increase national income by raising firms' profitability in imperfect markets (Krugman 1986). As Yoffie and Milner (1989) argued, greater scale economies and cumulative-experience effects make strategic groups[2] more dependent on access to foreign markets. If the Chinese government blocks access to its markets through protection, or subsidizes Chinese firms to compete effectively with US firms, US firms' preferred policies depend upon foreign rivals' choices. This interdependence leads to strategic trade policy where the firms place contingent demands that free trade at home depend on reciprocal access to foreign markets.

Since China joined the WTO in 2001, the opening of its markets for investment and trade has remained a major issue for foreign firms. In December 2006, the SASAC and China's State Council jointly announced the "Guiding Opinion on Promoting the Adjustment of State-Owned Capital and the Reorganization of State-Owned Enterprises." The policy statement identified seven strategic industries in which the state must maintain "absolute control through dominant state-owned enterprises," including armaments, power generation and distribution, oil and petrochemicals, telecommunications, coal, civil aviation, and shipping; foreign firms cannot participate in these industries or markets. The policy statement also identified five "heavyweight" industries in which the state will remain heavily involved, including machinery, automobiles, information technology, construction, and iron, steel, and nonferrous metals; foreign firms have restricted participation in these industries and experience heavy regulation (US-China Economic and Security Review Commission 2011).

Milner and Yoffie (1989) concluded that *ceteris paribus,* if a foreign government failed to create a competitive edge for its firms through subsidies and allowed foreign firms free entry into its markets, multinational corporations would avoid the potential costs associated with strategic trade policy, including retaliation and blocked access to foreign markets. But, if as has happened with China, foreign governments increase their firms' market shares in the United States, block access to domestic markets, and reduce US firms' profits through subsidizing their own firms, then rational multinational corporations would support protectionism at home.

Yoffie and Milner (1989) argued that strategic trade policy can potentially exploit three key market imperfections in traded sectors: large economies of scale with minimum efficient scales, steep learning curves that bestow first-mover advantages, and sizable R&D requirements that erect barriers to entry. When these market imperfections exist, domestic firms' access to foreign markets and foreign firms' and foreign governments' behaviors can directly affect domestic profits. Foreign subsidies or protectionism could give foreign competitors cost advantages that later entrants could not match. With an open US market and closed China market, Chinese firms could achieve more efficient scale via sales volume domestically and abroad while squeezing US competitors into a portion of their domestic market. Once firms fall behind in these industries, recovering profitability would become unlikely, and so strategic trade policy should rationally become their managers' top priority. As detailed later, these circumstances have emerged for US solar PV manufacturers (also see Haley and Haley 2012a, 2012b).

Yoffie and Milner (1989) also argued that the speed and intensity with which firms act become critical. Extending their arguments, a strategic group such as US solar PV manufacturers would only benefit from strategic trade policy before Chinese firms gain long-term sustainable advantages. Once the foreign firms achieve long-term sustainable advantages, the researchers concluded, foreign-market access would no longer benefit domestic firms, as they could not compete there. Under those conditions, domestic firms' choices would include only exit or unconditional protection. The level of industry segmentation into strategic groups affects speed and intensity. In the solar industry, at least two strategic groups have emerged with different competitive strategies: the Coalition of Solar Manufacturers (CASM), consisting of US manufacturers, has argued for strategic trade policy including countervailing and antidumping duties against illegally subsidized Chinese imports; the Coalition for Affordable Solar Energy (CASE), consisting of installers, Chinese manufacturers, and US importers, has argued for free trade and the ability to buy cheap, subsidized, imported Chinese solar panels. These distinctive strategic groups have hindered the development of a common industry response. In these fragmented industries with slow industry response, if foreign governments' intervention leads to rapid deterioration in domestic firms' net income and market shares, then the domestic industries will lose their first-mover advantages and become increasingly uncompetitive. If industrial competitiveness declines rapidly, only unconditional protection at home will allow these firms to survive.

Haley and Schuler (2011) proposed that in the solar PV industry, business strategies alter in response to production or consumption subsidies and include market or competitive (Porter 1985) as well as nonmarket or political (Baron 1995) strategies. Table 7.1 provides a static framework for profitable firms' market and nonmarket strategies in the solar PV industry. Haley and Schuler (2011) examined separately firms' strategic responses at the solar PV supply chain's three segments, upstream, midstream, and downstream, with distinct strategic groups that face diverse competitive environments, as elaborated in table 7.2. They also considered the initial policy environment "fixed" and focused on nonmarket actions that firms in particular localities (e.g., in California) could take toward the domestic federal and state governments of those same localities. They ignored the political actions that domestic firms might take toward foreign governments. Haley and Schuler (2011) proposed the following four quadrants of generic business strategies for solar firms, and these could apply to other industries as well.

Quadrant 1: No consumption or production subsidies. The first quadrant represents a policy environment that does not generally exist for this industry: solar power's high cost relative to other energy precludes the industry's

Table 7.1. FIRMS' STRATEGIES UNDER PRODUCTION AND CONSUMPTION SUBSIDIES

		Countries with production subsidies	
		No	Yes
Countries with consumption subsidies	Yes	II • Market strategies to access domestic markets • Nonmarket strategies to increase domestic content and block imports • *Proclivity to import*	IV • Market strategies of quality, differentiation and service • Nonmarket strategies to maintain government assistance & seek foreign-market liberalization • *Proclivity for niche strategies*
	No	I • Market strategies focusing on comparative national advantage, scale, efficient production, and market size • Nonmarket strategies to shield from pure competition • *Proclivity for shielding nonmarket strategies*	III • Market strategies to access foreign markets including expansion of production capacity • Nonmarket strategies to maintain government assistance, block imports & seek foreign-market liberalization • *Proclivity to export*

Source: Adapted from Haley and Schuler 2011.

development without government subsidies. However, challenging budget realities and many policies' high financial costs have created an uncertain regulatory environment, forcing many governments to diminish or to curtail subsidies to the solar PV industry, such as in Spain in 2008 and Germany in 2010.

Should production subsidies wane, firms in the upstream solar PV industry, such as those manufacturing polysilicon, would still operate in an oligopolistic, competitive environment. Advantages accrue to scale, so that profitable firms focus upon building scale and perfecting their operations (yields, quality, etc.). Firms may direct resources toward differentiation, distribution, and pricing. Firms address regulatory uncertainty by aiming nonmarket strategies at preserving the openness of markets to secure inputs and to sell outputs downstream into domestic and foreign markets. Thus, these upstream firms support trade-liberalization policies.

For midstream firms, the competitive environment would become fiercer, with over 100 firms making cells and over 400 making modules.

Table 7.2. THE SOLAR PV SUPPLY CHAIN

	Product	Process	Industry Characteristics	Technology	Generic Strategies
Upstream	Polysilicon	■ Quartz silica changed into silicon ingots	■ Oligopolistic • 5–10 companies • High entry barriers • Ample supply of inputs	■ Siemens trichlorosilane • Fluidized bed reactor • Upgraded metallurgical silicon • Vapor to liquid Deposition	■ Build scale economies • Establish quality control • Set price ceilings
Midstream	Wafer	■ Silicon ingots cut into wafers	■ Limited competition • About 50 companies • Medium entry barriers due to high investment • High dependence on polysilicon suppliers	■ Moncrystalline • Multicrystalline • String Ribbon	■ Access low-cost financing • Develop proprietary technology • Integrate midstream operations
	Cell	■ Circuitry put on wafer	■ Highly competitive • About 100 companies • Low entry barriers • Essential component of silicon-based power • Boom-bust exposure	■ Crystalline • Thin film (CIGS, CdTe, a-Si)	■ Establish proprietary technology • Integrate midstream operations
	Module	■ Cells placed on glass and made into panels	■ Highly competitive • More than 400 companies • Low entry barriers due to low investment • Boom-bust exposure	■ Low technology	■ Differentiation
Downstream	Installation	• Solar panels installed	■ Fragmented • Over 5,000 companies • Requires financing and connections	■ Low technology	■ Price • Nonmarket strategies

Source: Haley and Schuler 2011.

With lower barriers to entry than in upstream production, market competition derives from differentiation through technology, operational efficiency, delivery, and pricing. Nonmarket strategies toward enforcing intellectual property (IP) and maintaining open markets assume importance. But if domestic demand wanes and prices and profits fall, domestic firms may use nonmarket strategies to seek assistance such as trade protection against foreign rivals.

Over 5,000 firms also operate in the highly competitive and fragmented downstream segment. Firms compete on price as well as the delivery of systems (solar components, plus interconnections to grids, etc., as well as oftentimes financing). Nonmarket strategies may provide shelter from pure competition. Nonmarket strategies open avenues to diverse customers such as government agencies (e.g., municipal power companies), highly regulated entities (e.g., public utilities), or those subject to regulation (e.g., residential users currently purchasing electricity from regulated utilities). Nonmarket strategies may also help circumvent public opposition to restrictions such as roof-top installations in residential areas, another source of regulatory uncertainty.

Quadrant II: Consumption subsidies, but no production subsidies. While most countries extend both production and consumption subsidies, emphasis and institutional support for policies vary. Some countries, notably Germany and Spain, and a few US states have taken the lead in raising product awareness and providing incentives to consumers to purchase solar PV systems.

Upstream and midstream firms benefit from consumption policies, depending upon domestic markets' size. In large domestic markets, consumption subsidies create larger domestic drivers to pull products through the markets. Domestic producers of solar components with policy-created domestic demand, such as in California, Texas, and New Jersey, may also use nonmarket strategies to buffer against foreign competitors' encroachment. For example, Canadian midstream producers used nonmarket strategies to obtain a domestic-content requirement of 50 percent by 2010 and 60 percent by 2011 to Ontario's Feed-in-Tariff scheme for large solar projects.

Downstream firms become highly dependent on consumption subsidies to drive their business. These policies promote awareness of solar-energy products and more importantly reduce costs and increase availability to consumers, directly affecting marketplace participation. Downstream firms relying upon consumption policies use nonmarket strategies to address such dependence. In addition to lobbying public officials to maintain or to increase consumption assistance, downstream firms work cooperatively with nontraditional partners such as environmental groups and builders toward expanding such policies. Examples of such cooperation include Net-Zero affordable homes that come with solar panels as standard features in Arizona, California, Colorado, and Nevada. Domestic installers may favor policies that prohibit foreign installers from bidding on certain projects. Profitable domestic installers create networks of reliable suppliers from domestic and foreign locations. Consequently, firms in this segment support trade liberalization, as the modules they install often come from foreign countries.

As has occurred in Spain and some US states, we propose that a preponderance of consumption over systematic production policies results in a proclivity to import. From 2000 to 2010, the trade imbalance between the United States and China on solar cells made into modules steadily grew from $12 million to an estimated $1.12 billion, reflecting rising US imports from China, which grew from $13 million to an estimated $1.14 billion during that same period (Scott 2010).

Quadrant III: No consumption assistance, but production assistance. Governments attempt to spur the solar industry's development by offering subsidies to producers, including access to low-cost financing, direct grants, tax abatement, and other tax credits. As noted previously, China offers enormous and consistent production subsidies for solar PV producers, especially in the form of low-cost loans with easy terms for upstream and midstream firms, though assistance for consumption has lagged.[3]

Production assistance enables solar PV's upstream producers to achieve economies of scale and to erect barriers to entry. Polysilicon firms especially need plentiful and inexpensive capital to scale up production. Since governments mainly provide the cheap capital, firms deploy nonmarket strategies to mitigate financial risk. For example, since its inception, GCL Poly has employed nonmarket strategies to receive protection from top Communist Party leaders in its home province, Jiangsu, according to Chinese court and local media reports.[4] Midstream wafer, cell, and module producers also benefit from production subsidies. In highly competitive markets, domestic producers may pursue nonmarket strategies to direct production support toward themselves and away from foreign-owned or controlled firms. For instance, in 2010, China's Ministry of Finance chose Chinese firm Yingli to supply 70 percent of the modules for the Golden Sun project's first phase over foreign firms' higher bids. With its excellent government contacts, Yingli received $114 million in prepayments, or 35 percent of the total purchase price, in advance as an instant rebate. To meet capital shortfalls in the future, Yingli also cultivated political relationships to obtain additional low-cost loans from other state-owned banks, including the Export and Import Bank of China, ICBC, Bank of China, China Construction Bank, Bank of Communications, Citic, and Minsheng Bank.[5]

Furthermore, since midstream products trade in international markets, firms may pursue nonmarket strategies toward maintaining open markets for their products. Since many midstream firms attempt to differentiate through product innovation, they also may favor production-assistance policies that subsidize R&D as well as protect IP.

In the supply chain, downstream firms have the least direct interest in production subsidies. Their business strategies relate more to purchasing components and configuring them into systems. Downstream firms benefit indirectly from production subsidies that stimulate module production, increase quantities and choices in the market, and place downward pressure on prices. However, we would not expect that downstream producers invest heavily in nonmarket strategies to obtain production subsidies.

As has occurred in China, we propose that a preponderance of production over systematic consumption policies results in a proclivity to export. Excess capacities in their domestic markets, driven by production policies, encourage Chinese firms' exports.

Quadrant IV: Consumption and production assistance. We have shown that most countries utilize both consumption and production-subsidy policies. The relative emphasis and effectiveness of such policies vary across countries and across time and have global repercussions. Extensive and uncoordinated public policies across countries oftentimes lead to profound supply-demand imbalances, as shown with the excess supply in the solar industry. With production assistance, upstream producers position themselves to achieve economies of scale, as well as to move toward higher-grade polysilicon for higher-quality silicon wafers. Successful firms seek plentiful customers for their output as well as low-cost capital for investments in plants and production equipment. We expect these firms, which are highly dependent on government policies, to push aggressively for production assistance, including long-term and low-interest capital. Firms will also favor policies that expand product demand, subsidize users, and liberalize trade regimes to enable pursuit of foreign customers. Firms may also vertically integrate to have captive downstream markets to mitigate regulatory risk in case production assistance falls.

Midstream firms in this environment employ niche-market strategies of quality, differentiation, technology, service, and rapid distribution to compete for increased demand. For instance, cost and technology leader First Solar from the United States has expanded capacity and offered value-added services such as rapid construction and customized design for access to high-profile projects around the world. First Solar has also effectively used nonmarket strategies to sell projects and overcome nontariff barriers in emerging and developed markets. Midstream firms may pursue advantages through technological innovations and thus support governmental programs of R&D assistance and strong IP regimes to safeguard inventions. These firms will also favor public, preferably low-cost, financing, although domestic firms may pursue nonmarket strategies to limit recipients to domestically located or domestically owned and controlled firms. Midstream firms seek governmental schemes that spur demand for solar products, such as California's expanded mandates for solar use put into law in 2011. Midstream firms also pursue policies that open international markets to their products.

We expect that successful downstream firms will pursue public policies toward either mandating solar use or lowering its price to end users. For example, in Austin, Texas, the city-owned utility has a mandate to obtain 100 MW of electricity from solar power by 2020. We also expect that firms in this segment will support public policies that give tax incentives and production subsidies for solar projects and may partner with other organizations, such as environmental groups, that seek greater solar usage. Foreign firms will follow consumption subsidies that support higher internal rates of return, such as Chinese Suntech's expansion into Goodyear, Arizona. As foreign competitors move into domestic installation markets, domestic firms may use nonmarket strategies to limit the consumption-assistance programs to domestic installers.

TRADE POLICY

Most contributors to the economic analysis of strategic trade policy have viewed government attempts to apply policy as a Pandora's box (Brander 1995) partly because of very high informational requirements. These theorists also see lobbying and other forms of transfer seeking described in the previous section as resulting in major distortions. However as Brander (1995) indicated, interventionist policies in Japan, Korea, and France probably aided industries and companies from these countries in developing a strong international presence. Consequently, an understanding of strategic trade-policy instruments can explain some patterns of specialization ensuing from trade with China. As Eckhaus (2006) concluded in his empirical study, an overall positive relationship exists between Chinese industrial subsidies and Chinese exports. This relationship holds especially for SOEs and particularly for the coastal provinces, whose exports accounted for 92 percent of all Chinese exports in 1999.

Mattoo and Subramanian (2011) noted that from 2001 to 2009, China has loomed especially large in the most-protected sectors of major trading partners' markets. In 2009 in these most-protected sectors, share of imports from China greatly exceeded overall imports and dwarfed that of any other country. For example, China's share of the most-protected sectors in Japan was over 70 percent, in Korea over 60 percent, in Brazil about 55 percent, and in the United States, Canada, and the EU about 50 percent each. Even in these protected sectors, China's share increased dramatically over the course of the Doha Round of trade-liberalizing negotiations among WTO members. In many of the importing countries (e.g., Brazil, the EU, and the United States), China's share more than doubled. Indeed, China gained market share even in countries such as Canada, Mexico, and Turkey that have free-trade agreements with close and large neighbors. Thus, liberalization under the Doha agenda, especially in the politically charged, high-tariff sectors, resulted in other countries opening their markets to Chinese exports. For example, in the United States, China had by far the highest share of imports in 8 out of the 10 most-protected sectors, ranging from 22 percent in man-made fibers to 76 percent in footwear. But the Chinese market, despite China's far-reaching WTO-accession commitments, remained protected across several products (such as fertilizers, vehicles, and many manufacturing items) while the Chinese government simultaneously subsidized its manufacturers for increased exports. Consequently, industrial countries have increasingly resorted to contingent protection against imports from China. In March 2012, China's deputy minister of commerce, Zhong Shan, said at a conference that in each of the last 17 consecutive years, China has had more trade conflicts than any other country in the world, in more industries and with more countries. Since the beginning of 2012, eight trade complaints had been filed against China and over 100 had been filed in the previous 12 months. Since 2008, 600 trade complaints had been filed against China (*Beijing News* 2012). Table 7.3 lists the major trade disputes between the United States and China from full accession to the WTO in 2002 through 2011.

Developing-country's trade actions against China exceeded those of industrialized countries. For example, the share of developing-country antidumping actions against China (as a share of their total actions) increased from 19 percent in 2002 to 34 percent in 2009 (Mattoo and Subramanian 2011). The corresponding figures for industrialized countries approximated 11 and 27 percent, respectively. However, recourse to trade actions will become more difficult when China attains market-economy status in 2016. Additionally, the product-specific transitional safeguards that existing members negotiated at the time of China's WTO accession are

Table 7.3. REPRESENTATIVE US-CHINA TRADE DISPUTES, 2002–2011

Date	Complainant	Issue
March 2002	China	China joins other countries in a complaint about safeguard measures imposed by the US that increases duties on steel imports.
March 2004	US	The US complains Chinese semiconductor producers pay less tax than their foreign competitors.
March 2006	US	The US and other countries complain that China has imposed measures including tariffs that adversely affect their auto-parts exports.
February 2007	US	The US complains that China has granted tax refunds, reductions, and exemptions for companies that buy domestic goods.
February 2007	US	The US files a request for consultations regarding Chinese subsidies paid to foreign invested enterprises.
April 2007	US	The US lodges two cases with the WTO on intellectual property rights protection and market access for US movies, DVDs, books, and music.
April 2007	China	China complains against US duties on glossy paper used in packaging.
July 2007	US	A US study says China's steel industry has benefited over the past 10 years from the "pervasive influence" of financial transfers from central and local government bodies, some of which are alleged to have broken WTO rules.
March 2008	US	The US complains about China's attempt to put the financial information business of international news providers under the control of local rival and regulator, Xinhua News Agency.
September 2008	China	China files request for consultations regarding US policy to treat China as a nonmarket economy when imposing antidumping and countervailing duty safeguards.
December 2008	US	The US files request for consultations regarding subsidies promoting Chinese famous brands merchandise.
April 2009	China	China challenges a US law banning imports of processed Chinese poultry, saying the ban cannot be justified on health and safety grounds.
April 2009	China	China initiates antidumping investigation against imported nylon-6 chips from the US and other countries and regions.
June 2009	US	The US and EU complain that China grants raw materials to domestic manufacturers at below-market prices.
June 2009	US	The US imposes tariffs on certain passenger vehicle and light truck tires over a 3-year period of 55, 45, and 35 percent respectively.

Continued

Table 7.3. *(Continued)*

Date	Complainant	Issue
June 2009	US	The US complains that China constrains exports of raw materials.
June 2009	China	China imposes antidumping tariffs ranging from 5.7 percent to 35.4 percent on adipic acid from the US.
June 2009	China	China imposes a temporary antidumping duty of 10.9 percent to 37.5 percent on polyamide-6 imports from the US, Italy, the UK, France, and Taiwan.
June 2009	China	China begins antidumping investigation into grain-oriented flat-rolled electrical steel from the US.
August 2009	US	The US complains that China breaks WTO rules by requiring all imported media products to be channeled through state-run distributors.
September 2009	US	The US imposes safeguard duties of 35 percent on Chinese tires.
September 2009	China	China complains that US safeguard duties of 35 percent on Chinese tires are in excess of the rates permitted under US international obligations to China.
September 2009	China	China announces it will maintain antidumping measures on some imported polyvinylchloride (PVC) from the US, the Republic of Korea, Japan, and Russia.
September 2009	China	China launches antidumping and antisubsidy investigations into the imports of US car parts and chicken products.
September 2009	China	China's Ministry of Commerce launches study of antidumping investigations of US and EU on China's solar photovoltaic industry.
October 2009	China	China's Ministry of Commerce issues a preliminary ruling against the US and other countries, accusing them of dumping chemical fibers in China.
November 2009	US	The US imposes tariffs of 2 to 438 percent on Chinese-made wire decking.
November 2009	US	The US imposes antidumping duties ranging from 48.99 to 98.74 percent, and countervailing duties ranging from 13.66 to 53.65 percent on seamless steel pipe from China.
December 2009	US	The US slaps antidumping duties on Chinese steel-grating products.
December 2009	US	The US imposes duties of 10 to 16 percent on Chinese steel-piping imports.
December 2009	US	The US International Trade Commission slaps punitive penalties on $2.6 billion of oil company tubular goods from China.

Table 7.3. *(Continued)*

Date	Complainant	Issue
December 2009	China	China loses its appeal of a WTO ruling that its curbs on importing and distributing foreign publications and audiovisual products violate its WTO commitments.
January 2010	China	China extends antidumping measures by 5 years on imports of phenol from the US.
January 2010	US	The US starts antidumping and antisubsidy probe into Chinese steel drill pipes.
January 2010	US	The US imposes 175 percent antidumping duties on Chinese electric blankets and wire trays.
January 2010	US	The US slaps additional duties of 43 to 289 percent on imports of Chinese-made wire decking.
February 2010	China	China announces antidumping duties from 43.1 to 105.4 percent on imports of US chicken products.
February 2010	US	The US puts antidumping taxes of up to 231.4 percent on Chinese ribbons used for gift wrapping, hours after China announced the chicken duties.
February 2010	US	The US imposes preliminary duties ranging from 11 to 13 percent on steel pipes from China.
April 2010	US	The US imposes antidumping duties of up to 99.14 percent on imports of Chinese steel pipes.
April 2010	China	China slaps duties of as much as 64.8 percent on certain specialty-steel products from the US and Russia, following a preliminary ruling in December.
April 2010	US	The US Department of Commerce launches a probe into Chinese exports of aluminum products, with an initial determination scheduled for May 17.
April 2010	China	China starts two antidumping investigations into imports of optical fibers and a chemical product from the US and EU. It also levies tariffs on some nylon imports from the US and other countries.
April 2010	China	China's Ministry of Commerce imposes countervailing duties of up to 31.4 percent on some chicken products from the US.
April 2010	US	The US imposes preliminary antidumping duties of as much as 135.8 percent on glossy paper from China.
May 2010	US	The US Department of Commerce announces a final ruling to impose antidumping and countervailing duties of as much as 193.55 percent on imports of concrete steel wire from China. The duties will not come into effect until the International Trade Commission votes in June.
June 2010	US	The US Department of Commerce makes an initial ruling imposing tariffs of 15.72 percent on Chinese drill pipes.

Continued

Table 7.3. (*Continued*)

Date	Complainant	Issue
July 2010	China	China accepts the WTO ruling on importing and distributing foreign publications and audiovisual products.
September 2010	US	The US files for consultations regarding market access restrictions that prohibit foreign suppliers from handling renminbi-denominated card transactions.
September 2010	US	The US Department of Commerce makes a preliminary ruling imposing duties ranging from 6.18 to 137.65 percent on aluminum extrusions.
September 2010	US	The US Department of Commerce imposes duties ranging from 17.64 to 178.03 percent on Chinese coated paper for high-quality graphics.
October 2010	US	The US sets final duties of up to 61 percent on copper pipe and tube from China.
October 2010	US	The US begins investigation following petition filed by the USW.
February 2011	US	The US accuses China of creating a monopoly in its electronic payments market, allowing China Union Pay to handle most credit and debit card transactions made by Chinese consumers.
February 2011	US	The US asks WTO to rule on its allegation that Chinese imposed antidumping and countervailing duties of more than 2 percent on imports of grain-oriented flat-rolled electrical steel without sufficient evidence of unfair pricing practices or government subsidies.
March 2011	China	WTO overturns, on China's appeal, a ruling supporting US antidumping and antisubsidy tariffs against Chinese steel pipe, woven sacks, and off-road tires on the basis that the US could not simultaneously use other markets to determine the fair price of goods made in China, a nonmarket economy, and penalize it for state subsidies. The WTO did rule in favor of the US view that discounted land, electricity, and loan prices could be considered subsidies. It also found that while not all state-owned enterprises are "public bodies," state-owned banks can be so considered.
June 2011	China	China agrees to stop subsidizing wind power firms that use domestic equipment in place of imports, after the US requested WTO consultations over the Chinese subsidies.
July 2011	China	WTO rules that China's export restrictions on several raw materials unfairly raise world prices.
September 2011	US	The US sets antisubsidy and antidumping duties ranging up to 313.8 percent on coated paper from China.

Table 7.3. (*Continued*)

Date	Complainant	Issue
September 2011	China	China loses its appeal of the US imposition of 35 percent safeguard duties on Chinese tires.
October 2011	US	The US Department of Commerce sets preliminary anti-dumping duties of up to 193.54 percent on steel wheels from China.
October 2011	US	The US Senate, targeting China, passes bill allowing companies to seek countervailing duties on goods from countries with undervalued currencies.
November 2011	US	The US announces an investigation into Chinese-made solar panel sales.
November 2011	China	China announces an investigation into US policy and subsidies for renewable energy, wind, solar, and hydro-technology products.
December 2011	US	The US Department of Commerce announces preliminary countervailing duties of 22.34 percent and additional preliminary duties of 5 to 26 percent on high-pressure steel cylinders from China.
December 2011	China	China's Ministry of Commerce set punitive duties of up to 22 percent on large cars and sport utility vehicles exported from the United States.
December 2011	US	The US asks WTO to strike down China's heavy anti-dumping duties on US chicken products.
January 2012	US	President Obama announces plan to establish a Trade Enforcement Unit to investigate unfair trade practices.

Source: Compiled with information from *CNN Money*, March 13, 2012; *GOV.cn*, December 27, 2010; *Financial Times* Global Economy, October 8, 2009–May 18, 2010; Reuters Factbox, December 15, 2012; US-China Business Council, October 26, 2010.

due to expire in 2013. These circumstances leave China's trading partners even more anxious about competition from China. The appendix indicates how the research included this book on steel, glass, paper, and auto-parts has been used in US negotiations on trade with China (see also expert congressional testimony at U. Haley 2006, 2007; G. Haley 2007, 2009).

In the 10 years since China joined the WTO, the US trade deficit with China has grown by 330 percent. While the overall US trade deficit with the world grew from $376.7 billion in 2000 to $500 billion in 2010, China's share nearly tripled during the period, from 22 percent in 2000 to 55 percent in 2010. These data suggest that the growth in the US global trade deficit reflects growth in the US trade deficit with China, and that China is replacing other emerging economies as the final supplier of finished exports to the United States (US-China Securities and Exchange Commission 2011).

The more significant trend deals with the composition of traded goods. Over the last decade, Chinese manufacturing has undergone a dramatic restructuring away from labor-intensive goods toward investment-intensive goods. Increasingly, low-cost capital rather than low-cost labor has driven production as subsidies build next-generation manufacturing facilities and produce advanced-technology products for export. In 2000, exports of labor-intensive products constituted 37 percent of all Chinese exports; by 2010, this percentage fell to 14 percent. The global shifts in specialization have serious welfare implications for the US economy. From 2004 to 2011, US imports of Chinese advanced-technology products grew by 16.5 percent on an annualized basis, while US exports of those products to China grew by only 11 percent. In August 2011, US exports of advanced-technology products to China stood at $1.9 billion, while Chinese exports of advanced-technology products to the United States reached $10.9 billion, setting a record one-month deficit of more than $9 billion. On a monthly basis, in 2011 the United States imported more than 560 percent more advanced-technology products from China than it exported to that country (US-China Economic and Security Review Commission 2011). By contrast, the monthly US trade surplus in scrap and waste reached a record high of $1.1 billion in August 2011. The annual US trade surplus in scrap and waste grew from $715 million in 2000 to $8.4 billion in 2010, representing an increase of 1,187 percent, or 28 percent per year on an annualized basis.

The US trade deficit with China, which has ballooned to account for more than half of the total US trade deficit with the world, has had welfare implications, including lost US jobs. Researchers have disputed the exact number of US jobs lost to China trade but not that jobs have been detrimentally affected—in testimonies to the US-China Economic and Securities Review Commission (2011), the Peterson Institute's C. Fred Bergsten has estimated 600,000 jobs lost on the low end, while the Economic Policy Institute's Robert Scott has estimated 2.4 million jobs lost on the high end.

By mid-2011, the United States had brought seven cases against China at the WTO concerning subsidies or grants. Of the seven, four were settled through consultation, two were decided in favor of the United States, and one remained undecided (US-China Economic and Security Review Commission 2011). The cases dealt with integrated circuits (settled), auto parts (holding for US sustained on appeal), taxes (settled), intellectual property rights (held for US), financial services (settled), grants and loans (no resolution), and wind power (settled).

This section covers three government policies surrounding subsidies that we can broadly classify as focusing on domestic consumption or on domestic production. The WTO permits certain responses from importing nations that can prove they suffered material injury due to unfair trade practices. Trade remedies that shield domestic markets through affecting consumption primarily include antidumping and countervailing duties. The Chinese government has also adopted another policy of indigenous innovation that subsidizes high-technology production as well as identifies technology transfer as a prerequisite for foreign companies to access China's large government-procurement market. We discuss each of these policies in turn.

Consumption: Antidumping and Countervailing Duties

Antidumping duties constitute the most popular trade remedy in worldwide trade disputes. US law defines dumping as foreign products exported to the US at prices below fair value, that is, either below the prices of comparable goods sold in the exporters' home market or below the costs of production. When dumping can be shown to have occurred, antidumping duties can be applied. For economic analyses of antidumping and countervailing duties see Feenstra (1995).

Since 2002, China has concluded nine free-trade agreements and started negotiations for five more. A precondition to negotiation has been agreement by the other country to grant China market-economy status (US-China Economic and Security Review Commission 2011). These preconditions target eliminating certain restrictions placed upon China during accession to the WTO: In particular, countries that institute antidumping proceedings against China can draw price comparisons from third-party countries, in lieu of China, to show dumping by Chinese companies. Similarly, to identify illegal subsidies and to calculate countervailing measures, instituting countries may refer to prices and conditions in third-party countries in lieu of China. Under the terms of the Accession Protocol, however, China's nonmarket-economy status will expire in 2016, when these provisions will cease to have effect. However, applicable US domestic law will continue to have effect beyond 2016, adding pressure to the trade filings.

In 2005, Canada became the first country to impose countervailing duties on Chinese products under the WTO system, raising the issue of the permissibility in WTO law of using such duties against nonmarket economies (Zhao and Wang 2008). In 2007, the United States joined Canada by imposing its own countervailing duties against China. In 2007, the United States Department of Commerce altered a long-standing policy of not applying countervailing-duty law to nonmarket economies and initiated eight countervailing and antidumping duty investigations on Chinese imports (U. Haley 2006, 2007; G. Haley 2007, 2009). The change has brought heated debate on trade-remedy policies and nonmarket economy issues among lawyers and policymakers.

Governments resort to countervailing duties less often than antidumping duties. From January 1, 1995, to December 31, 2006, WTO reporting members were notified of 3,048 antidumping and 191 countervailing initiations (Zhao and Wang 2008). The United States had not applied countervailing duties to China, as China had been classified as a "nonmarket economy" since 1981. This policy rested on two principles advanced in 1984 and confirmed by a federal appeals court. On November 21, 2006, the US Department of Commerce announced its decision to initiate an antidumping and countervailing-duty investigation on imports of coated free-sheet paper from China. This decision changed the long-standing precedent that the nonmarket economies had exemption from US countervailing-duty investigations, as the government could not identify or measure the extent of subsidies in these markets. In the case of coated free-sheet paper, the US Department of Commerce found several countervailing subsidies provided by the Chinese government, but the US International Trade Commission found no injury to US industry, and the first case ended in 2007 without a countervailing-duty order. However, the change in the Department of Commerce's policy opened the gate for more successful countervailing-duty cases on China, including the solar industry (see Haley and Haley 2012b).

On October 19, 2011, a strategic group of seven US solar manufacturers, founding members of CASM, filed petitions with the USITC and Department of Commerce's International Trade Administration seeking relief for the US domestic producers injured by Chinese imports of crystalline silicon photovoltaic (CSPV) products. On March 20, 2012, Commerce announced its affirmative preliminary determination in the countervailing-duty investigation. Suntech Power received a preliminary countervailing duty of 2.9 percent, Trina Solar 4.7 percent, and all other Chinese manufacturers 3.6 percent. On May 17, 2012, Commerce announced preliminary antidumping duties on Chinese manufacturers of CSPV cells. Commerce assessed preliminary tariffs against Suntech Power and Trina Solar of 31.22 and 31.14 percent, respectively. Commerce also assessed preliminary tariffs against other Chinese manufacturers, including JA Solar, Yingli, Hanwha SolarOne, Canadian Solar, LDK Solar, and Jiawe Solar China of 31.18 percent. All other Chinese manufacturers received a preliminary tariff of 249.96 percent. On November 7, 2012, the US International Trade Commission voted unanimously in favor of the duties, clearing the way for the Department of Commerce to issue five-year anti-dumping and countervailing duty orders on Chinese imports (Palmer 2012).

In May 2012, China filed WTO cases challenging US antisubsidy tariffs on 22 Chinese goods. Beijing appeared to be challenging Washington's general approach to subsidies and dumping as well as specific policies on individual industries. China accused the United States of improperly using antidumping and countervailing duties to shield US companies from competition. "The relevant practices constitute the abuse of trade remedy measures which undermines the legitimate interests of China's enterprises," Beijing's mission to the WTO stated (Associated Press 2012). The Chinese statement argued that the US trade measures affected Chinese exports to the United States worth $7.3 billion and included steel, paper, and solar cells.

Production: Indigenous Innovation

In 2006, Beijing announced plans to increase R&D spending from 1.5 percent of GDP to 2.5 percent by 2020 in an effort to move China into higher-value-added and innovative manufacturing. A nationwide network of regulations and plans known loosely as "indigenous innovation" identified the subsidies that encouraged domestic high-technology production. Indigenous innovation closely ties to the Chinese government's procurement, including 16 megaprojects that the National Medium- and Long-Term Plan for the Development of Science and Technology (2006–2020) (MLP) described as "assimilating and absorbing" advanced imported technologies to "develop a range of major equipment and key products that possess proprietary intellectual property rights." The government's procurement market and subsidies have become the key drivers for these projects.

Because of opaque ownership, no definitive published value for Chinese government procurement exists; however, by all accounts, the government in some form remains China's largest consumer. The US-China Economic and Security Review Commission (2011) identified some problems with measuring government procurement in China. In China's official statistics, SOEs include only wholly state-funded firms and exclude shareholding cooperative enterprises, joint-operation enterprises, limited-liability corporations, and shareholding corporations owned mostly by the government, public organizations, or the SOEs. In 2009, the Chinese government estimated that its procurement market surpassed $100 billion. That same year, the Organization for Economic Cooperation and Development, using data from 2006, estimated the SOEs' share of China's GDP at 29.7 percent, but the private sector did not account for the remaining 70 percent. A US-China Economic and Security Review Commission study conducted in 2011 concluded that the state's share of the Chinese economy exceeded 50 percent. The European Union Chamber of Commerce (2011) in China estimated the size of China's government procurement market at $1 trillion. The US government has argued that SOEs and provincial and local government agencies form part of China's governmental procurement. China has responded that central, provincial, and local SOEs and provincial and local government agencies do not form part of governmental procurement, thereby hindering China's accession to the WTO's 40-member "Agreement on Government Procurement."

Hout and Ghemawat (2010) indicated several subsidies that China is using to propel indigenous innovation, such as tax incentives, including accelerated depreciation of investments in R&D facilities and tax breaks on returns from venture-capital investments in technology-based start-ups; cheap loans, and special-funding of domestic technologies to replace imported technologies; and national, provincial, and municipal procurement policies to favor indigenously developed technologies.

McGregor (2011) detailed several of the underlying policies and institutions behind China's indigenous innovation. In December 2009, China's Ministry of Science and Technology (MOST), Ministry of Finance, Ministry of Industry and Information Technology, and SASAC codified a catalog of 240 types of industrial equipment into 18 categories that received governmental tax incentives, science and technology subsidies, and priority listings for domestic production. In November 2011, the State Council released a draft of the Government Procurement Law defining a "domestic product" as one made within China's borders with "domestic manufacturing costs exceeding a certain percentage of the final price." As patent filings became part of SOEs' performance evaluations, local governments gave subsidies to pay for patent filings that often exceeded budgeted costs. If one accepts the European Chamber's figures, China's indigenous-innovation policies and official procurement catalogs wall off 17 percent of China's $5.9 trillion economy from foreign participation.

McGregor (2011) sketched how China's domestic wind industry responded to the indigenous innovation regulations on domestic content and government procurement. In 2005, the NDRC required 70 percent domestic content in all wind turbines in China. The 2006 Renewable Energy Law increased subsidies for wind-energy projects and domestic capacity expanded. The 2007 Foreign Investment Industry Guidance

Catalogue listed wind-turbine manufacturing as an encouraged industry for foreign participation, but foreign firms that manufactured wind turbines over 1.5 MW had to engage in domestic joint ventures (JVs) or partnerships. Vestas, Gamesa, and Suzlon still decided to operate independently, but others, such as GE, entered into JVs. The Chinese government encouraged technology transfers, provided financial subsidies, instituted preferential tax policies, and provided preferential treatment in project tendering and bidding to fan domestic companies' growth. In 2004, foreign wind-turbine manufacturers held 75 percent of the Chinese market. By 2009, the three largest domestic players, Sinovel, Goldwind, and Dongfang alone held 60 percent of the domestic market, while foreign firms held 14 percent.

Various Chinese governmental agencies disburse indigenous-innovation subsidies; MOST funds science parks, research labs, and the megaprojects. The China Development Bank provides soft loans for projects. The Export-Import Bank of China creates special accounts for innovative enterprises. In November 2008, China responded to the global financial crisis with RMB 160 billion for indigenous innovation, including RMB 27 billion for the first phase of work on three megaprojects: core electronic devices, semiconductors, and wireless broadband. In a few months, stimulus money launched another five Chinese megaprojects.

In the auto-parts industry, the Chinese government has withheld subsidies from foreign firms to obtain cutting-edge technology. For example, the Chevrolet Volt, a plug-in hybrid manufactured by the largest foreign auto company in China, General Motors (GM), incorporates three important technologies sought by the Chinese government: electric motors, complex electronic controls, and power-storage devices, including batteries and fuel cells. The Chinese government has withheld a $19,300 per car subsidy from GM, while bestowing it on Chinese competitors of plug-in electric cars such as BYD, until GM provides its core technology to a Chinese car company. GM has refused to comply so far. However, without the subsidy, the company has difficulty competing in the Chinese market (Bradsher 2011c; US-China Economic and Security Review Commission 2011). GM has denied that it experienced any pressure from the Chinese government (*Automotive News China* 2011a, 2011b).

IMPLICATIONS AND FUTURE RESEARCH

China's state capitalism resembles what Hancke (2010) termed a coordinated-market economy where correctly calibrated, complementary institutions across states, provinces, and municipalities reinforce one another and determine market efficiencies. Hancke indicated that coordinated market economies showed greater willingness to invest in worker skills and narrower market niches than firms in liberal market economies such as the United States and the United Kingdom. Consequently, Hancke argued that high-skill and high-productivity activities will concentrate in core, coordinated market economies. Lower-value-added, lower-skill, and lower-price activities will move to liberal market economies. Subsidies to Chinese manufacturing have spawned many implications for firms, the global economy, and researchers.

For Firms

Haley and Schuler (2011) saw Hancke's (2010) observations reflected in how global consumption and production subsidies affected firms' manufacturing location and technology development in the solar PV industry. China's consistent production subsidies, coupled with other countries' more uncertain ones, shaped firms' location decisions on development of R&D and on manufacturing, with unintended effects on employment. Consistent government subsidies for R&D had helped the United States become the technology leader in solar PV; yet massive Chinese production subsidies had encouraged many to move manufacturing to China after developing their technology in the United States. The urge to reduce end-user costs could also affect firms' future investments in technology, leaving US consumers with no option but to buy older and more-established technology products from China (Haley and Haley 2012a, 2012b).

Shipping costs constitute more than 5 percent of the cost of goods sold for US solar manufacturers like First Solar and less than 3 percent for a leading Chinese firm. This could lead to a bifurcation in manufacturing for some processes (e.g., c-Si): firms could make lightweight cells in China and ship them to the United States (or Mexico) for assembly into modules. Essentially, higher-value manufacturing would move to Asia, while lower-value, lower-technology manufacturing would remain in the United States. Higher-technology firms, such as cell manufacturers, would continue to stay in China. Firms using thin-film technologies would see the United States as a more appealing manufacturing base, as large percentages of thin-film cells and modules are manufactured together. The manufacturing facilities for cells on superstrates/substrates that form the modules must also include the higher-technology facilities. Firms manufacturing thin-film cells independently from modules (e.g., Energy Conversion Devices, which manufactures cells in the United States and is moving module manufacturing to Mexico) could also bifurcate manufacturing, affecting US competitiveness.

However, firms' cost calculations also need to incorporate political resistance. As we stated at the beginning of chapter 1, in 2011, responding to Chinese production subsidies, primarily loans, Evergreen Solar, the third-largest US panel manufacturer, withdrew its production to China, with the goal of exporting production back to the United States. On a wintry morning in February 2011, when moving operations from Massachusetts to China, Evergreen Solar's senior manager in charge of government and public relations communicated to us his perceptions of the importance of market strategies: "You are a business professor. You should know that we made the right business decision. Capital seeks the highest rate of return. This is something we learn in business schools, and that is what we are doing as a well-run company."

Yet Evergreen's market strategy has had unintended nonmarket ramifications and encountered varied political opposition (Haley and Schuler 2011). Understanding that outsourced production may satisfy US demand but create value and jobs elsewhere, key stakeholders such as the United Steel Workers labor union have argued convincingly for domestic-content legislation.[6] The National Defense Authorization Act for 2011, signed into law by President Obama, includes a new provision citing that the US Department of Defense, the world's largest government purchaser of solar panels, can only purchase PV modules manufactured in the United States or in countries that have signed the WTO's government-procurement agreement. As noted earlier, China has not accepted this agreement. Consequently, China-based firms will have to adjust their market strategies to accommodate the Buy America provisions that support US-based employment by setting up manufacturing facilities in the United States.[7] The Massachusetts state government is suing Evergreen for some its money back. Local media has highlighted how the firm took Chinese subsidies with promises to create jobs in China after receiving the largest production grant in Massachusetts's cash-strapped history.[8]

The managers of non-Chinese firms need to understand the role of subsidies in the competitiveness of Chinese firms and approaches to systematic measurement of that role. In their formulations of competitive strategy, these firms should either attempt to overcome the competitive advantages stemming from Chinese subsidies or should choose to target market segments where these advantages have less significance.[9]

Firms, too, have to incorporate subsidies into a long-term, interactive planning process, including competitors' and foreign governments' behaviors. Political forces can abruptly affect subsidies (see Haley and Haley 2008). For example, the November 2007 WTO subsidy-reduction agreement between the United States and China cut export subsidies to foreign firms located in China but maintained subsidies to Chinese firms. This shows how subsidy-based cost advantages of foreign firms located in China can suddenly evaporate. Second, firms that offshore to, or source or import from, China may suffer price shocks if they fail to discount fluctuating, subsidy-based cost advantages. Our research (Haley and Haley 2008), showed that under scrutiny, subsidies from Beijing often dry up, only to be replaced to varying degrees by subsidies from provincial and local governments that use them to support employment, build self-sufficiency, and promote import-substitution locally. Firms should establish relationships with industry and government officials in China so that they know the source of subsidies and can calculate interactively the risk of reduction and subsequent price increases. Before foreign companies cut other suppliers loose in favor of lower-priced Chinese sources, they should be mindful that Chinese firms' prices may fluctuate abruptly as subsidies shift. Rational foreign firms should therefore retain at least some original supplier relationships and cultivate alternate ones until Chinese suppliers prove reliable over the medium term. For effective strategies, foreign firms' managers should initiate serious efforts to understand the political forces at work impacting Chinese subsidies to gauge the probabilities of their actual reduction or removal.

For the Global Economy

The Chinese subsidy practices we cover have impacted the global economy beyond the boundaries of the steel, glass, paper, auto-parts, and solar industries on which we focus. For example, the substantial indirect energy subsidies that benefit the Chinese steel industry also lower costs in varying degrees for other Chinese manufacturing firms. Our findings contradict the widespread belief that China's enormous success in the past two decades as an exporting nation derives primarily, if not exclusively, from low labor costs and from its government's deliberately undervaluing its currency. Chinese labor costs may continue rising as they have done and trading partners' pressures may result in marginally increasing the value of the yuan, thereby making Chinese products more expensive to foreigners. However, Chinese producers' low costs stemming from extensive, systemic government subsidies will continue, contributing substantially to their competitiveness in global markets.

The extent of Chinese industrial subsidies, the political processes that underlie their disbursement, and the meshing of Chinese production into global supply chains also augur a period of heightened uncertainty as well as international booms and busts. In August 2012, the *New York Times* (Bradsher 2012) reported on some of the effects of these subsidies on Chinese industries and the intertwined, global economy. Unsold goods were piling up in China at the fastest rate since surveys of inventories began in April 2004. The glut of products, which included steel, glass, paper, autos, and solar panels, had produced price wars and led manufacturers to redouble efforts to export what they could not sell domestically. As we have highlighted in previous chapters, the overcapacity that stems from government subsidies appears a primary source of these developments. In the auto industry, manufacturers refused to cut production and were pressuring financially struggling dealers to accept delivery of cars under their franchise agreements. The Chinese government responded by blocking or adjusting economic data so the severity of inventory overhang would not affect investors' confidence. China's Public Security Bureau, for example, halted the release of data on falling demand in autos reflected in new-car registrations. In 2012, the government also repeatedly revised data on the steel industry after a new method showed a steeper downturn than the government had acknowledged. Similarly, the government had not released information about the number of empty apartments (which affected new construction and therefore glass demand) since 2008. Enormous and unpredictable amounts of steel, glass, and paper on the global market, and the commoditization of products such as cars, appear inevitable. The price for solar PV cells fell 66 percent from mid-2010 to the mid-2012, mostly because of Chinese overproduction and worldwide glut. In the United States over 13 firms went bankrupt (Haley and Haley 2012b). The impact has extended to Germany, Australia, India, and China. Jigar Shah, who put together CASE, said all major Chinese solar companies expected economic difficulties because of overproduction. "Everything's crashing right now. The Chinese are maybe overplaying their hand" (Kilzer 2012).

The subsidies provided by the central, provincial, and local governments have inhibited the consolidation of manufacturing facilities and the reduction of excess capacity that normally would result from Chinese firms' efforts at lowering costs to increase competitiveness in global markets. The provision of lower costs through subsidies has removed firms' incentives to lower costs through economically sound actions that result in achieving economies of scale and in shedding excess production capacity. Thus, many Chinese firms are economically inefficient in relation to their non-Chinese competitors, but Chinese subsidies overcome those inefficiencies and make those firms globally competitive (see Doom 2012).

When the central government removes subsidies—for whatever reason—the provincial and local governments fill in the gaps. We have attempted to discuss some of the political dynamics of state capitalism in chapter 1. The provincial and local governments want to support employment, promote import substitution, and build self-sufficiency locally through the use of subsidies, just as the central government wanted to do nationally when initially providing subsidies. While China's central government now wants to position certain domestic firms as price makers, rather than price takers, by moving them up the value chain, local governments do not want to bear the restructuring costs that these efforts entail. The central government may remove a subsidy or subsidies because of trading partners' pressures. However, provincial and local governments replace them, resulting in pursuit of the same objectives by the same means, although in each instance with narrower, geographic focus. This might explain the apparently high tolerance of inconsistent policies between the levels of government in China. The central government can point to national compliance with international trade agreements, with knowledge that much of what it really wants to happen will occur at provincial and local governmental levels.

Government officials from national and regional trading blocs should understand Chinese subsidies' extensive contributions to Chinese firms' global competitiveness, the difficulties of obtaining reliable data on these subsidies, and the frequent replacement by the provincial and local governments of subsidies removed by the central government. Recognition and understanding of these realities about Chinese subsidies should result in national and regional blocs' government officials expending greater effort to identify and to measure them, in setting a very high priority on addressing them, and in including provincial and local governments' policies as well as the central government's policies in trade negotiations with China.

For Researchers

Future research could incorporate some dynamism into our understanding of both governments' and firms' strategic behaviors. Brander (1995) showed that most economic models of strategic trade policy rely heavily on one-shot or static models of both oligopoly and government-policy formulation. However, long-term interactions and retaliations between firms and governments appear the rule. Economic models, however have not captured the appropriate differential-game versions of strategic interactions with rational calculations.

Researchers drawing on strategic-management concepts can explore the long-term ramifications of subsidies for several of the industries highlighted in this book (steel, glass, paper, auto parts, and solar) as they affect firm, governmental and national interests. Retaliation appears as a regular cry when governments use some of the policy instruments we have identified (see Haley and Haley 2012b). However, as we have argued, retaliation does not seem rational, and neither the United States nor China has engaged consistently in retaliatory policies. Our research however, has largely been static so far. More realistic scenarios must incorporate interactive elements that mold strategic intent and action not only of domestic firms, but also of foreign firms and governments.

Future research could also augment our measurement of subsidies through adding more variables. Though we included in our measurements of subsidies direct, firm-level data hitherto ignored, we also excluded many variables that researchers have noted as providing subsidy effects to firms. The variables we considered but did not incorporate in our research include the subsidy effects of an undervalued currency and of brand-building subsidies (see G. T. Haley 2009). Consequently, our measurement of subsidies represents the tip of the iceberg, awaiting the inclusion of many more variables to capture more fully a complex and highly influential global reality.

NOTES

1. In economics, rent-seeking deals with obtaining excess returns in competitive markets through manipulating social or political environments in which economic activities occur, rather than through creating new wealth.
2. Yoffie and Milner (1989) defined a strategic group as one or more firms following similar international-trade, manufacturing, and competitive strategies.
3. Mercom Capital showed that the solar PV industry's top five debt deals in 2010 emanated from the state-owned China Development Bank to Chinese firms, including a credit facility of $8.9 billion to LDK Solar; a loan facility of $7.3 billion to Suntech; a loan of $6.3 billion to Yingli; a loan of $4.4 billion to JA Solar; and a loan facility of $4.4 billion to Trina Solar.
4. See *Leshan News*, March 23, 2008. http://www.leshan.cn/lsnews/news/bwsd/userobject1ai153105.html.

5. Brean Murray, Carret and Co.
6. On September 9, 2010, the USW filed a petition under Section 302(a) of the Trade Act of 1974 with the USTR accusing China of illegally subsidizing and protecting firms that export green-tech products, including solar PV.
7. In 2010, China's NDRC publicly issued a call for China's energy industry to broaden operations overseas.
8. See Sato's (2011a, 2011b, 2011c) three-part investigative report for the *Lowell Sun on Evergreen Solar and our research*.
9. We are indebted to an anonymous reviewer for this observation and for other ideas that we have woven into this subsection.

APPENDIX

United States Senate

WASHINGTON, DC 20510

October 27, 2009

The Honorable Gary Locke
Secretary of Commerce
1401 Constitution Ave., NW
Washington, DC 20230

The Honorable Ron Kirk
United States Trade Representative
600 17th Street, NW
Washington, DC 20208

Dear Secretary Locke and Ambassador Kirk:

We write to you today to urge you to address the increasing harmful effects of Chinese policies on the American manufacturing sector when you meet with your Chinese counterparts as part of the Joint Commission on Commerce and Trade (JCCT).

Since 2001, the American manufacturing sector has lost over 2 million jobs as a result of the trade deficit with China, which over 2007 and 2008 exceeded $526 billion. The dramatic increase in the trade deficit is a direct result of Chinese subsidization, which drives down the cost of their exports and prevent American companies from competing on a level playing field. Industries across the country have been affected by these unfair policies, including steel, tires, textiles, solar energy and glass.

Recently, a study was completed on the negative effects Chinese policies have caused the American glass industry. The study by Dr. Usha Haley of Harvard University, *Through China's Looking Glass: Subsidies to the Chinese Glass Industry from 2004-08*, documents the industry's growth and exports, and the Chinese government subsidies that have bolstered such industry. Specifically, Dr. Haley makes the following findings:

- Since 2003, glass production in China has more than doubled. Concurrently, production capacity in China has doubled since 2003 and increased more than three-fold since 2000.
- China has become the largest exporter of flat glass and glass fiber in the world. The Chinese glass industry experienced a three-fold increase in exports to the United States from 2000 to 2008; correspondingly, the U.S. trade deficit with China on glass also tripled in the same period.
- China's glass and glass-products industry received at least $30.3 billion in subsidies from 2004 to 2008. These subsidies spanned heavy oil, coal, electricity, and soda ash and have been growing steadily in this period, reaching about 35% of gross industrial output value of glass in 2008.

As a direct result of China's policies, glass production in the U.S. has suffered in recent years, with plant closings and as many as 40,000 lost jobs throughout the country. While our domestic glass industry is the most efficient in the world, it cannot compete against production that is heavily subsidized.

At a time when we need job growth, not loss, we strongly urge you to raise the issues mentioned in this letter with your Chinese counterparts. Thank you for your attention to this important issue. We have enclosed a copy of Dr. Haley's report for your reference.

Sincerely,

Robert P. Casey, Jr.
United States Senator

Arlen Specter
United States Senator

Mary L. Landrieu
United States Senator

Charles E. Schumer
United States Senator

Evan Bayh
United States Senator

Debbie Stabenow
United States Senator

Sherrod Brown
United States Senator

Kirsten E. Gillibrand
United States Senator

01/20/10 15:45 FAX

002/002

EXECUTIVE OFFICE OF THE PRESIDENT
THE UNITED STATES TRADE REPRESENTATIVE
WASHINGTON, D.C. 20508

January 19, 2010

The Honorable Robert P. Casey, Jr.
United States Senate
Washington, D.C. 20510

Dear Senator Casey:

Thank you for your letter regarding Chinese government subsidies to its glass industry, and for the study that you provided to me by Dr. Usha Haley of Harvard University.

I share your concerns about the large job losses in the U.S. manufacturing sector. Especially during the current trying economic times, it is critical to maintain existing jobs and put those who are unemployed back to work. That is this Administration's highest priority.

I can assure you that the Administration understands the problems caused by China's industrial policies, including those affecting the glass sector. In our discussions with our Chinese counterparts, Secretary Locke and I have emphasized the need for China to increase its domestic consumption and reduce its overall economic reliance on exports. We have also raised, and will continue to raise, concerns regarding China's use of export-oriented fiscal and regulatory policies, including government financial support and policies to promote low-cost inputs.

My staff is also engaged on this matter. Last month, after Dr. Haley issued her study, my staff met with her to discuss in more detail her findings on Chinese government subsidies being provided to China's glass industry. My staff has also been consulting with subsidies experts at the Department of Commerce. We intend to raise our concerns during upcoming U.S.-China Joint Commission on Commerce and Trade working group meetings focusing on China's industrial policies.

Thank you again for sharing your concerns with me.

Sincerely,

Ambassador Ron Kirk

01/20/2010 3:39PM

Congress of the United States

Washington, DC 20510

July 28, 2010

The President
The White House
Washington, DC

Dear Mr. President:

We write to bring to your attention the damage caused to American manufacturing by the subsidies that China's paper industry receive, which are significant and market-distorting.

A recently released study by the Economic Policy Institute (EPI) documents the known subsidies that China's government provides its paper industry and the ensuing exponential growth of production and export sales of Chinese paper. These events correspond to an increasing U.S. trade deficit with China in paper. The EPI study shows that paper production in China tripled over the last ten years, despite global overcapacity, saturated markets, and no inherent advantage in the marketplace. It is clear to us that the rise of China's paper industry is less related to market forces than to a decision by China's government to implement an industrial policy that promotes domestic paper production.

America's paper industry is the most efficient in the world and is part of a supply chain that promotes sustainable forestry practices and good-paying jobs. This industry should not be asked to continue to compete on the unlevel playing field that China has constructed through heavy subsidization of domestic production. This is a critical period of time for the U.S. paper industry. Production in the U.S. has declined while China's surged. From 2002 through the end of 2009, U.S. employment in the paper and paper products sector dropped 29 percent, from roughly 557,000 workers to 398,000. In each of our states and districts, hardworking Americans still rely on the paper industry – both directly and indirectly – for their livelihoods and the chance for a decent, middle-class wage.

To that end, we urge you to carefully examine the practices employed by the Chinese government to provide its paper industry an artificial and unfair advantage in the U.S. market, and determine the extent to which these practices cause or threaten to cause harm to American producers. Such an analysis should be conducted to identify China's unfair trade practices in the paper industry and apply all appropriate and necessary remedies to combat those identified. Thank you for your attention to this important issue.

Sincerely,

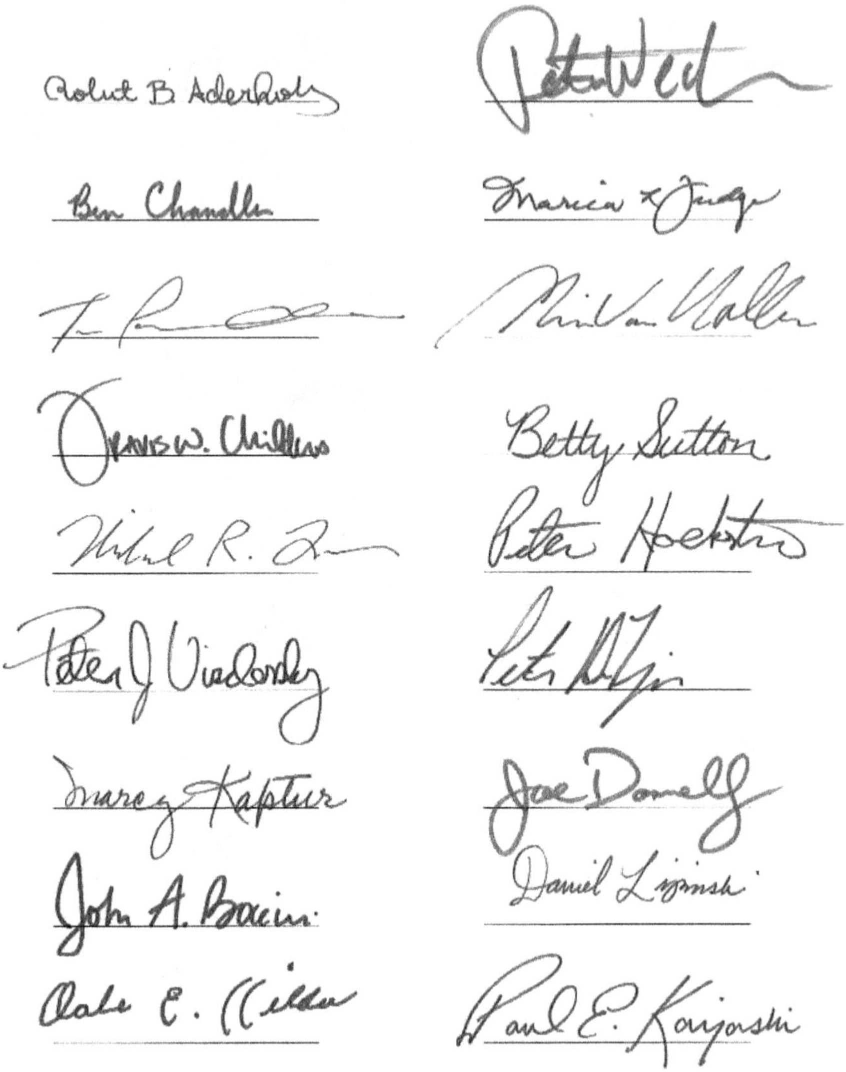

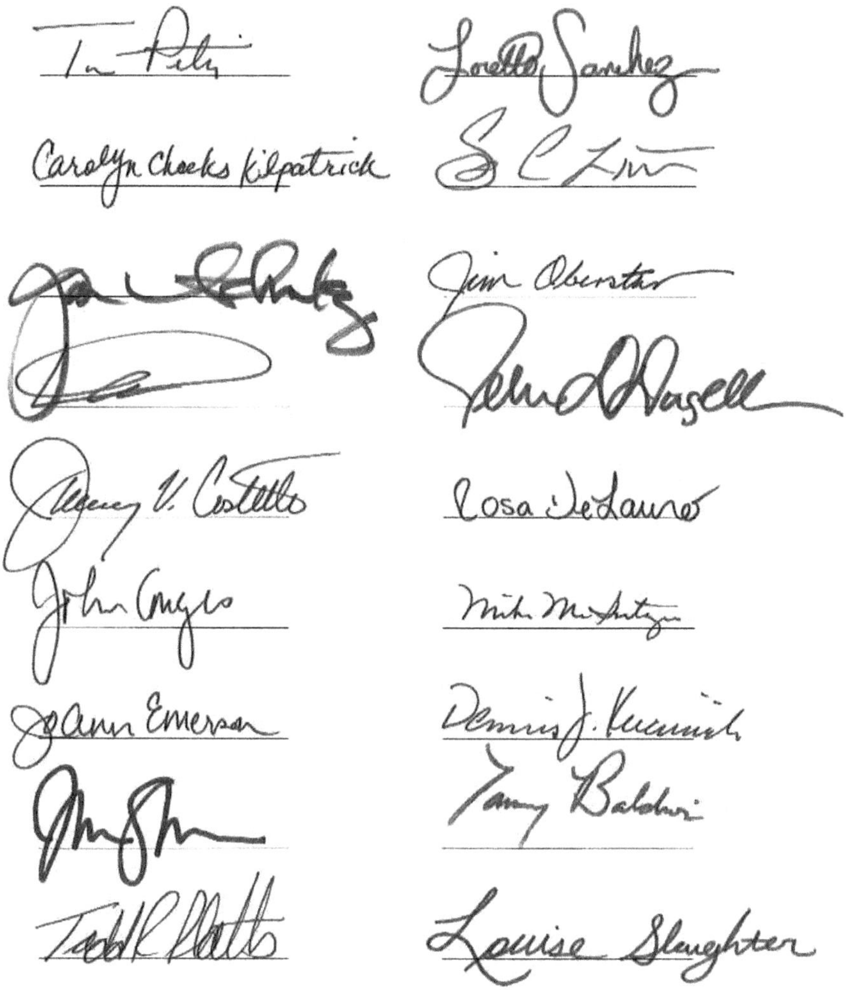

Congress of the United States
Washington, DC 20515

March 16, 2012

President Barack Obama
The White House
Washington, DC 20500

Dear Mr. President:

We are writing to express serious concern about China's unfair practices in the auto parts sector, and to encourage your Administration to use all existing authority under the law to preserve and protect U.S. production and jobs.

Recently released reports have highlighted the vast array of policies China's government uses to advantage its producers, such as limiting our exports to their market, subsidizing their exports to ours, and assisting their producers to the disadvantage of ours. The Chinese Government also imposes restraints on the export of key raw materials needed for the production of parts. In that regard, the United States recently won a major decision challenging some of those restraints at the World Trade Organization. We must build on this victory and begin addressing other restraints on materials, including those critical to the production of autos and auto parts. China also coerces U.S. companies in China to transfer their technologies to Chinese partners.

These tactics are working. Chinese auto parts exports are rapidly growing and have increased almost 900 percent since 2000. An unfortunate result of China's predatory and protectionist policies in the auto parts sector has been to begin to sever the traditional link between auto assemblers, parts producers, and aftermarket producers. Thus, while our nation's auto producers are recovering, the auto parts sector faces serious challenges.

We cannot wait until further damage is done. China has signaled its commitment to continue this approach in its recently released twelfth Five-Year Plan and other government directives. To level the playing field for U.S manufacturers and their workers, we must develop and implement a much more assertive and comprehensive strategy. Your announcement of the Interagency Trade Enforcement Center to promote a more coordinated, effective response to China's unfair trade practices is a major step toward such strategy. Addressing Chinese predatory policies in auto parts should be one of the Enforcement Center's first and highest priorities.

Seventy-five percent of the jobs in the automotive sector are in auto parts, and these jobs are at risk in every state in the nation. China has virtually closed its market to our auto parts exports and continues to take actions to further limit access. Given its importance, the Administration's vigilance in addressing China's harmful policies now, while we can still change this one-way street in trade, is essential. American companies and workers can compete anywhere when the playing field is level.

Sincerely,

March 16, 2012 Auto Parts Letter

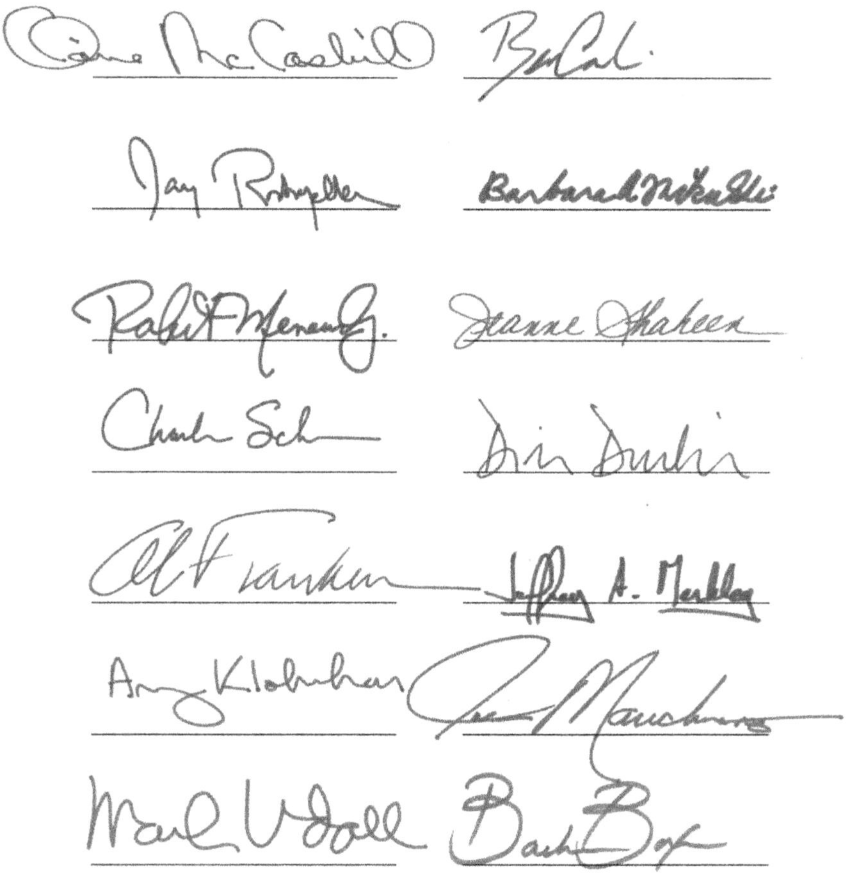

March 16, 2012 Auto Parts Letter

March 16, 2012 Auto Parts Letter

March 16, 2012 Auto Parts Letter

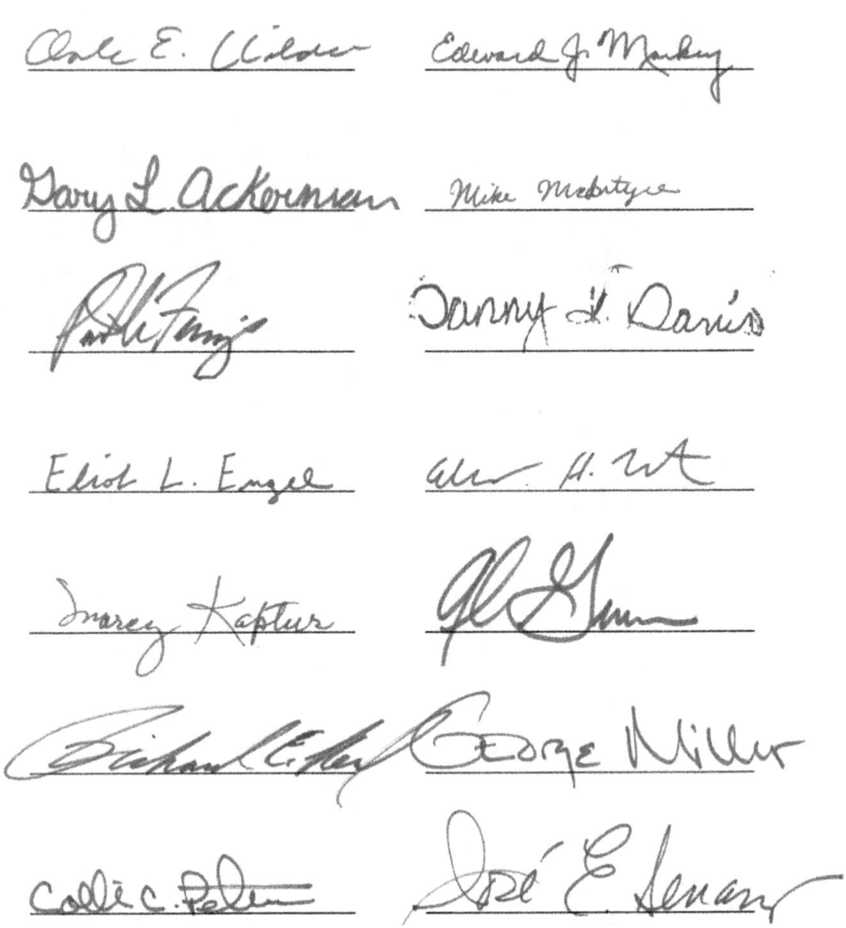

March 16, 2012 | Auto Parts Letter

March 16, 2012 Auto Parts Letter

March 16, 2012 Auto Parts Letter

March 16, 2012 Auto Parts Letter

March 16, 2012 Auto Parts Letter

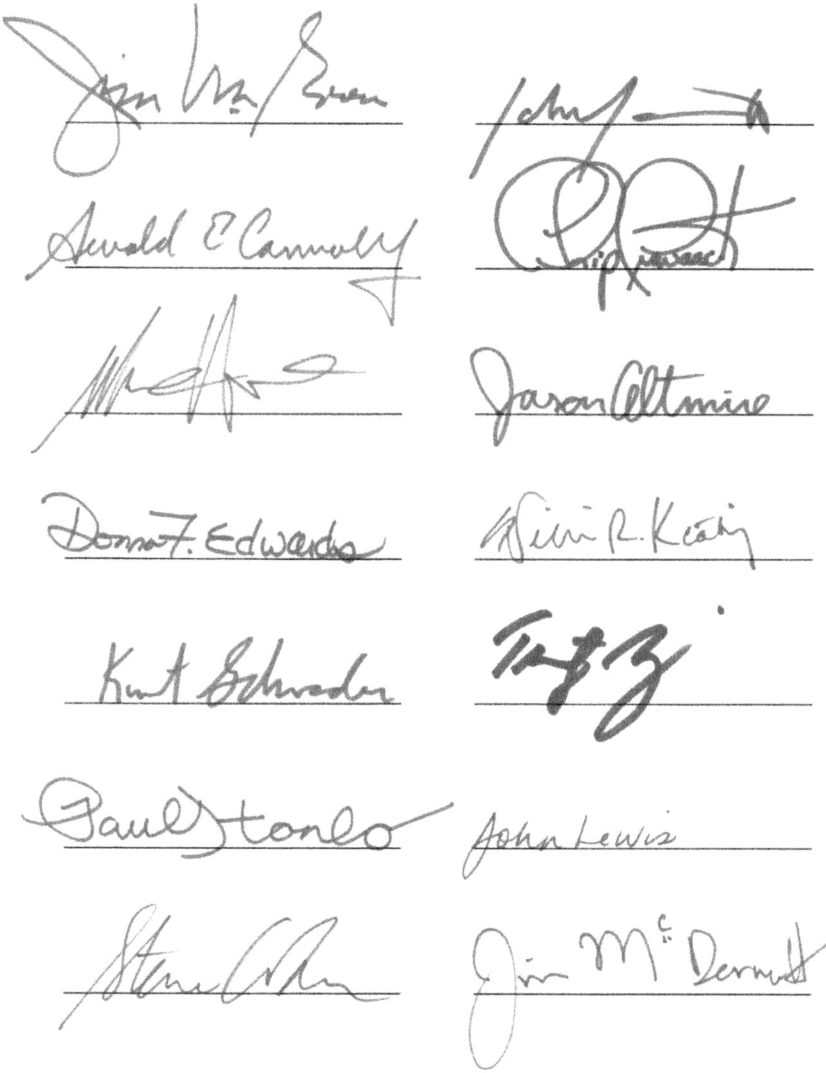

March 16, 2012 | Auto Parts Letter

March 16, 2012 Auto Parts Letter

March 16, 2012 Auto Parts Letter

March 16, 2012 Auto Parts Letter

Senators:
Sen. Mark Begich
Sen. Michael F. Bennet
Sen. Richard Blumenthal
Sen. Barbara Boxer
Sen. Sherrod Brown
Sen. Ben Cardin
Sen. Robert P. Casey, Jr.
Sen. Richard J. Durbin
Sen. Al Franken
Sen. Kirsten E. Gillibrand
Sen. Tom Harkin
Sen. John F. Kerry
Sen. Amy Klobuchar
Sen. Mary L. Landrieu
Sen. Frank R. Lautenberg
Sen. Patrick J. Leahy
Sen. Carl Levin
Sen. Joe Manchin, III
Sen. Claire McCaskill
Sen. Robert Menendez
Sen. Jeff Merkley
Sen. Barbara A. Mikulski
Sen. Mark L. Pryor
Sen. Jack Reed
Sen. John D. Rockefeller, IV
Sen. Bernard Sanders
Sen. Charles E. Schumer
Sen. Jeanne Shaheen
Sen. Debbie Stabenow
Sen. Jon Tester
Sen. Mark Udall
Sen. Sheldon Whitehouse

Representatives:
Rep. Gary L. Ackerman
Rep. Jason Altmire
Rep. Robert E. Andrews
Rep. Joe Baca
Rep. Tammy Baldwin
Rep. John Barrow
Rep. Karen Bass
Rep. Xavier Becerra
Rep. Shelley Berkley
Rep. Sanford Bishop
Rep. Timothy Bishop
Rep. Earl Blumenauer
Rep. Suzette Bonamici
Rep. Leonard Boswell
Rep. Robert Brady
Rep. Bruce Braley
Rep. G.K. Butterfield
Rep. Lois Capps
Rep. Michael Capuano
Rep. Russ Carnahan
Rep. John C. Carney
Rep. Andre Carson
Rep. Ben Chandler
Rep. Judy Chu
Rep. David Cicilline
Rep. Hansen Clarke
Rep. Yvette Clarke
Rep. William Clay
Rep. Emanuel Cleaver
Rep. Steve Cohen
Rep. Gerald Connolly
Rep. John Conyers, Jr.
Rep. Jim Costa
Rep. Jerry F. Costello
Rep. Joe Courtney
Rep. Chip Cravaack
Rep. Mark Critz
Rep. Joseph Crowley
Rep. Elijah Cummings
Rep. Danny Davis
Rep. Peter DeFazio
Rep. Diana DeGette
Rep. Rosa DeLauro
Rep. John Dingell
Rep. Lloyd Doggett
Rep. Joe Donnelly
Rep. Michael Doyle
Rep. Donna Edwards
Rep. Keith Ellison
Rep. Elliot Engel
Rep. Sam Farr
Rep. Chaka Fattah
Rep. Bob Filner
Rep. Barney Frank
Rep. Marcia Fudge
Rep. John Garamendi
Rep. Al Green
Rep. Gene Green
Rep. Raul Grijalva
Rep. Louis Gutierrez
Rep. Janice Hahn
Rep. Martin Heinrich
Rep. Brian Higgins
Rep. James Himes
Rep. Maurice Hinchey
Rep. Kathleen Hochul

March 16, 2012 Auto Parts Letter

Rep. Tim Holden
Rep. Rush Holt
Rep. Duncan Hunter
Rep. Steve Israel
Rep. Jesse Jackson, Jr.
Rep. Henry C. Johnson
Rep. Walter Jones
Rep. Marcy Kaptur
Rep. William Keating
Rep. Dale Kildee
Rep. Adam Kinzinger
Rep. Larry Kissel
Rep. Dennis Kucinich
Rep. James Langevin
Rep. John B. Larson
Rep. Steven LaTourette
Rep. Barbara Lee
Rep. Sander M. Levin
Rep. John Lewis
Rep. Daniel Lipinski
Rep. David Loebsack
Rep. Zoe Lofgren
Rep. Nita Lowey
Rep. Steven Lynch
Rep. Carolyn Maloney
Rep. Donald Manzullo
Rep. Edward Markey
Rep. Carolyn McCarthy
Rep. Betty McCollum
Rep. Thaddeus McCotter
Rep. Jim McDermott
Rep. James McGovern
Rep. Mike McIntyre
Rep. Jerry McNerney
Rep. Gregory Meeks
Rep. Michael Michaud
Rep. Brad Miller
Rep. George Miller
Rep. Tim Murphy
Rep. Jerrold Nadler
Rep. Grace Napolitano
Rep. Richard E. Neal
Rep. Eleanor Holmes-Norton
Rep. John Olver
Rep. William Owens
Rep. Frank Pallone
Rep. Bill Pascrell
Rep. Ed Pastor
Rep. Ed Perlmutter
Rep. Gary Peters
Rep. Collin Peterson
Rep. Chellie Pingree
Rep. Mike Quigley
Rep. Nick Rahall
Rep. Charles B. Rangel
Rep. Laura Richardson
Rep. Cedric Richmond
Rep. Mike Ross
Rep. Steven Rothman
Rep. Lucille Roybal-Allard
Rep. C.A. Dutch Ruppersberger
Rep. Bobby Rush
Rep. Tim Ryan
Rep. Linda Sanchez
Rep. John P. Sarbanes
Rep. Janice Schakowsky
Rep. Kurt Schrader
Rep. Allyson Schwartz
Rep. Robert "Bobby" Scott
Rep. David Scott
Rep. Jose Serrano
Rep. Terry Sewell
Rep. Brad Sherman
Rep. Albio Sires
Rep. Louise Slaughter
Rep. Jackie Speier
Rep. Pete Fortney Stark
Rep. Betty Sutton
Rep. Bennie Thompson
Rep. Mike Thompson
Rep. John Tierney
Rep. Paul Tonko
Rep. Adolphus Towns
Rep. Nikki Tsongas
Rep. Chris Van Hollen
Rep. Peter Visclosky
Rep. Timothy Walz
Rep. Peter Welch
Rep. Lynn C. Woolsey
Rep. John Yarmuth

BIBLIOGRAPHY

Aghion, P., and P. Howitt. 1992. A model of growth through creative destruction. *Econometrica* 60: 323–51.

American Forest and Paper Association. 2004. China's subsidization of its forest products industry. Unpublished report.

Amsden, A. H. 1992. *Asia's Next Giant: South Korea and Late Industrialization*. New York: Oxford University Press.

Asia Pulse. 2007. China halts preferential pricing of 14 provinces. April 17.

Asia Pulse. 2009. Analysis—China auto industry expands with overcapacity worries. November 19.

Associated Press. 2012. China files WTO case challenging US trade penalties over 22 products, widening trade battle. May 25.

Auer, R., and A. M. Fischer. 2010. The effect of low-wage import competition on U.S. inflationary pressure. *Journal of Monetary Economics* 57: 491–503.

Automobile Industry Development Policy, People's Republic of China. 2004. Decree of the State Development and Reform Commission, No. 8. June 28. Available at hktdc.com.

Automotive Industry Development Policy, People's Republic of China. 2009. Revised, Decree of the State Development and Reform Commission. Promulgated August 15, effective September 1. Translation through *China Law & Practice, Euromoney*, October 9.

Automotive News China. 2011a. GM upgrades vehicle R&D efforts in China. February 19.

Automotive News China. 2011b. GM says China has not pressured it to share Volt technology. September 9.

Barboza, D. 2010. Report warns of risks to China's bank system. *New York Times*, July 14.

Baron, D. P. 1995. Integrated strategy: Market and non-market components. *California Management Review* 37(2): 47–65.

Batson, A., and J. Zhang. 2011. Public debt: The magic mountain. *China Economic Quarterly*, June, 41–47.

BBC News. 2001. China joins the WTO—at last. December 11.

Behboodi, R. 1994. *Industrial Subsidies and Friction in World Trade*. New York: Routledge.

Beijing News. 2012. Ministry of Commerce: China has the Most Trade Conflicts in the World. March 24.

Berkowitz, B., K. Krolicki, and L. C. Yee. 2011. Special report: Warren Buffett's China car deal could backfire. Reuters, March 9.

Birol, F., and J. H. Keppler. 1999. World Energy Outlook: Looking at energy subsidies: Getting the prices right. Paris: Organization for Economic Co-operation and Development.

Bloomberg. 2009. China's vehicle sales top U.S. tally for first time. February 10.

Bo, K. 2007. Ending oil subsidies serves China's oil security. *ChinaStakes.com*, December 26.

Bradsher, K. 2009. Recovery picks up in China as US still ails. *New York Times*, September 29.

Bradsher, K. 2011a. Solar panel maker moves work to China. *New York Times*, January 14.

Bradsher, K. 2011b. Chinese foreign currency reserves swell by record amount. *New York Times*, January 11.

Bradsher, K. 2011c. Hybrid in a trade squeeze. *New York Times*, September 5.

Bradsher, K. 2012. China confronts mounting piles of unsold goods. *New York Times*, August 23.

Brander, J. A. 1995. Strategic trade policy. In G. M. Grossman and K. Rogoff, eds, *Handbook of International Economics*, vol. 3, 1395–1455. Amsterdam: Elsevier Science.

Brander, J. A., and B. J. Spencer. 1985. Export subsidies and international market share rivalry. *Journal of International Economics* 18: 83–100.

Brandt, L., and X. Zhu. 2000. Redistribution in a decentralized economy: Growth and inflation in China under reform. *Journal of Political Economy* 108: 422–39.

Bremmer, I. 2010. *The End of the Free Market*. New York: Portfolio.

Cable, J. 2010. Automakers see China as an engine of growth. *IndustryWeek*, December 29.

CEIC. Various years. http://www.ceicdata.com/.

China Association of Automobile Manufacturers. 2008–2011. .http://www.caam.org.cn.

China Automotive Review. 2006. The genes of China's auto industry are changing. January, 34.

China Automotive Technology & Research Center (CATARC). 2009. China drafts strategies to boost auto and auto parts exports. December 7.

China Automotive Technology & Research Center (CATARC). 2011. New strategy to help automakers. *CATARC—Analysis and Forecasts on China Automotive Industry*, March 7.

China Daily. 2009. BeijingWest gets control of Delphi's key units. April 2.

China Economic Information Network. 2004–2009. *China Statistical Databases*.

China Economic Information Service. 2009. China to cut back paper industry support. October 20.

China Electric Power Yearbook 2008 China Electric Power Press (in Chinese)

China Market Pulp Report. 2005–2009. ChinaPaperOnline. Pacific Net Holding Corporation, Beijing.

China Recovered Paper Report. 2005–2009. ChinaPaperOnline. Pacific Net Holding Corporation, Beijing.

Citigroup Global Markets. 2005. Metals-Steel. August 30.

Claro, S. 2006. Supporting inefficient firms with capital subsidies: China and Germany in the 1980s. *Journal of Comparative Economics* 34: 377–401.

Coady, D., R. Gillingham, R. Ossowski, J. Piotrowski, S. Tareq, and J. Tyson. 2010. Petroleum product subsidies: costly, inequitable and rising. IMF Staff Position Note, SPN/10/05. International Monetary Fund, Fiscal Affairs Department, Washington, DC, February 25.

Communist Party of China. 2007. Socialism with Chinese characteristics. The Seventeenth National Congress of the Communist Party of China. Available at http://english.peopledaily.com.cn/90002/92169/92211/6275043.html#.

Cooney, S. 2006. Steel: Price and policy issues. CRS Report to Congress, August 31.

Corden, M., 1957. The calculation of the cost of protection. *Economic Record* 33: 29–51.

Credit Suisse. 2007. US steel sector. May US steel imports—China imports rise. June 26.

Cull, R., and L. C. Xu. 2003. Who gets the credit? The behavior of bureaucrats and state banks in allocating credit to Chinese state-owned enterprises. *Journal of Economic Development* 71(2): 553–59.

Directorate for Science Technology and Industry Steel Committee. 2006. Current situation of the Chinese steel industry. OECD, Joint India/OECD/IISI Workshop, New Delhi, India, May 16–17.

Dixit, A. 1983. International trade policy for oligopolistic industries. Discussion paper 48, Woodrow Wilson School, Princeton University.

Dean, J., A. Browne, and S. Oster. 2010. China's "state capitalism" sparks a global backlash. *Wall Street Journal Online*, November 16.

Deyo, F. C., ed. 1987. *The Political Economy of the New Asian Industrialism*. Ithaca, NY: Cornell University Press.

Doom, J. 2012. Suntech "not solvent" without Chinese assistance, Maxim says. *Bloomberg News*, August 1.

Dyer, G. 2006. Ford to double China procurement. *Financial Times*, October 26.

Eckaus, R. S. 2006. China's exports, subsidies to state owned enterprises and the WTO. *China Economic Review* 17: 1–13.

The Economist. 2001. From bamboo to bits and bytes. April 7, 13.

The Economist. 2002. How cooked are the books? March 14.

The Economist. 2006. Dim sums. November 2.

The Economist. 2007. Cultural revolution. January 11.

The Economist. 2007. A less fiery dragon? November 29.

The Economist. 2011. The rise and rise of the cognitive elite. January 20.

Economist Intelligence Unit. 2010. China risk: Alert shortages of workers push up wages. April 6.

European Automobile Manufacturers Association. 2010. *The Automobile Industry Pocket Guide*. 2nd ed. Available at http://www.ace3a.be/images/uploads/files/2010924_Pocket_Guide_2nd_edition.pdf.

European Chamber of Commerce in China. 2009. *Overcapacity in China: Causes, Impacts and Recommendations*. Special Report in partnership with Roland Berger Strategy Consultants, Beijing, November.

European Chamber of Commerce in China. 2011. *Public Procurement in China: European Business Experiences Competing for Public Contracts in China*. Beijing, April.

Evans, P., D. Rueschemeyer, and T. Skocpal, eds. 2002. *Bringing the State Back In*. New York: Cambridge University Press.

Feenstra, R. C. 1995. Estimating the effects of trade policy. In G. M. Grossman and K. Rogoff, eds., *Handbook of International Economics*, vol. 3, 1553–95. Amsterdam: Elsevier Science.

Ferri, G. and L.-G. Liu. 2009. Honor thy creditors before thy shareholders: Are the profits of Chinese state-owned enterprises real? HKIMR Working Paper 16/2009, Hong Kong Institute for Monetary Research, Hong Kong.

Fitch Ratings. 2010. Chinese banks: Informal securitization increasingly distorting credit data. *China Special Report*, July 14.

Fligstein, N. 1996. Markets as politics: A sociological view of market institutions. *American Sociological Review* 61: 656–73.

Fligstein, N. 2001. *The Architecture of Markets: An Economic Sociology of Twenty-First-Century Capitalist Societies.* Princeton, NJ: Princeton University Press.

Fligstein, N., and J. Zhang. 2011. A new agenda for research on the trajectory of Chinese capitalism. *Management and Organization Review* 7(1): 39–62.

Flynn, R. 2006. China's pulp and paper industry: What low cost advantage? Presentation at the conference "China's Boom: Implications for Investment and Trade in Forest Products and Forestry," Vancouver, Canada, January 18.

French, H. W. 2007. Beijing seeks energy cuts; localities find loopholes. *New York Times*, November 24.

GaveKal Dragonomics. 2009. BYD: China's electric car pioneer. Special report, September.

General Administration of Customs, People's Republic of China. 2009. Decree of the General Administration of Customs of the People's Republic of China, No. 175. June 16. Available at http://english.customs.gov.cn/publish/portal191/tab3972/info174200.htm.

Girma, S., Y. Gong, H. Gorg, and Z. Yu. 2007. Can production subsidies foster export activity? Evidence from Chinese firm-level data. Working Paper Series No. 6052, Centre for Economic Policy Research, London, January.

Girma, S., Y. Gong, H. Gorg, and Z. Yu. 2009. Can production subsidies explain China's export performance? Evidence from firm-level data. *Scandinavian Journal of Economics* 111(4): 863–91.

GM Media. 2010. GM China breaks ground for advanced technical center in Shanghai. Press release, July 19.

Grant, J. 2012 Chinese subsidies prop up steel mills. The commodities note, *FT.com*, September 7.

The Guardian. 2010. China overtakes US as world's biggest car market. January 8.

Guthrie, D. 2000. Understanding China's transition to capitalism: The contributions of Victor Nee and Andrew Walder. *Sociological Forum* 15(4): 727–49.

Haley, G. T. 2007. Overview of China's pillar and strategic industries. Expert testimony to US-China Economic and Security Review Commission's hearing "The Extent of the Government's Control of China's Economy, and Its Impact on the United States," May 25.

Haley, G. T. 2009. State-owned enterprises: Vehicles of industrial policy implementation. Expert testimony to U.S.-China Economic and Security Review Commission's Hearing "China's Industrial Policy and Its Impact on U.S. Companies, Workers and the American Economy," Washington, DC, March 24.

Haley, G. T., and U. C. V. Haley. 2007. Understanding subsidies to the Chinese steel industry from 2000–2007: Spotlight on energy. Invited presentation to the US International Trade Commission, Industry Seminar Series, Washington, DC, December 5.

Haley, G. T., and U. C. V. Haley. 2012a. Bringing solar manufacturing back. *The Hill's Congress Blog*, February 7. Available at http://thehill.com/blogs/congress-blog/energy-a-environment/209239-bringing-solar-manufacturing-back.

Haley, G. T., U. C. V. Haley, and C. T. Tan. 2004. *The Chinese Tao of Business: The Logic of Successful Business Strategy*. Singapore: John Wiley & Sons.

Haley, G. T., U. C. V. Haley, and C. T. Tan. 2009. *New Asian Emperors: The Business Strategies of the Overseas Chinese*. Singapore: John Wiley & Sons.

Haley, G. T., and C. T. Tan. 1996. The black hole of South-East Asia: Strategic decision-making in an informational void. *Management Decision* 34(9): 37–48.

Haley, U. C. V. 2001. *Multinational Corporations in Political Environments: Ethics, Values and Strategies*. 2nd ed. Singapore: World Scientific Press.

Haley, U. C. V. 2003. Assessing and controlling business risks in China. *Journal of International Management* 9: 237–52.

Haley, U. C. V. 2006. Chinese economic planning and the role of subsidies. Expert testimony to US-China Economic and Security Review Commission's Hearing "China's WTO Compliance and Industrial Subsidies," Washington, DC, April 4.

Haley, U. C. V. 2007. Support for the Non-market Economy Trade Remedy Act. Expert testimony to the Committee on Ways and Means, Subcommittee on Trade's hearing "The Non-market Economy Trade Remedy Act of 2007," 110th Congress, Washington, DC, March 15.

Haley, U. C. V. 2009. Through China's looking glass: Subsidies to China's glass industry from 2004–2008. Briefing Paper No. 242, Economic Policy Institute, Washington, DC.

Haley, U. C. V. 2010. The Pandora's box of trade with China. *Huffington Post*, August 27. Available at http://www.huffingtonpost.com/usha-haley/the-pandoras-box-of-trade_b_695662.html.

Haley, U. C. V., and G. T. Haley. 2008. The real source of the China price. *Harvard Business Review*, June, 25–26.

Haley, U. C. V., and G. T. Haley. 2012b. The case for US tariffs on Chinese solar panels. *Financial Times*, BeyondBrics, May 25. Available at http://blogs.ft.com/beyond-brics/2012/05/25/guest-post-the-case-for-us-tariffs-on-chinese-solar-panels/.

Haley, U. C. V., and D. A. Schuler. 2011. Government policy and firm strategy in the solar photovoltaics industry. *California Management Review* 54(1): 17–38.

Hancke, B. 2010. Varieties of capitalism and business. In D. Coen, W. Grant, and G. Wilson, eds., *The Oxford Handbook of Business and Government*, 123–46. New York: Oxford University Press.

Hobson, J. M. 1997. *The Wealth of States*. Cambridge: Cambridge University Press.

Hout, T. M., and P. Ghemawat. 2010. China vs the World. Whose technology is it? *Harvard Business Review*, December, 94–103.

Huang, Y. 2003. *Selling China*. New York: Cambridge University Press.

Huang, Y. 2008. *Capitalism with Chinese Characteristics*. New York: Cambridge University Press.

Huang, Y., and B. Wang. 2010. Cost distortions and structural imbalances in China. *China & World Economy* 18(4): 1–17.

Hudec, R. 1990. "Mirror, mirror on the wall": The concept of fairness in United States trade policy. Paper presented at the Annual Meeting of the Canadian Council of International Law, Ottawa, October 19.

Hufbauer, G. C., and J. S. Erb. 1984. *Subsidies in International Trade*. Washington, DC: Institute for International Economics.

HKTDC. 2010. Kimberly-Clark to build new plant in China. January 27.

IKEA. 2009. *Sustainability Report 2008*. January 7.

IBISWorld. Various years. Industry Reports. http://www.ibisworld.com.

Information Office of the State Council, People's Republic of China. 2007. China's energy conditions and policies. White paper, Beijing, December.

Interfax. 2007. *China Metals Weekly*, October 26.

Interfax. 2008a. *China Energy Report Weekly*, March 20–March 26.

Interfax. 2008b. *China Energy Report Weekly*, August 28–September 3.

International Energy Agency. 1999. *Looking at Energy Subsidies: Getting the Prices Right*. World Energy Outlook Insights Series. Paris: OECD.

International Energy Agency. 2006. *World Energy Outlook*. Paris: OECD.

International Energy Agency. 2007. *China and India Insights*. World Energy Outlook Insights Series. Paris: OECD.

International Trade Administration. 2009. *U.S. Automotive Parts Industry Annual Assessment*. Office of Transportation and Machinery, US Department of Commerce, Washington, DC, April.

International Trade Administration. 2010. *On the Road: U.S. Automotive Parts Industry Annual Assessment*. Office of Transportation and Machinery, US Department of Commerce, Washington, DC, April.

ISI Emerging Markets. Various years. http://www.securities.com.

ISI Emerging Markets Analytics. Various years. http://www.securities.com.

Iwagaki, M. 1986. The state of China's automobile industry. JETRO. *China Newsletter*, no. 63.

Jaruzelski, B., and K. Dehoff. 2007. The customer connection: The global innovation 1000. Resilience Report, *Strategy+Business*, Booz-Allen-Hamilton.

Jaruzelski, B., and K. Dehoff. 2009. Profits down, spending steady. The global innovation 1000. *Strategy+Business*, Issue 57, Winter.

JD Power & Associates. 2007. *China Automotive Components Outlook*. Automotive Resources Asia.

Johnson, C. 1995. *Japan: Who governs? The Rise of the Development State*. New York: Norton.

Just-Auto. 2010. China: Auto parts exports up 44%. December 10.

Kahn, J., and J. Yardley. 2007. As China roars, pollution reaches deadly extremes. *New York Times*, August 26.

Katz, L., and L. Summers. 1989. Can interindustry wage differentials justify strategic trade policy? In R. Feenstra, ed., *Trade Policies for International Competitiveness*, 85–124. Chicago: University of Chicago Press.

Kilzer, L. 2012. Solar cell industry in free fall. *Pittsburgh Tribune Review*, July 28.

Komesaroff, M. 2009. Too much size matters. *China Economic Quarterly* 13(4): 39–44.

Kornai, J. 1990. *The Road to a Free Economy: Shifting from a Socialist System. The Example of Hungary*. New York: Norton.

Kornai, J. 1992. *The Socialist System: The Political Economy of Communism*. Princeton, NJ: Princeton University Press.

Krueger, A. 1974. Political economy of the rent-seeking society. *American Economic Review* 64(3), 291–303.

Krugman, P. 1986. *Strategic Trade Policy and the New International Economics*. Cambridge: MIT Press.

Krugman, P. 2010. *Taking on China*. Opinion. *New York Times*, March 14.

LaHaye, L. 2008. Mercantilism. *The Concise Encyclopedia of Economics*. Library of Economics and Liberty. Available from http://www.econlib.org/library/Enc/Mercantilism.html.

Lavergne, R. P. 1983. *The Political Economy of US Tariffs: An Empirical Analysis*. New York: Academic Press.

Law, F., and J. Chiu. 2011. Nine Dragons shares hit as S&P pulls rating. *Wall Street Journal Online*, June 15.

Lenway, S., R. Morck, and B. Yeung. 1996. Rent seeking, protectionism and innovation in the American steel industry. *Economic Journal* 106 (March): 410–21.

Lesprom Inform. 2009. China forest industry revitalization. *Timber News*, December 14.

Liao, W. 2007. Foreign joint venture partners urged to fulfill contract commitments. *China Automotive Review*, March, 12.

Lin, B., and Z. Jiang. 2011. Estimates of energy subsidies in China and impact of energy subsidy reform. *Energy Economics* 33: 273–83.

Lin, N. 2011. Capitalism in China: A centrally managed capitalism (CMC) and its future. *Management and Organization Review* 7(1): 63–96.

Liu L. 2008. Local government and big business in the People's Republic of China—Case study from Shandong Province. *Asia Pacific Business Review* 14(4): 473–89.

Liu, Y. 2001. An explanation on the efficiency puzzle of China's SOEs. In R. Yang, ed., *An Economic Analysis on the Innovation of Corporate Governance*. Renmin: University of China Press.

Liu, W., and H. W. Yeung. 2008. China's dynamic industrial sector: The automobile industry. *Eurasian Geography and Economics* 49(5): 523–48.

Luo, H., and R. Golembiewski. 1996. Budget deficits in China: Calculations, causes, and impacts. *Public Budgeting and Financial Management* 8: 305–333.

Lovasz, A., and S. White. 2007. Dollar hits low against the euro. *Bloomberg News*, November 7.

Macquarie Research. 2007. Steel sector—China continues to Export Aggressively. January 12.

Mathur, A. 2007. Chinese steel exports boom despite curbs. *Business Standard*, November 24.

Mattoo, A., and A. Subramanian. 2011. China and the world trading system. Policy Research Working Paper No. 5897, Development Research Group, World Bank, Washington, DC, December.

McCrone, G., 1962. *The Economics of Subsidizing Agriculture: A Study of British Policy*. Toronto: University of Toronto Press,

McGregor, J. 2011. China's drive for indigenous innovation: A web of industrial policies. US Chamber of Commerce report, February.

McGregor, R. 2010. *The Party: The Secret World of China's Communist Rulers*. New York: HarperCollins.

Melanie, J., R. Curtotti, M. Saunders, K. Schneider, L. Fairhead, and Y. Qian. 2002. *Global Coal Markets*. ABARE Research Report 02.2, Canberra, Australia.

Melanie, J., and A. Austin. 2006. China's coal sector: Recent developments and implications for prices. *Australian Commodities* 13(3): 542–54.

Meyer. M. W. 2011. Is it capitalism? *Management and Organization Review* 7(1): 5–18.

Milner, H. V., and D. B. Yoffie. 1989. Between free trade and protectionism: Strategic trade policy and a theory of corporate trade demands. *International Organization* 43(2): 239–72.

Ministry of Machinery, People's Republic of China. 1994. Dangdai zhongguo guoji jiaoche gongye fazhan yu zhongguo jiaoche gongye fazhan zhanlue [The development of the contemporary Chinese international auto sedan industry and the Chinese auto sedan development strategy]. Symposium, Beijing.

Mysteel. Various years. http://www.mysteel.net.

National Bureau of Statistics, China. 2000–2012. *Yearly Statistics*.

National Bureau of Statistics, China. 2000–2012. *Monthly Statistics*.

Nee, V. 1989. A theory of market transition: From redistribution to markets in state socialism. *American Sociological Review* 54: 663–81.

Nee, V. 1992. Organizational dynamics of market transition: Hybrid forms, property rights, and mixed economy in China. *Administrative Science Quarterly* 37: 1–27.

Nee, V. 1996. The emergence of a market society: Changing mechanisms of stratification in China. *American Journal of Sociology* 101: 908–49.

Nee, V. 1998. Norms and networks in economic and organizational performance. *American Economic Review* 88(2): 85–89.

Ni, C. C. 2006. China's electric power industry and its trends. Institute of Energy Economics, Nuclear Power and Coal Group, Industrial Research Unit, Japan, April.

Nolan, P. 2001. *China and the Global Economy: National Champions, Industrial Policy, and the Big Business Revolution*. New York: Palgrave.

OECD. 2003. *China: Progress and Reform Challenges*. OECD Investment Policy Reviews. Paris: OECD.

Oliver, C. 2008. Warren Buffet looks to electric car in BYD stake. *MarketWatch*, October 9.

Palmer, D. 2012. Trade panel approves duties on China solar products. *Reuters*, November 7.

Papease. 2009. http://www.papease.com.

People's Daily Online. 2000. Bank backs Shanghai Auto Industry. July 8. Available at http://english.peopledaily.com.cn/ english/200007/08.html.

People's Daily. 2006. Following central government orders and paying attention to national interests. August 8, 1. (In Chinese.)

Polanyi, K. 1944. *The Great Transformation*. Boston: Beacon Press.

Polanyi, K., C. M. Arensberg, and H. W. Pearson. 1957. *Trade Market in the Early Empires*. Glencoe, IL: Free Press.

Porter, M. E. 1985. *Competitive Advantage: Creating and Sustaining Superior Performance*. New York: Free Press.

Porter, M. E. 1990. *The Competitive Advantage of Nations*. New York: Free Press.

Price, A. H., T. C. Brightbill, C. B. Weld, and D. S. Nance. 2007. *Government Ownership and Control of China's "Private" Steel Producers*. Wiley-Rein LLP, Washington, DC, October.

Rabinovitch, S., and J. Anderlini. 2011. Extent of local debts in China laid bare. *Financial Times*, June 27.

Rawski, T. G. 2001. What's happening to China's GDP Statistics? *China Economic Review* 12: 347–54.

Ray, E. 1981. Determinants of tariff and nontariff trade restrictions in the U.S. *Journal of Political Economy*, February, 105–21.

Reynolds, A. 1993. *The Political Economy of a North American Free Trade Agreement*. Vancouver: Hudson Institute and Fraser Institute.

Reuters. 2009. Chinese loans surge as output and sales slow. March 12.

RISI. 2007–9. *Asian Pulp and Paper Monitor*, various monthly issues.

RNCOS Industry Research Solutions. Various years. http://www.rncos.com.

Rodrik, D. 1995. Political economy of trade policy. In G. M. Grossman and K. Rogoff, ed., *Handbook of International Economics*, vol. 3, 1457–94. Amsterdam: Elsevier Science.

Rodrik, D. 2006. What's so special about China's exports? *China & World Economy* 14(5): 1–19.

Romer, P. 1990. Endogenous technological change. *Journal of Political Economy* 98: S71–S102.

Rosen, D. H., and T. Houser. 2007. China energy: A guide for the perplexed. Peterson Institute for International Economics, May.

Sato, H. 2011a. Can U.S. factories take on China? *Lowell Sun*, March 1.

Sato, H. 2011b. Capital, not labor, is key to China manufacturing. *Lowell Sun*, March 2.

Sato, H. 2011c. Evergreen Solar shifts focus, but tough challenges lie ahead. *Lowell Sun*, March 3.

Scott, R. E. 2010. Appendix: Comments on the USTR investigation of China's subsidies to green industries and their impacts on U.S. producers of clean energy products and other green technology goods. Economic Policy Institute, Washington, DC.

Scott, R. E. 2010. Unfair China trade costs local jobs. Briefing Paper No. 260, Economic Policy Institute, Washington, DC, March 23. Available at http://epi.3cdn.net/91b2eeeffce66c1a10_v5m6beqhi.pdf.

Segerstrom, P. S. 2000. The long-run growth effects of R&D subsidies. *Journal of Economic Growth* 5: 277–305.

Schneider, K., Q. Ye, R. Curtotti, A. Ball, X. Liu, Z. Wu, S. Gao, X. Jiang, and Z. Su. 2003. Natural gas in eastern China: The Role of LNG. ABARE Research Report 03.1, Canberra, Australia, March.

Shanghai Securities News. 2007. Execs refuse to co-operate. October 18.

Sinofile Information Services. 2010. Auto parts trade surplus expanded. November 8.

Swartz, S., and S. Oster. 2010. China tops U.S. in energy use. *Wall Street Journal Online*, Business section, July 18.

Shih, V. C. 2008. *Factions and Finance in China*. New York: Cambridge University Press.

Shirk, S. L. 1993. *The Political Logic of Economic Reform in China*. Berkeley: University of California Press.

Smith, A. 1776. *The Wealth of Nations*. Available at Bibliomania, http://www.bibliomania.com/2/1/65/112/frameset.html.

Specialty Steel Industry of North America. 2008. *China's Specialty Steel Subsidies: Massive Pervasive and Illegal*. October.

Spence, J. D. 1997. Deng Xiaoping as past and prologue. *Time*, March 3.

Spencer, B. J. 1988. Countervailing duty laws and subsidies to imperfectly competitive industries. In R. E. Baldwin, C. B. Hamilton, and A. Sapir, eds., *Issues in US-EC Trade Relations*, 315–48. Chicago: University of Chicago Press.

Stanway, D. 2009. Fuel prices: New, improved—and higher. *China Economic Quarterly*, March, 10–12.

Starbuck, W. H. 2006. *The Production of Knowledge: The Challenge of Social Science Research*. New York: Oxford University Press.

State Forestry Administration, People's Republic of China. 2009. Three banks including State Development Bank release favorable policies to serve forestry clients. Ministry of Commerce, People's Republic of China. Available at http://www.english.mofcom.gov.cn, posted August 25.

Stewart, T. P. 2007. China's support programs for selected industries: Wood and wood products. Trade Lawyers Advisory Group, June.

Sun, L. 2010. China's development and policies of new energy auto industry. ITEC Working Paper Series 10-02, Institute for Technology, Enterprise and Competitiveness, Doshisha University, Japan, March.

Sykes, A. O. 2005. Subsidies and countervailing measures. In P. F. J. Macrory, A. E. Appleton, and M. G. Plummer, eds., *The World Trade Organization: Legal, Economic and Political Analysis*, Part III, A, 1682–1706. New York: Springer.

Szamosszegi, A. 2007. How chinese government subsidies and market intervention have resulted in the offshoring of U.S. auto parts production. Case Study, American Iron and Steel Institute and Steel Manufacturers Association.

Tang, R. 2010. China's steel industry and its impact on the United States: Issues for Congress. Congressional Research Service, September 21.

Taube, M., and T. in der Heiden. 2009. The state-business nexus in China's steel industry—Chinese market distortions in domestic and international perspective. European Confederation of Iron and Steel Industries, January.

Thun, E. 2004. Industrial policy, Chinese style: FDI, regulation, and dreams of national champions in the auto sector. *Journal of East Asian Studies* 4: 453–89.

Trade Lawyers Advisory Group. 2007. China's laws, regulations and practices in the areas of technology transfer, trade-related investment measures, subsidies and intellectual property protection which raise WTO compliance concerns. US-China Economic and Security Review Commission, September. Available at http://www.uscc.gov/researchpapers/2008/TLAG%20Report%20-%20China's%20Laws,%20Regulations,%20Practices%20in%20Areas%20of%20Technology%20and%20WTO%20Non-Compliance.pdf.

Trebilcock, M. J., D. Hartle, R. Prichard, and D. Dewees. 1982. The choice of governing instrument. Economic Council of Canada, Ottawa.

Turnbull, J. W. 2007. Development of sustainable forestry plantations in China: A review. Impact Assessment Series Report No. 45, Australian Centre for International Agricultural Research, Canberra, June.

Uchitelle, L. 2010. Glassmaking thrives offshore, but is declining in U.S. *New York Times*, January 18.

US-China Economic and Security Review Commission (USCC). 2007. Report to Congress. November. Available at http://www.uscc.gov/researchpapers/2008/TLAG%20Report%20-%20China's%20Laws,%20Regulations,%20Practices%20in%20Areas%20of%20Technology%20and%20WTO%20Non-Compliance.pdf.

US-China Economic and Security Review Commission. 2011. 2011 Report to Congress. 112th Congress, first session, November. Washington, DC: US Government Printing Office.

US International Trade Commission. 2010. USITC Interactive Tariff and Trade DataWeb.

Wade, R. 1990. *Governing the Market: Economic Theory and the Role of Government in East Asian Industrialization*. Princeton, NJ: Princeton University Press.

Walder, A. G. 1992. Property rights and stratification in socialist redistributive economies. *American Sociological Review* 57: 524–39.

Walder, A. G. 1995. Local governments as industrial firms: An organizational analysis of China's transitional economy. *American Journal of Sociology* 101(2): 263–301.

Waldmeir, P. 2009a. Government stimulus gives China car sales surprise boost. *Financial Times*, February 11.

Waldmeir, P. 2009b. China auto sales increase 90 percent. *Financial Times*, September 9.

Wallerstein, I. 1979. *The Capitalist World Economy*. Cambridge: Cambridge University Press.

Wan, Y. 2006. China's energy efficiency policy in industry. Expert Group Seminar with the OECD Global Forum on Sustainable Development, Paris, March.

Weiss, L. 1998. *The Myth of the Powerless State*. Ithaca, NY: Cornell University Press.

Wesiman, S. R. 2007. China agrees to remove certain subsidies. *New York Times*, November 30.

Wen, J. 2008. Interview on *Fareed Zakaria GPS*, CNN, September 28. Available at http://transcripts.cnn.com/TRANSCRIPTS/0809/28/fzgps.01.html.

White, R. E., R. E. Hoskisson, D. W. Yiu, and G. D. Bruton. 2008. Employment and market innovation in Chinese business group affiliated firms: The role of group control systems. *Management and Organization Review* 4(2): 225–56.

Wiley Rein LLP. 2007. Money for metal: A detailed examination of Chinese government subsidies to its steel industry. July. Washington, DC.

Wong, J. 2004. The adaptive developmental state in East Asia. *Journal of East Asian Studies* 4: 345–62.

World Bank. 1997. Expanding the measure of wealth: Indicators of environmentally sustainable development. Environmentally Sustainable Development Studies and Monograph Series, No. 17, Washington, DC.

World Trade Organization. 2006. *World Trade Report: Exploring the Links between Subsidies, Trade and the WTO*. Available at http://www.wto.org/english/res_e/booksp_e/anrep_e/world_trade_report06_e.pdf.

Xie, S. X., and Y. F. Chen. 2009. On non-public forestry subsidies policies. *China Forestry Economy*, issue 2, March, 5–7. (In Chinese.)

Xinhua News Agency. 2010. Investment in China's auto parts industry to peak in 2010. January 25.

Xinhua News Agency. 2011. China 2011 steel output go higher than expected on price rise. September 26.

Xu, J., and A. G. Yeh. 2005. City repositioning and competitiveness building in regional development: New development strategies in Guangzhou, China. *International Journal of Urban and Regional Research* 29(2): 283–308.

Yang, J. 2012. Why cities' subsidies will hurt domestic automakers in the long run. *Automotive News China*, August 24.

Yee, L. C. 2011. China tops U.S., Japan, to become top patent filer. Reuters, December 21.

Yeh, A. 2005. China raises price of natural gas. *Financial Times*, December 27.

Yoffie, D. B., and H. V. Milner. 1989. An alternative to free trade or protectionism: Why corporations seek strategic trade policy. *California Management Review* 31(4): 111–31.

Yu, W. 2009. An analysis of government subsidies. *Journal of Huangshan University* 11(3): 108–11. (In Chinese.)

Yuwei, Z. 2011. Firm that grew from ridiculous blueprint. *China Daily*, January 14.

Zhang, J. 2011. Shadow finance. *DragonWeek*, February 28, 2.

Zhao, L., and Y. Wang. 2008. Trade remedies and non-market economies: Economic implications of the first US countervailing duty case on China. Policy Research Working Paper No. 4560, Poverty Reduction and Economic Management Division, World Bank, Washington, DC, March.

Zheng, X. 2010. Chinese model forum and investment priorities during the 12th Five-Year Plan forum. Speech, Investment Association of China and Central University of Finance and Economics, Beijing, December.

Zhongxiu Z., and L. Zhi. 2009. Global supply chain and the Chinese auto industry. *Chinese Economy* 42(6): 27–44.

Zhou, E. Y., and B. Stembridge. 2010. Patented in China: The present and future state of innovation in China. *World IP Today*, Thomson Reuters.

Zhu, C., R. Taylor, and G. Feng. 2004. *China's Wood Market, Trade and the Environment*. Beijing: World Wild Life Fund & Science Press.

Ziliak, S. T. (2011) Haiku Economics: Money, Metaphor, and the Invisible Hand,, *Poetry*, 197 (5), 314–316

Zubko, N. 2008. General Motors to increase sourcing in China. *IndustryWeek*, January 1.

INDEX

Note: Material in figures or tables is indicated by italic page numbers. Endnotes are indicated by n. after the page number.